SYSTEMS DESIGN OF EDUCATION:
A JOURNEY TO CREATE
THE FUTURE

SYSTEMS DESIGN OF EDUCATION

A Journey to Create the Future

BELA H. BANATHY

EDUCATIONAL TECHNOLOGY PUBLICATIONS
ENGLEWOOD CLIFFS, NEW JERSEY 07632

Library of Congress Cataloging-in-Publication Data

Banathy, Bela H.
  Systems design of education : a journey to create the future /
Bela H. Banathy.
      p. cm.
  Includes bibliographical references (p.) and index.
  ISBN 0-87778-229-6 : $29.95
  1. School management and organization--United States.
  2. Educational planning--United States. 3. Educational change-
-United States. I. Title.
  LB2805.B264 1991
  371.2'07--dc20   90-19155
                                                              CIP

Printed in the United States of America.

Library of Congress Catalog Card Number:
90-19155.

International Standard Book Number:
0-87778-229-6.

First Printing: January, 1991.

TO MY WIFE, EVA

AND

FUTURE GENERATIONS OF BANATHYS

ACKNOWLEDGMENTS

The Far West Laboratory has provided the primary creative context—over the last two decades—in which I developed program ideas, proposed and received grant and contract support from various sources, and provided leadership to programs and projects in which systems and design thinking was applied in the functional contexts of societal and educational systems. More recently, our cooperative venture with Lynn Jenks in the educational systems design program has been particularly productive.

Working with graduate students at U.C. Berkeley and Saybrook has provided me the opportunity to appreciate how systems and design learning can empower creative human potential. During the last three decades, working with my colleagues in the international systems science and design communities has been always an enriching learning experience.

I am grateful to Larry Hutchins, Lynn Jenks, and Charlie Reigeluth for their careful review and comments on the manuscript of this book, and for their contributions presented in the appendices. I thank Jane Shelly for her excellent editorial help. It has been particularly rewarding to work with the publisher, Lawrence Lipsitz, who so quickly recognized the contribution that the systems idea and systems design approach can make to the creation of future systems of learning and human development.

INTRODUCTION

Systems design in the context of human activity systems is a future-creating disciplined inquiry. People who constitute a human activity system engage in design in order to create and implement a new system, based on their vision of "what that system should be." Or, they may redesign their existing system in order to realize their own aspirations and respond to the changing conditions and expectations of the environment in which their system is embedded. These USER DESIGNERS aim to create a system that has a "goodness of fit" with their own purposes and expectations as well as those of the larger society. When the term "systems design" is used in this text, it is used to stand for the kind of inquiry described here.

Current educational change efforts start with an analysis of the existing system. Problems are identified and a plan is developed by which to correct and improve the system. Systems designers, on the other hand, start by exploring the overall societal context in order to formulate the purposes and define the societal function of education. They envision an ideal image of a system with the characteristics and the potential to attain those purposes and attend to those functions. Next they design and describe the system that will have the organizational capacity and the human capability to realize that image.

Design is a journey to create the future. Education creates the future. Whatever a future generation will become as individuals and collectively as a society, they become so primarily on account of the learning experiences in their lives. These experiences are available in a great variety of forms, shapes, and modes. They are provided formally, informally, in public or private settings, in schools, in the home, through the media, on the street, wherever one experiences life. It is a central task of the society to DESIGN SYSTEMS that will offer opportunities, arrangements, and resources for learning and human development by which future generations will be enabled and empowered to attain their full potential and become competent in shaping their own future and developing their society. The task of this

work is to MAP THE JOURNEY FOR THE DESIGN OF SUCH SYS-
TEMS.

At the beginning of the journey a "design lens" is used to
demonstrate the current educational reform scene and aid us to
realize that we have to go beyond RE-FORM, we have to TRANS-FORM
education. Next, new thinking and new approaches are proposed that
enable us to envision new images of education. Then, the journey
leads us into an exploration of how systems design can be used by our
communities in creating new systems of learning and human development.

TABLE OF CONTENTS

PART ONE: IMPROVEMENT OR TRANSFORMATION?

CHAPTER ONE: Why Systems Design? 5

CHAPTER TWO: A Call for New Thinking, a New
Approach, and a New Strategy 21

CHAPTER THREE: Creating Images of Future
Educational Systems 41

PART TWO: EXPLORING ALTERNATIVE IMAGES

CHAPTER FOUR: Selecting the Scope of the Inquiry . . .59

CHAPTER FIVE: The Focus of the Inquiry 85

CHAPTER SIX: Organizing Society's Resources for
Learning 105

CHAPTER SEVEN: Creating the Image: An Example . . . 123

PART THREE: DESIGN THINKING AND DESIGN PRACTICE

CHAPTER EIGHT: Change by Design 135

CHAPTER NINE: The Design Journey 153

CHAPTER TEN: The Process and Products of
Design 173

REFERENCES 195

APPENDICES

    INTRODUCTION 199

    APPENDIX A: A Third-Wave Educational System
                Charles M. Reigeluth 201

    APPENDIX B: The Application of Design to School
                Planning
                C.L. Hutchins 223

    APPENDIX C: Experience-Based Career Education:
                A Secondary School Program
                C. Lynn Jenks 229

INDEX: 237

SYSTEMS DESIGN OF EDUCATION: A JOURNEY TO CREATE THE FUTURE

PART ONE

IMPROVEMENT
OR TRANSFORMATION?

The question raised above reflects a decade of honest struggle with the issue of a "nation at risk." The struggle with this question has intensified recently, as we have realized that the successive waves of improvement, the unprecedented interest and efforts invested in educational reform, have not produced the expected results, and the nation is still at risk. In Chapter One the current problem situation of educational reform is characterized, leading to the realization that improvement of the existing system will not do in our vastly changed society, and only transformation by design and the self-transcendence of education offer promise.

In Chapter Two, new ways of thinking about education are called for. The theoretical foundations of a new mindset are established, and a new intellectual technology—systems design—is proposed by which the new thinking and theory can be put into practice for the transformation of education. In Chapter Three, a framework is created that enables our educational communities to establish the boundaries of design inquiry, and create and explore options for the redesign of their educational systems.

Chapter One

WHY SYSTEMS DESIGN?

"If Rip Van Winkle would wake up today, the only place he would feel at home is the classroom." (From a conversation with the superintendent of a large school district.)

INTRODUCTION

This chapter has three interconnected sections. The first section presents a brief overview of the educational improvement/restructuring scene of the last several years; describes and reflects upon the successive "waves" of the various educational reform proposals, reports, and programs; and identifies their common features. Next, statements are highlighted that represent an assessment of these reform attempts. For example, the current consensus seems to be that the nation is still "at risk" and the "crisis of education" continues. Some reformers are now calling for a radical redesign and transformation of education. It seems, however, that most of those who call for redesign do not know how to go about it.

The second section develops a comprehensive view of the current educational predicament and examines it through a "systems design lens." This predicament has two major sources. The first is the set of approaches we have applied in our attempts to improve or reform/restructure education. These include: (1) a piecemeal and incremental approach; (2) a failure to integrate problem solution ideas; (3) a discipline-by-discipline study of education; (4) a reductionist orientation; and (5) staying within the existing boundaries of the system. The second, and far more significant, source is at the very heart of the problem. It is a lack of realization of the ever-widening developmental gap between the current state of education and the rapidly changing society — and, consequently, a lack of realization that the current design of schooling is still grounded in the industrial societal model of a bygone era. It is outdated and has lost its viability and usefulness.

In the third section, the conclusion is drawn that we have to go beyond reform. Improving or restructuring an obsolete system will not do; it is counterproductive. We have to realize that the crisis in education is first and foremost a "crisis of perception," which IS the genesis of the "crisis of performance" of the existing system. What is needed today is a major shift in the way we think about education, in the way we approach educational inquiry, and in the kind of intellectual technologies we use in changing and renewing our educational systems.

I. THE NATION IS STILL "AT RISK"

The ship of education is sailing on troubled waters. One national report after another has highlighted the current "crisis" of a "nation at risk," pointing out dangerous currents and menacing shoals. There is an ever-increasing realization that unless we change the course, the ship will sink. But people are still trying to "rearrange the chairs" on the deck of the sinking ship, a la THE TITANIC. In this section the educational reform movement of the last decade is reviewed briefly and its impact assessed.

The eighties have been one of the most intensive and active decades in terms of educational reform attempts. The highly acclaimed genesis of the current reform movement was the report of the National Commission on Excellence in Education. The commission was created because of "the widespread public perception that something is seriously remiss in our educational system." Entitled *A Nation at Risk: The Imperative of Educational Reform* (1983), the report states that "for the first time in the history of our country, the educational skills of one generation will not surpass, will not equal, will not even approach, those of their parents" (p. 11). The most troubling conclusion was that "if an unfriendly foreign power had attempted to impose on America the mediocre educational performance that exists today, we might well have viewed it as an act of war" (p. 5). The commission's report and many other reports since have brought home the realization that "we have met the enemy and it is us."

Since the commission's report, we have seen a groundswell of public and private energy and enthusiasm for educational improvement (Harvey and Crandell, 1988). The amount of sustained activity directed towards this end has been unprecedented. All the states have accepted the challenge and initiated improvement efforts. New funds have been allocated, new policies have been established, and many school improvement programs have been implemented. We have seen the proliferation of commissions, forums, task forces, professional groups — at national, state, and local levels—publishing and reviewing reports and books. They all have been genuinely concerned about the "crisis."

The reform efforts and recommendations have come in waves. The SCHOOL IMPROVEMENT wave, initiated by the commission's report, insisted upon doing MORE OF THE SAME. More classroom instruction, more of the "basics" and science, more discipline, more teacher training, more control, more parent participation, more pay for teachers. A follow-up modification of this first wave called for doing basically the same but DOING IT BETTER. In this early period, the focus was on EFFICIENCY. But assessments of the push for improvement found it to be far from adequate to meet the challenges of the "crisis."

Reviewing the outcomes of this period, George Leonard's (1984) comments are most telling. He concluded that there is no reason to believe that the improvement efforts would change the basic nature of schooling. Even if all the recommendations were implemented, "the resulting school would be fundamentally no different from the schools of today. In fact, it would be pretty much the same as the school of a hundred years ago." In the space age, "the reformers are offering the nation an educational horse-and-buggy. They would improve the buggy, keep the passengers in it longer, and pay the driver more" (Leonard, pp. 49-50).

The second wave, still in motion, suggests that nothing less than RESTRUCTURING THE SYSTEM is adequate. We should focus on the EFFECTIVENESS of schooling by rearranging its components and realigning the distribution of responsibilities. The structuralists believe (Kniep, 1989) that we need to bring about fundamental changes in the EXISTING organization of schooling. "They are largely silent about the substance of the school program. Even their most influential voices virtually ignore this issue, focusing instead on the form and structure of schools and teaching" (*ibid.*, p. 44). Some scholars have used the term "restructuring" in the sense of "redesign" (Branson, 1988; Perelman, 1987; Reigeluth, 1988). Three recent publications highlight the need for change, but still focus on the existing system. Elmore (1990) presents an analysis of varied and often conflicting programs for restructuring, explores their strengths and weaknesses, and examines their implications for policymakers, administrators, and teachers. Barth (1990) focuses on the internal relationships among adults within the school, and makes proposals for how schools can be restructured from within by empowering teachers and building a collegial atmosphere. Schlechty (1990) calls upon schools to adapt to their changing environment; restructure by altering rules, roles, and relationships; and develop strong leadership.

Summing up, the two waves described above represent remedies for fixing or rearranging the current system. Whatever terms are used, "improve," "reform," "renew," "restructure," the host of recommendations and projects focus on MAKING ADJUSTMENTS IN THE EXISTING SYSTEM, rather than thinking about a new one. In the course of the last several years, the states have spent up to 70 percent more on education, supporting piecemeal improvements that have resulted at best in minuscule gains. In January 1990, the Secretary of Education presented a gloomy summary report on the state of education, saying that "frankly, there has been very little educational progress made." Criticizing the educational reform efforts of the eighties, he said that the nation "has gone through the motions," but the situation is "virtually unchanged and the achievements are dreadfully inadequate." The only conclusion that can be drawn at this juncture of the educational reform movement is that in spite of the massive and costly efforts of the eighties, the nation is still "at risk" and the "crisis" is ever more threatening. But there is hope — we are beginning to see the "light at the end of the tunnel."

Some of the observations that have been made in the last several years are beginning to point toward the need for new thinking and approaches very different from those of the first two waves. It seems that a new wave is emerging. These observers point to the need to look at the total SYSTEM and seek NEW DESIGNS. The National Governors' Association's report (1986) says that despite all the attempts to reform education, "we are afraid that the states are working for more of the same without taking a hard look at the SYSTEM itself" (*ibid.*, p. 12). The Department of Education Task Force's report (1986) and the Carnegie Forum report (1986) call for a "FUNDAMENTAL REDESIGN" of the entire system of education. A recent article in the WALL STREET JOURNAL points to this new direction: "Now, after five years of the most sustained school reform movement in U.S. history, it's becoming clear to many that the U.S. educational factory is obsolete. It needs to be rebuilt from the ground up in an entirely different way, under entirely different operating assumptions." The purpose of this book is to set forth new assumptions for a NEW DESIGN of education and propose SYSTEMS DESIGN as an entirely different way of rebuilding our educational systems. An exploration of the sources of our current predicament will help us to gain some new insights and shape new assumptions.

II. SOURCES OF THE CURRENT PREDICAMENT

Analysts of the educational predicament of the last decade have come up with a number of specific problems that should be corrected. We are now beginning to realize that there is much more to the genesis of the current crisis in education than specific deficiencies. I suggest that this crisis has two major sources. One is rooted in our prevailing "mindset," the way we think about and study education, and consequently the way we have approached educational change and reform. The other, which I believe is at the very heart of the problem situation, is a lack of realization of the wholly outdated "design" of the current educational system and the ever-widening gap between rapidly changing societal developments and the persisting (basically unchanged) nature of education. It is the still prevailing "mindset" that hinders and blocks such realization.

A CHARACTERIZATION OF THE CURRENT MINDSET AND SCHOOL REFORM APPROACHES

Our prevailing "mindset" is rooted in the fragmented study of education and in the traditional scientific orientation of educational scholarship. It is these two orientations that have shaped approaches to school reform.

A. THE FRAGMENTED STUDY OF EDUCATION

The fragmented and disconnected view prominent in studying education is inherent in the prevailing approach to social-systems inquiry. This approach depends on scholarship in a variety of disciplines that can provide only a partial interpretation of the system studied and sets forth descriptions based on disparate theoretical frameworks. For example, in education, we study the sociology of the classroom, the psychology of instruction, the economics of education, the anthropology of school culture, and the politics of governance. This way of trying to understand education brings to mind the parable about a group of blind men who try to describe an elephant by touching its various parts. Compartmentalized inquiry, combined with the use of widely differing orientations, methods, and languages of the separate disciplines, results in unintegrated and incomplete knowledge and characterization. Thus, the disciplines-based theoretical frameworks currently in use in educational scholarship cannot conceptualize and depict education as a total system. A particular discipline addresses only a narrow aspect of the whole. It focuses on a small number of variables conducive to being studied by the discipline. This approach tends to disregard complex interactions and the systemic connectedness among the various components of the system. It cannot adequately portray the mutually interacting and recursive dynamics of systems processes. To sum up, the orientation described here holds little promise of providing a theoretical basis for reconceptualizing education as a SYSTEM, and consequently it cannot offer useful approaches and strategies for its purposeful REDESIGN.

B. TRADITIONAL SCIENTIFIC INQUIRY STILL PREVAILS

Inspired by the Cartesian-Newtonian scientific worldview, disciplined inquiry during the last three hundred years has sought understanding by taking things apart, seeking the "ultimate part," and groping to see or reconstruct the whole by viewing the characteristics of its parts. Implicit in this approach is an exclusive commitment to defining elementary cause-and-effect relationships, which led to a deterministic perception of the world. (This particular problem in education is brought about by this particular "cause." Fix the cause and the problem will disappear.) The "mechanistic" scientific worldview, by its technological applications, was best manifested in the Industrial Revolution. Its essential characteristics — namely, analytical thinking, reductionism, and determinism — still prevail in current educational scholarship. We have failed to implement the massive scientific "paradigm shift" that has occurred in the course of the last several decades. Our inquiry is still dominated by controlled reductionist experiments, the application of quantitative measures (which greatly limit the scope of inquiry), observational "objectivity," and deterministic models. No wonder this approach cannot possibly cope with the complexity, mutual causality, purpose, intention, uncertainty, ambiguity, and ever accelerating dynamic changes that characterize our systems and the larger societal environment.

* * *

It is the "mindset" of the fragmented and traditional scientific worldview described above that is the conceptual basis of (and which is so clearly reflected in) the approaches we have applied in the educational reform movement of the last decade. Three of these approaches are highlighted here: (1) the piecemeal/incremental approach, (2) the failure to connect and integrate solution ideas, and (3) staying within the boundaries of the existing system.

1. The Piecemeal and Incremental Approach

The efforts to change and improve education during the last two or three decades (with increasing intensity and urgency more recently) demonstrate the same part-oriented, fragmented, reductionist scientific view discussed above. These improvement efforts can be (and have been by many observers) characterized as "piecemeal," "incremental," "disjointed," "corrections at the margin," "nibbling at the edges," "tinkering with parts," etc. The results and documentations of educational innovation and improvement R&D surely fill whole libraries. Yet, the metaphor applies of a warehouse full of vehicle parts, parts that do not fit into a whole. There is no blueprint for integrating the parts. The myriad of educational improvement programs and products do not "map" into the system we call education. In fact, no map of this system exists.

2. Failure to Integrate Solution Ideas

The various recommendations and reports have proposed many improvement ideas but have failed to organize them into a comprehensive system of reform. For example, the Governors' Conference report (1986) recommended a dozen major improvement ideas without integrating them into an internally consistent program. A two-year study funded by the Carnegie Corporation labeled the existing system an outdated assembly line and made 58 specific unintegrated proposals to "radically transform" schools. This "failure to connect" again harks back to a lack of systemic orientation in education in general and in educational reform specifically. Mitchell (1989) arrived at the same conclusion of a lack of integration as he reviewed a variety of reform strategies that has been tried, such as: (1) standard-setting strategies, (2) staff development strategies, (3) curriculum improvement strategies, (4) organizational strategies, and (5) environmental change strategies.

3. Staying Within the Boundaries of the Existing System

This shortcoming has yet to be recognized by the educational community. Without exception, recent improvement and reform inquiries have focused on the system "as it exists" and have stayed

within its boundaries, with only occasional attention to selected societal issues. These improvement inquiries stipulated changes at the
margin. Few of the reports have taken a broader societal perspective.
As a rule, they have failed to recognize the complexity of current issues
surrounding education and have not grappled with the essential
nature of education as a societal system; a system interacting with other
societal systems, a system which is embedded in the rapidly and
dynamically changing larger society. Limiting the scope of inquiry to
the existing system is the main reason for the failure to recognize that
the design of the current educational system is outdated.

The improvement/planning approach so widely practiced in
recent years follows traditional social planning. It reduces the problem to manageable pieces and seeks solution to each. It is believed
that solving problems piece by piece ultimately will correct the larger
issue of the current crisis. But, GETTING RID OF WHAT IS UN-
DESIRABLE WILL NOT ENSURE THE ATTAINMENT OF WHAT IS
WANTED.

LOOKING AT THE RECENT EDUCATIONAL REFORM
MOVEMENT THROUGH A SYSTEMS DESIGN LENS

In sharp contrast with the prevailing approach described above, the
SYSTEMS DESIGN APPROACH proposed here seeks to understand
the current crisis in education as an issue for systems design. It views
the educational problem situation as a system of interconnected,
interdependent, and interacting problems, seeking to create the
design solution as a system of interconnected, interdependent, interacting, AND internally consistent solution ideas. The systems design
approach seeks to envision educational arrangements and the entities
that attend to those arrangements as a WHOLE SYSTEM that emerges
and should be designed in view of the synthesis of its interacting parts.
A SYSTEMS VIEW suggests that the essential quality of the part resides
in its relationship to the whole. Furthermore, a social system—such
as education—should be designed from the perspectives of the system
itself, its environment, and its component parts. And, the purpose of
the system should be defined in view of those three levels. The system
should serve the purpose for which it was designed, it should serve
the purpose(s) of people in the system—the learners in our case—and
it should serve the purpose of the environment, the larger societal
system that created the system. It is this last level, the requirements of
the larger society, that failed to receive adequate attention in the
reform movement. By staying within the boundaries of the existing

educational system and trying to reform it from the inside, reformers have failed to recognize the ever-widening gap between recent massive changes in the larger society's design and the unchanging design of education.

The whole systems design notion requires both COORDINATION and INTEGRATION. We need to design all parts operating at a specific system level of the organization interactively and simultaneously. This requires coordination. The requirement of designing for interdependency and internal consistency across all system levels invites integration.This "simultaneous, all-over, whole-system" approach is the hallmark of systems design. It is totally different from the "incremental-piecemeal," "disjointed," "part-oriented," "inside-focused" approach practiced by the recent reform movement.

III. BEYOND REFORM:
THE CALL FOR TRANSFORMATION BY DESIGN

In this third section of Chapter One, the stage is set for a consideration of the need for a new design in education and, consequently, the use of systems design as the new intellectual technology in education. Around the middle of this century we entered what is often called the "post-industrial information/knowledge age," a new stage in the evolution of humanity. This stage has unfolded new thinking, new perspectives, a new scientific orientation, new technologies, and a new planetary worldview. It has brought about massive changes and discontinuities in all aspects of our lives, requiring changes in the way we think about education, the way we define its societal functions, and the way we provide arrangements for learning and human development. In facing the realities of current societal transformations and understanding their educational implications, we have no other choice but to call for a NEW DESIGN and the TRANSFORMATION of education by DESIGN. Such a call has been voiced in several recent proposals.

NEW EDUCATIONAL DESIGN:
AN EMERGING REQUIREMENT

In his call for a "Third-Wave Educational System," Reigeluth (1988) suggested that it is the design of our current system that is at the heart of the current problem situation. "As the one-room schoolhouse, a 'first-wave' educational system, was appropriate for what Toffler (1980) calls a first-wave agrarian society, so our present, second-wave educational system has a structure and philosophy that were appropriate for a second-wave industrial society" (*ibid.*, p. 5). The current system clearly shows the assembly line thinking and practice of the industrial machine age, as a highly regimented, rigidly controlled, lockstepped, group-based, rotational, top-down designed, time-oriented, and isolated within a building of the 'educational factory.'"

Reigeluth, like some others, uses the metaphor of the evolution of transportation systems. As we entered into the industrial age, the transportation needs of society changed, and the many attempts made to improve the horse-and-buggy system resulted in minuscule gains compared with the development of the railroad. (Note that the railroad was NOT extrapolated from the horse-and-buggy, it was a new design.) "The railroad was far faster, more comfortable, more reliable, and more efficient than the horse. It could transport many more people much greater distances far more effectively. But, like our current educational system, it was much less flexible. You were greatly restricted as to where you could go and when" (*ibid.*, p. 4). Recent changes in the society have brought about new transportation needs. "Fine tuning" the railroad did not meet these needs. The current space-age transportation systems represent a quantum leap in all dimensions of transportation design. In the same sense, as we entered the post-industrial information age, the industrial age-based design of our educational system will no longer suffice, regardless of how much effort and money we invest in its "fine tuning." Reigeluth suggests that only a "third-wave" system will provide the quantum leap for "meeting the changing needs of our society" (*ibid.*, p. 5). His design is reviewed in Appendix A.

"There are times in history when what seems like an endless cycle comes to an end; when the closed path is broken and events veer off on a new trajectory. There ARE rare moments of true transformation" (Perelman, 1987 p. 5). There is little doubt, says Perelman, that a basic transformation in education is coming. It is difficult to believe, he says, that traditional education "can be sustained much longer in the face of historic transformations. We are living in a time and place for which the past is NOT prologue. The most outstanding and disconcerting aspect of our age, whether we call it the 'Post-industrial Society' or the 'Third Wave,' is that it confronts us with threats and opportunities that are utterly unprecedented, they are unlike anything that ever happened before" (*ibid.*, p. 6). He concludes that whether we lead in the transformation of education or play "catch-up" with other cultures will "determine whether the United States will continue to play an international leadership role in the 21st century," or slide into the "impoverished nostalgia" of earlier empires (*ibid.*, p. 7).

In a milestone-setting new design for achieving educational excellence, Hutchins (1990) suggests that what prevents us today from attaining excellence is the still-prevailing (old) design of schooling. Reviewing the evolution of the current educational design, Hutchins says that its shape was outlined as early as the 1830s. It was created from the perspectives of employers. "They wanted a work force that would meet the needs of the industrial society; they wanted workers who would work long hours, follow orders without answering back, do repetitive work, and be on time" (*ibid.*, p. 41). The design of the 1830s was modified in the 1890s when the "Committee of Ten" recommended a textbook-controlled new curriculum for the twentieth century. The old design reached its final form a half a century later, when James Conant advocated the introduction of industry/business-type management models and the creation of the comprehensive high school of the 1950s.

In his analysis Hutchins says, "The old design worked relatively well for the society it served; it brought schooling to millions of immigrants whose skill and conformity were needed to stoke the engines of the industrial society. Today's society no longer requires such a work force. We need people who can think creatively and solve problems using information and technology" (*ibid.*, p. 1). Commenting on recently proposed reforms, Hutchins notes that they are only "bandages on the old design." "Lengthening the school day won't change outcomes when barely 25 percent of the typical school day is spent with students learning successfully. Testing teachers won't make any difference if they weren't taught well in the first place. Tightening standards for students and testing them won't make any difference if the standards and the requirements are irrelevant to the requirements of the 21st century" (*ibid.*, p. 2). The new design is introduced by Hutchins in "A⁺chieving Excellence." It will be outlined in Appendix B.

THE TRANSFORMATION IMPERATIVE

At times of accelerating and dynamic societal changes, when a new stage is unfolding in societal evolution, inquiry should not focus on improving existing systems. A "focus within" limits perception in education to the old societal image (of the machine age) in which the system is still rooted. A design rooted in an outdated image is useless. Locked in an old design, such as we are now in education, we must break the old frame of thinking and reframe our "mindset." We should "jump out from the system," explore educational change and renewal from the larger vistas of the transformed society, and envision a new design. Starting design from the perspectives of the overall societal context, we extend our horizon and develop the LARGEST POSSIBLE PICTURE of education within the LARGEST POSSIBLE SOCIETAL CONTEXT.

An assessment of recent educational reform attempts and recommendations leads us now to the following conclusion. Making adjustments, restructuring, or improving our educational system, which is still grounded in the assembly-line thinking and practices of the industrial/machine age, will not do at the current stage of societal development. Thus, our challenge today is to create a new design of education that will guide the transformation of education in the nineties and beyond.

ASKING NEW AND DIFFERENT QUESTIONS

Educational reform inquiries over the last several years have probed the adequacy of our educational system from the inside. Focusing on the existing system, we have asked such questions as:

What is wrong with the system?

How can we improve it to make it more efficient? or

How can we restructure it to make it more effective?

How can we provide more instructional time?

How can we improve student and teacher performance?

How can we establish better standards, and how can we test for those better standards?

How can we attain more discipline in the classroom and have a drug-free school?

How can we increase achievements in the basics and in science?

How can we ensure more parent and community involvement?

Many more questions like these have been asked. Such questions might be appropriate in times of relative stability, when adjustments and piecemeal improvements in an existing system could bring it in line with slow and gradual changes in the environment. However, in the time of turbulence, accelerating and dynamic changes, and discontinuities that characterize the current era, when a new and very different stage is unfolding in societal evolution, it is time to ask new questions, questions very different from those we have asked in the course of the eighties. For instance:

What is the nature, and what are the characteristics, of the current post-industrial information age?

What are the educational implications of those characteristics?

What should be the role and function of education in this new era of societal development?

What new image (of education) is emerging from the answers to the above questions, and what values and beliefs might guide us in the creation of a new design of education?

What approach and what strategies will enable us to realize the image, create a new design, and devise a system that will best represent the design in the real world?

What approach and what strategies can be used to develop, implement, and institutionalize that system?

The questions proposed here shift the direction of our inquiry from exploring the existing system as a source of its improvement, to working from the larger perspective of a societal and future-generation-focused design. The questions also mark the milestones of the design journey. They define the major stages of systems design and set forth the agenda of this work.

PREPARING FOR THE JOURNEY

Before designers of future educational systems can start their journey toward creating their new design, they have to grapple with the issues of the "mindset" and the creation of a framework of thinking for contemplating design options. The "mindset," often called a view of the world, is the paradigm we use to perceive and explain. It is at the very core of any design. Earlier in this chapter we explored the mindset of the old design. That mindset guided generations of educational communities who wrote and kept on rewriting and revising the "old story" of education. The latest revision is the product of the recent reform movement. But we know now that the "old story" does not work for us anymore. We now realize that we have to write a "new story" based on the new design that we should now create.

"WE CANNOT POUR NEW WINE IN AN OLD WINE SKIN"

The new wine metaphor in the Bible was used to represent the "New Testament," which cannot just be plugged into the old design of religious practice. The new thinking we speak of is the "new wine" that once defined and made explicit will guide the creation of the new image and the new design of education.

On the current world scene we are witnessing an unfolding drama in Europe, where nations are in search of a new design that they are now forging based on "new thinking" that has emerged in their collective consciousness during the historical events of 1989-90. In his eloquent speech to the US Congress, President Havel voiced his vision for the world in which history has accelerated, and we should believe that once again "it will be the human mind that will notice this acceleration, give it a name, and transform those words into deeds" (Havel, 1990). His message is a message to us who seek a new vision of education. Once we become open to the emergence of "new thinking" by a conscious and purposeful exploration of the new worldview that has guided the accelerated emergence of the new stage of societal evolution, then we can "give a name" to a new image of education, develop new core ideas about education. The image will then guide us in the creation of the new design, so that we can transform the image and the design "into deeds."

Two additional issues must be addressed before design can proceed. The first is how to think about change, change that is directed by design. The second issue is the construction of a framework, the scope of which is large enough to allow designers to explore various images and design options. These issues are marked as stations of the design journey.

Now we can develop a map of the journey. The map is pictured in Figure 1.1. Two circles represent the contours of the map. In the inner circle, at the center of the map, is placed "new thinking," "core ideas," and "core values." In the outer circle we display the questions that mark the milestones of the design journey. The thinking and ideas indicated in the inner circle are continuously evolving as we proceed with the journey. They guide the journey and are enriched and informed by it. The journey is not linear. Its stages are interactive and recursive. One stage informs the next and a later stage may lead to the reformulation of an earlier one. It is important for us to understand and appreciate this open nature of design.

FIGURE 1.1. THE MAP OF THE DESIGN JOURNEY

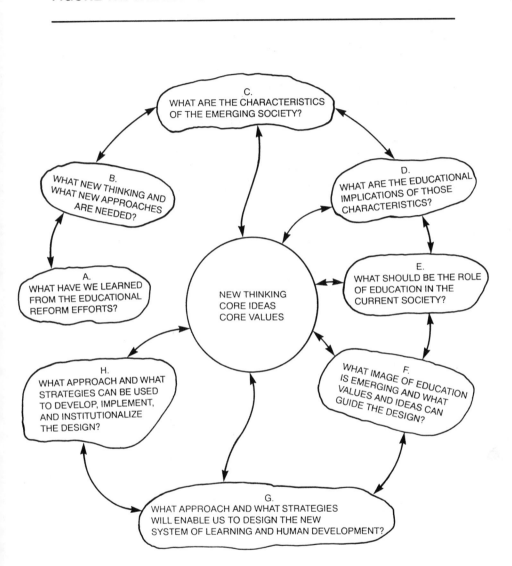

REFLECTIONS

The title of this book is SYSTEMS DESIGN OF EDUCATION: A JOURNEY TO CREATE THE FUTURE. In this chapter a rationale has been developed for the creation of a new image and design of education and for the use of a new intellectual technology: systems design. This technology is viewed here as a journey to create a new educational system for future generations. The task of this work is NOT to create or describe a new system. Such is the task of our communities across the nation. The task is to describe the approach and the strategies by which the design can be accomplished. Still, I will introduce some examples that demonstrate possible outcomes of the application of the approach and the strategies.

Chapter Two

A CALL FOR NEW THINKING, A NEW APPROACH, AND A NEW STRATEGY

"To ask larger questions is to risk getting things wrong. Not to ask them at all is to constrain the life of understanding." (George Skinner)

INTRODUCTION

From a review of the educational reform movement and from an understanding and analysis of the sources of the educational predicament of the day, a new insight emerged in Chapter One. This insight tells us that the current "crisis" in education first and foremost is a "crisis of perception." This crisis now calls for a major shift in our "mindset." It calls for "asking larger questions" and searching for answers different from what we have developed heretofore. It calls for new thinking in—and a new vision of—education. It calls for a new approach and a new strategy in educational inquiry. In this chapter, I develop an example of the notion of new thinking, approaches, and strategies.

The new thinking proposed in this chapter reflects my involvement over more than three decades in educational R&D, systems science, and the application of systems and design thinking in real-world settings, coupled with teaching all these in a variety of contexts. This experience yielded organized knowledge, understanding, and possibly wisdom, which suggests that a new design of education should be based on "new thinking" that is rooted in an appreciation of societal evolution and development, and in systems and design thinking.

There are obviously others in the educational reform movement who
reach into some other domains for enlightenment and guidance. The
point I wish to make is that we have to have access to some source of
guidance, and that we should make that guidance explicit to ourselves
and others.

In the first part of this chapter, I review societal evolution and seek
to understand our individual and collective role in it. Evolutionary
thinking and a societal developmental perspective will lead us to ask
those "larger questions." Furthermore, evolutionary consciousness
and competence are essential conditions of envisioning and creating
new educational systems designs. In the second part, I weave into the
discussion "design thinking" as part of the emerging new thinking.
The application of design thinking in educational reform will help us
to create the new design of education we need to bring about. In the
third part, systems thinking is introduced as another essential component of "new thinking," and its application in education is highlighted.

I. EVOLUTIONARY AND DEVELOPMENTAL THINKING

*"We humans are integral agents of evolution: we spearhead it on our
planet and perhaps in our entire solar system. We are evolution and
we are—to the extent of our power—responsible for it."*   (Erich Jantsch)

As we approach the end of the 20th century, the worldwide changes
that have been brought about by unrestrained growth, technological
advancements, and the knowledge explosion are no longer viewed as
a route to a better future for humanity. These changes have occurred
at a much faster rate than corresponding changes in our social
systems. This discrepancy is the main source of our current predicament in the overall society as well as in various societal systems, such
as education. To better understand this predicament, we should
examine human evolution. Unlike other living systems, humans are
involved in biological AND cultural evolution. Cultural evolution is
very recent in the evolutionary time scale, and it is constantly gaining
momentum. The more we develop, the more we enhance our capacity
for further development. To better understand this phenomenon we
should look at the time scale of cultural evolution and the key markers
of its various evolutionary stages (Curtis, 1982).

- STAGE ONE spanned over a half million years. Its genesis was
  the evolution of human consciousness, coupled with the
  greatest human creation: speech. Speech made it possible for

us to expand the boundaries of human experience in time and space as hunting-gathering tribal cultures emerged and oral tradition embraced the past. Magico-religious myth became the all-embracing paradigm of perception and explanation.

- STAGE TWO emerged about ten thousand years ago, as we entered the agricultural age and developed writing as our new communication technology. These developments brought about the extension of spatial boundaries into city-states and even empires. Through writing, the time boundary was further extended into the past and future. Several major religions and the logico-philosophical paradigm emerged.

- STAGE THREE started five hundred years ago. Print, our new communication technology, enhanced the establishment of nation-states and the emergence of national consciousness. In this age of the beauty of Renaissance and the "enlightenment" of modern science, a mechanistic and deterministic worldview emerged. Science-based technology culminated in the industrial revolution, which greatly extended our physical power through machine technology. In the latter part of the last century, telecommunication brought about the realization of global connectedness and the promise of the emergence of global consciousness.

- STAGE FOUR is our current evolutionary stage. It emerged around the middle of this century. Its genesis is marked by the introduction of the greatest destructive force, the atomic bomb; the creation of the United Nations, a new hope for a global humanity; and the formulation of the cybernetic/systems paradigm and its technological application in the computer, which greatly extended our cognitive power. We designate the new era that has emerged as the "post-industrial society," the "information/knowledge age," the "systems age," the "space age." Table 2.1 displays the key evolutionary markers of the various stages and dramatizes our current predicament.

Recognizing the great disproportion of the time span of the various evolutionary stages—five hundred thousand years, ten thousand, five hundred, fifty years—we realize that the synergic effect of the speed and intensity of developments during stage four has resulted in a perilous evolutionary imbalance (Banathy, 1987). In earlier times,

Table 2.1. KEY EVOLUTIONARY MARKERS

STAGE ONE	STAGE TWO	STAGE THREE	STAGE FOUR
hunting gathering groups	agricultural societies	industrial society	post-industrial society
HALF MILLION years	TEN THOUSAND years	FIVE HUNDRED years	FIFTY years
speech	writing	print	cybernetic technology
wandering tribes	communities city-states	nation-states	potential of a global society
magico-myth paradigm	logico-philosophical paradigm	deterministic scientific paradigm	systemic paradigm
survival technology	fabricating techology	machine technology	intellectual technology

when societal evolution was rather slow and gradual, it allowed time for the various systems of the society to co-evolve and keep a well-balanced space across all systems of the society. The intellectual and social mechanisms of attaining such a state were adjustment and adaptation. During the last hundred years, however, mankind has experienced an unleashing of unprecedented scientific, technological, and material advancement. In the first part of this century, we were still able to manage change brought about by those advancements on acceptable terms. During the last several decades, however, the technological revolution, while giving us power, earlier unimagined, has accelerated to the point where we have lost control over it. We have failed to match the advancement of technological intelligence with an advancement in socio-cultural intelligence and wisdom, which are required to give direction to and guide technological developments for the benefit of all mankind (Peccei, 1977). The development and nurturing of such intelligence and wisdom will be proposed as THE key challenge to education. (Today we are still preoccupied—single-mindedly—with the promotion of technological intelligence.)

Furthermore, while earlier we tended "to view change as an attribute of reality and see the world as changing," we now "understand that the world is itself but a moment in a more fundamental process of change" (Morgan, 1986, p. 234). Understanding such a change in the nature of change tells us that adaptation and adjustment are NOT adequate anymore. Rather than adjusting to or adapting to changes, our systems now have to co-change and coevolve with their constantly changing environments. The mechanism for this kind of change is ongoing design. We shall now examine how evolutionary consciousness enables and fuels the creating process of design.

THE POWER OF EVOLUTIONARY CONSCIOUSNESS

In evolution, the most advanced state of existence is human consciousness. It is expressed in its highest forms in those who are most developed in terms of their relationship to others and in their ability to interact harmoniously with all else in their sphere of life. They have the greatest capacity to shape change. Evolutionary consciousness empowers us to collaborate actively with the evolutionary process and use the creative power of our mind to guide our systems and our society toward the fulfillment of their potential. Salk (1983) remarked that evolutionary consciousness can motivate action toward giving direction to our future by consciously guiding evolution, provided we have a clear vision and image of what we wish to bring about. Conscious evolution, says Jantsch (1981), provides a sense of direction for cultural and social development by illuminating it with guiding images. And the faster we go—as we do at our current evolutionary stage—the further we have to look for images to guide our movement. I am reminded of Csanyi (1982, p. 427), who said, "Evolution on earth, and within it the history of mankind, is a unique story,"..."man can create his own evolution, choose his own history, and this is his freedom."

The human race has profoundly changed the parameters of the evolutionary process. Our unlimited capacity for learning and the explosive rate at which we produce knowledge and design artifacts and systems have had an extraordinary—and often unintended—impact on societal evolution. The question that confronts us is: For what purpose are we going to use this limitless capacity for learning and our creating power? We can use them to create a better future and give a hopeful direction to societal development. This, however, is dependent on our meeting four conditions (Banathy, 1989): (a) the development of evolutionary consciousness; and based on it (b) the creation of guiding images for the future; (c) the acquisition of competence needed to design our systems based on those images: and, (d) the application of this competence in designing our systems. It is through this process that evolutionary images can be transformed into societal development. What follows is a description of how this transformation works, how to apply the intellectual technology of systems design in societal development, and in the design of systems of learning and human development.

II. DESIGN THINKING AND DESIGN ACTION

> *"Intentions are fairly easy to perceive, but frequently do not come about. Design is hard to perceive. It is design and not intention that creates the future."*
> (Kenneth Boulding)

Kenneth Boulding's admonition is surely on target in regard to the current reform movement, which has produced a large number of sets of intentions without considering the design of systems that can realize those intentions. Most recently, the States' governors presented a set of ambitious goals to be attained by the end of the century. They also intend to present some strategies by which to approach these goals. Rephrasing Boulding, goals and strategies are easy to perceive. But, it is design that creates the system that enables us to attain those goals and carry out the strategies.

In evolution, the most advanced state of existence is consciousness. It has a self-reflective cognitive aspect and a creative aspect of a sense of shaping the future. These two aspects are manifested in two complementary and recursive functions (Banathy, 1988b).

SELF-REFLECTIVE CONSCIOUSNESS is contemplating the here and now. It creates an image—a cognitive map—of the self, the world around the self, and one's role in the world. Through this process, individuals, groups, organizations, and societies make representations of their perceptions of the world—and their understanding of their place in the world. They map "WHAT IS" in their individual and collective minds. Such a representation is implicit in the mind. It can be inferred from the behavior of the map makers, and it can be made explicit by its expression through a variety of mediations. These maps are "alive." They are created, confirmed, disconfirmed, elaborated, changed, redrawn...

CREATING CONSCIOUSNESS focuses on "WHAT SHOULD BE." By constructing an image—a cognitive map—of the desired future, it guides individual, social, and societal evolution and development. This creation is based on the belief that although the future is influenced by the past and present, it is NOT determined by what has been or what is. It remains open to conscious and purposeful intervention, and it can be realized by systems design.

The creating inquiry of design draws normative maps, based on the ideas, expectations, and the designers' vision of what the future should be. Such maps are constructed for and by human activity systems of all kinds. Such construction is achieved by (a) creating a vision of the future state of the system, (b) elaborating this vision in the form of an image (cognitive map), and (c) engaging in the design (and the eventual development) of the system that has the organizational capacity and collective human capability to realize the image. The table below displays the relationship of these stages.

Table 2.2. VISION-IMAGE-DESIGN

VISION ⟶	IMAGE ⟶	DESIGN
the grand ideal, the underlying philosophy, the inspiration that guide imaging	a system of core values and core ideas that elaborate the vision and guide system design	the model of the future system that realizes the image

The image of a desired future state of the system guides designers in their creation of the DESIGN or the MODEL of the FUTURE SYSTEM. This systems creation includes the formulation of PURPOSES and the CORE DEFINITION of the system, the specification of the desired CHARACTERISTICS of the future system, the selection and systemic arrangement of FUNCTIONS that have to be carried out by the system in order to attain the stated purpose, the design of the SYSTEM that will guide us in carrying out the identified functions, and the design of the ORGANIZATION that has the capacity and human talent and competence to attend to those functions.

The design or the model of the system also serves additional functions. It endows people in the system with a common purpose, assists them in understanding their specific contributions in the attainment of the purpose, and guides them in operating their system as a collective venture. Furthermore, the design or model of the system, once made public, informs the environment that embeds the system, and other systems in the environment, about what the system does, how it works, and how it is related to the environment and other systems.

THE SIGNIFICANCE OF SYSTEMS DESIGN
AT THE CURRENT STAGE OF SOCIETAL DEVELOPMENT

In the context of specific societal systems, the need to engage in the creative process of envisioning, imaging, and designing emerges from the realization that the cognitive map we are now using has ceased to represent or mirror the now-existing state of the society. It has become outdated. It no longer projects the true picture of the environment in which our system is embedded; therefore, it cannot and should not be used to guide our actions. Such self-reflective realization usually creates a great deal of anxiety and uncertainty. (The condition just described characterizes well the current educational predicament.) However, if channeled in a positive direction and guided by creating consciousness, such anxiety and uncertainty can become the genesis of the reconstruction of our cognitive map. This reconstructive process has utmost significance today. Let me explain.

When a new era develops in a society, a developmental gap opens up between the overall society and those societal systems that are still guided by the old design of an earlier society. Any attempt to adjust to new realities while still holding on to the old design brings about confusion. A case in point: Societal systems, such as our educational system, that still operate based on the outdated image of the industrial society of the bygone machine age are losing their viability. They operate in a continuous crisis mode unless they are prepared to re-create their image, redesign their systems, and transform themselves. The transformation of such systems means engaging in a three-pronged inquiry:

- RE-VISION their societal functions in view of their understanding of the characteristics and emerging features of the larger society that has gone through major changes and transformations.

- Develop CORE IDEAS for their systems that represent those changes and transformations, and create a new IMAGE that is compatible with the changed and changing society.

- Describe the new image and engage in the DESIGN of their future system based on the new image.

The new image and the new design that the designers of the system create will bring the system in harmony with the larger society and other systems in the society. The discussion above portrays a general transformation model of societal systems. In the context of the discussion in Chapter One, its applicability to the redesign of education should become obvious and transparent. The section that follows further elaborates the point made here.

EDUCATION AND THE SOCIETY: AN EMERGING CO-EVOLUTIONARY RELATIONSHIP

Education in any society is the reflection of the collective beliefs, aspirations, and cultural and ethical norms of its members. This reflection is articulated in terms of purposes, expectations, and propositions that define the content and the form of the educational experience. The beliefs, values, aspirations, and competence of society's members, on the other hand, are shaped by the educational experiences provided to them. Thus, education creates the future generation, and that creation is shaped by the society of that generation. We can say that EDUCATION AND THE SOCIETY ARE IN A CO-EVOLUTIONARY RELATIONSHIP.

There are times when an evolutionary imbalance exists between education and the society. Such is the case today. The education we offer reflects perceptions and practices based on the societal image of the industrial age.

An "image of man," as Markley and Harman (1982) noted, is a gestalt perception of humankind, both the individual and the collective, in relation to self, others, society, and the cosmos. The image that the current educational system represents is still grounded in the societal image of the industrial age. As a new stage emerges in societal evolution, as happened around the middle of this century, the continuing use of old images creates more problems than it solves. And this is precisely what characterizes the current educational scene. The present "crisis" driven reform efforts have been rooted in an outdated image. No wonder assessments of these efforts have found little or no improvement but often an intensification of the crisis.

On the other hand, when a new image leads socio-cultural evolution, it can exert—as Polak (1973) called it—a "magnetic pull" toward the future. As a society moves toward the realization of that image, and the various societal systems capture it, the congruence increases between the development of the society and the re-visioned societal systems, and internal consistency and harmony will prevail (Markley and Harman, 1982).

We desperately need a new image of education that is in congruence with and is reflective of the societal image of the current age. Only if such a state comes about will a co-evolutionary relationship between society and education be reestablished. If such an image can be created by our educational community, it will exert that "magnetic pull" which is needed to guide education into the nineties and beyond.

In the two previous sections, evolutionary and design thinking were introduced as constituents of the new thinking we need in education. In the next section, the third strand, the systems view is woven into our "new thinking."

III. THE SYSTEMS VIEW AND SYSTEMS THINKING

"We witness today another shift in ways of thinking: the shift toward rigorous but holistic theories. This means thinking in terms of facts and events in the context of wholes, forming integrated sets with their own properties and relationships. Looking at the world in terms of such sets of integrated relations constitutes the systems view." (Ervin Laszlo)

In the first part of this chapter we explored two salient aspects of "new thinking": evolutionary and design thinking, and wove these into an integrated strand of thought that has guided us to see the issue of school reform in a new light. Enlightened by this new thinking, education is now thrust into the very center of society's development and is seen as a key agent in the transformation of the society. To assume such a role, however, education itself has to be transformed and not merely reformed. The process by which this can be accomplished is the disciplined inquiry of design, a process by which we can create a new evolutionary image of education, develop a new design of a future system of education, and implement the design.

In this part, we weave a third strand into our "new thinking": Systems Thinking. As we speak of the design of an educational system that carries out societal functions, we can no longer use the term "system" loosely as we do in our daily lives. (Everything is a system today, thus the meaning of the term is trivialized.) Systems thinking will provide us with new insights into what the real meaning of a system is. It will empower us to approach educational reform with a new "mindset," from the perspective of a systems view of the world. From this perspective education is defined as:

> a deliberately constructed complex human activity system, operating at several system levels, embedded in and co-evolving with the larger society, interacting with other social service systems, and designed to carry out the specific societal function of nurturing learning and human development.

The above definition exemplifies the definition of any social system. What follows is a brief characterization of systems inquiry and its relevance to and application in education.

SYSTEMS INQUIRY

Over the last four or five decades, we have been faced with increasingly more complex and pressing problem situations, embedded in interconnected systems which operate in dynamically changing and turbulent environments. In addressing these problem situations and working with their relevant systems, we have learned to recognize the limitations of the perspectives, methods, and tools of traditional scientific orientation. This orientation reigned during the industrial age and was the genesis of its explosive machine technology. But it has been found less than useful in the context of the new era that emerged around the middle of this century. Thus, by necessity, a new kind of orientation, a new kind of scientific thinking, a new approach to disciplined inquiry have emerged: systems thinking and systems inquiry.

Systems inquiry has demonstrated its capability in dealing effectively with highly complex and large-scale problem situations. It has orchestrated the efforts of various disciplines within the framework of systems thinking. It has introduced systems approaches and methods to the analysis, design, development, evaluation, and management of systems of all kinds.

Systems inquiry has three interconnected aspects: systems theory, philosophy, and methodology. SYSTEMS THEORY pursues the scientific exploration and understanding of systems that exist in the various realms of experience, in order to arrive at a general theory of systems: an organized expression of sets of interrelated concepts and principles that apply to all systems.

In contrast to the reductionist, deterministic, and uni-directional cause-and-effect thinking of classical science, SYSTEMS PHILOSOPHY brings forth a reorganization of ways of thinking. It creates a new worldview, a new paradigm of perception and explanation, which is manifested in integration, holistic thinking, purpose-seeking, mutual causality, and process-focused inquiry.

Applying systems thinking and systems theory, SYSTEMS METHODOLOGY has developed approaches, strategies, and methods of analysis, design, and development in the context of complex systems. It has also developed approaches to and methods for the management and change of systems, and the management of problem situations.

THE APPLICATION OF SYSTEMS THINKING AND SYSTEMS INQUIRY

The need for the kind of thinking and inquiry introduced above is nowhere more obvious than in professions involved with studying and working with social and societal systems, such as systems of education and human development. In these systems the prevailing approach is usually dependent on the disparate methods and frameworks of a number of disciplines, resulting in unintegrated and incomplete understanding and descriptions. As already discussed in Chapter One, this is the approach that is still used in educational scholarship and practice.

SYSTEMS THINKING and SYSTEMS INQUIRY help us to understand the true nature of education as a complex and dynamic system that operates in ever-changing environments and interacts with a variety of other societal systems. The application of systems inquiry enables us to explore and describe (Banathy, 1988a):

- The embeddedness of education as it is nested in the community and the larger society. (From this exploration and description we can develop an understanding of the educational implications of the changes in the society, leading to a reformulation of the societal function of education.)

- The purposes and the boundaries of education systems as those emerge from an examination of the relationship and mutual interdependence of education and the society, and the exploration of interactions between the two.

- The nature of education as a purposeful and purpose-seeking complex open system, composed of interacting components woven into a pattern of multiple connectedness, and operating at various interdependent and integrated system levels. Here we are faced with three questions: (a) Given that education is organized at various system levels—such as the institutional, administrative, instructional, and the learning-experience levels—which of these levels is designated as the primary system level? (b) What or who is the key entity around which—and in response to which—we shall design the system? (c) How can we design a system that provides the variety of learning experiences required by the variety of its clients, the learners?

- The behavior of education as a living system, and the changes that are manifested in its functions, components, and interactions through time.

Systems thinking generates insights into ways of knowing and reasoning that empower us to pursue the kinds of inquiry described above and organize the findings of our inquiry in the form of comprehensive systems descriptions (models) of educational organizations and arrangements.

The generation of comprehensive systems descriptions or models of education is particularly significant as we contemplate the systems design of education. Such descriptions enable us to portray the system as it IS now, and then—as the outcome of design—describe the system as it SHOULD BE. Thus, having such descriptions, developed from the same systemic frame of reference, we shall be able to plan how to move from the current state to the desired (and described) future state. Next, I introduce an approach that enables us to portray educational systems.

THE USE OF SYSTEMS MODELS

Systems models are useful frames of reference within which we can examine and talk about societal systems that the models represent. Using the same frame of reference, we enhance communication among us. I constructed three models that represent systems concepts and principles pertinent to (a) systems-environment relationships, (b) the functions/structure of systems at a given moment in time, and (c) the behavior of systems through time (Banathy, 1973). These models are "lenses" that we can use to look at an educational organization, and understand, describe, and analyze it as a system. The three models are introduced next.

The use of the SYSTEMS-ENVIRONMENT lens enables us to take a BIRDS-EYE-VIEW, and describe an educational system in the contexts of the community and the larger society. We can define the "rules of the game" that govern systems-environment relationships, interactions, and mutual interdependence. A set of inquiries helps us to make an assessment of the environmental adequacy and responsiveness of the educational system and, conversely, the adequacy of the responsiveness of the environment toward the system.

The FUNCTIONS/STRUCTURE lens focuses on what the system IS at a given moment in time. It projects a "STILL PICTURE" image of the system. It enables us to describe (a) the goals of the system, (b) the functions it carries out to attain those goals, (c) the relational arrangement of those functions, (d) the components that engage in carrying out those functions, and (e) how those components are organized and integrated to constitute the structure of the system. The use of this lens produces a "snapshot" model of the educational system. Coupled with the model is a set of inquiries that probes into the functions/structure adequacy of the system.

The PROCESS/BEHAVIOR lens concentrates inquiry on what the education system DOES through time. It helps us to project a "MOTION PICTURE" image. It helps us to understand how the system behaves as a changing, dynamic societal system: How it (a) receives, screens/assesses, and processes input; (b) transforms input for use in the system; (c) engages in operations that attend to the purposes of the system and transforms the input into output; (d) assesses and processes the output; and (e) makes adjustments and changes, and, if needed, how it transforms itself, based on information (feedback) coming from within and from the environment. A set of inquiries helps users of this model to assess the process/behavioral adequacy of the system.

What is important to understand is that no single lens can provide us with a true representation of an educational organization as a system. Each lens portrays certain characteristics but not all we need to have to describe the whole system. Only if considered jointly, as if overlaid upon each other, do these lenses reveal the real story of education as a system. The three lenses will be used by designers as they present a description of the new system they have created.

CONSIDERING DIFFERENCES IN SYSTEM TYPES AND UNDERSTANDING THE UNIQUENESS OF SYSTEMS

Two of the most helpful insights that come from systems thinking are an understanding that there are DIFFERENT TYPES of systems and that each system is UNIQUE. While the uniqueness of individual systems is by now somewhat understood—"systems are not like machines"—an understanding of the uniqueness of systems suggests that the design of educational systems should be accomplished in each and every community. Each community is unique. Its uniqueness calls for a systems design of education that matches that uniqueness. A design that was created in community "A" cannot be transported into community "B."

An understanding of the notion of differences in systems types and its implications for educational inquiry is not yet appreciated by the educational community. Such understanding, however, is particularly important in systems design. There are several types of human activity systems (Banathy, 1988c). The types can be mapped on four continua, based on the degree of (a) their closed versus open nature, (b) their simplicity versus complexity, (c) their mechanistic versus systemic characteristics, and (d) the degree to which they are unitary or pluralistic in their purposes. The significance of system type in design is two-fold. First, designers should have a clear idea as to the type of system they wish to design. Second, they should select the design approach, method, and tools that are appropriate to the type of system they are designing. Next, four dimension pairs are introduced that enable us to differentiate five types of systems.

CLOSED refers to a system operating within well-defined and guarded boundaries, with limited and well-regulated interaction with the environment. OPEN does not mean complete openness and no boundaries, but a great deal of interaction and exchange between the system and its environment, coupled with flexible and fuzzy boundary conditions.

RESTRICTED indicates a system with few and clearly defined variables and few (usually not more than two) levels of decision making. COMPLEX indicates a system with a large number of variables and components, with multiple levels of embeddedness and decision making.

MECHANISTIC implies a system in which the parts are of primary significance, are stable, and operate in a fixed relationship. SYS-TEMIC indicates a dynamic relationship among the components of the system, where the interactions—and whatever emerges as a result of those interactions—are the most significant properties of the system.

UNITARY refers to a system having a clearly designated purpose or goal. PLURALISTIC indicates a system in which there is diversity or even conflict of purposes and goals.

Based on the above dimensions, five types of human activity systems can be differentiated: rigidly controlled, deterministic, purposive, heuristic, and purpose-seeking. The map of systems types is pictured in Figure 2.1 and a definition of the types is presented below the figure.

FIGURE 2.1. A MAP OF SYSTEM TYPES

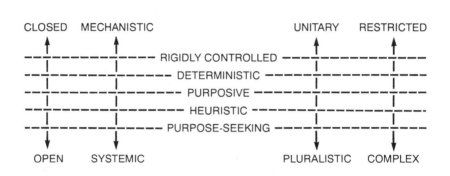

RIGIDLY CONTROLLED systems are rather CLOSED and have only limited and well-guarded interactions with their environment. These types are RESTRICTED, have few components, operate with a limited degree of freedom, are UNITARY (singleness of purpose), and behave MECHANISTICALLY. Examples: man-machine systems, assembly-line work groups.

DETERMINISTIC systems are MORE OPEN to their environment, they are UNITARY with clearly defined goals, with some degree of freedom in selecting ways and means of operating; thus they are less MECHANISTIC. They have several levels of decision making, thus they are more complex. Some minor changes may happen through time in components and their relationships. Examples: traditional bureaucracies, centralized (national) educational systems, small businesses.

PURPOSIVE systems are still UNITARY (have their goals set), but have freedom in the selection of operational objectives and methods. Their state changes are gradual, influenced by their environments, thus they are moderately OPEN. They have multi-level hierarchies (are COMPLEX and SYSTEMIC), and are controlled from top-down. Examples: corporations, industry, public service agencies, our current public education systems.

HEURISTIC systems formulate their own goals under some overall policy (are somewhat PLURALISTIC). They are OPEN to changes based on interaction with their environment. They are COMPLEX and SYSTEMIC in their functional/structural arrangements. Examples: corporations developing new ventures, R&D agencies, non-traditional (experimental) educational systems.

PURPOSE-SEEKING systems are ideal-seeking, guided by their vision of the future. They are OPEN and capable of co-evolving with the environment. They are COMPLEX and SYSTEMIC, define their own policies/purposes and are in constant search for new purposes and new niches in the environment. They are PLURALISTIC. Examples: corporations seeking societal service roles, communities seeking renewal by the integration of their systems, societies establishing regional integrated systems.

In designing new educational systems, the consideration of what system type is the most appropriate in our rapidly changing and transforming society is indeed a crucial issue. Most likely, designers will identify with either the heuristic or the purpose-seeking system type.

A COMPREHENSIVE SYSTEM OF INQUIRY

During the past two or three decades, we have applied systems thinking and systems inquiry in education and in other societal systems. As a result of those applications, we now have available to us approaches and methods that are capable of coping with—and responding to—the dynamic, open, and complex nature of education as a purpose-seeking human activity system. These approaches and methods empower us to carry out inquiry in four complementary domains of disciplined inquiry (Banathy, 1988d):

- The ANALYSIS and DESCRIPTION of educational systems, applying the three systems models described earlier.

- SYSTEMS DESIGN, design inquiry with the use of design models and methods, appropriate to the type of system we wish to create.

- IMPLEMENTATION of the design by SYSTEMS DEVELOPMENT and the INSTITUTIONALIZATION of the new system.

- SYSTEMS MANAGEMENT, the management of systems operations and change and issues management.

Figure 2.2 below depicts these four domains of organizational inquiry. In the center of the figure is an integrating cluster. This cluster articulates sets of core ideas, core values and beliefs, and organizing perspectives that collectively guide our inquiry.

FIGURE 2.2. A COMPREHENSIVE SYSTEM OF ORGANIZATIONAL INQUIRY

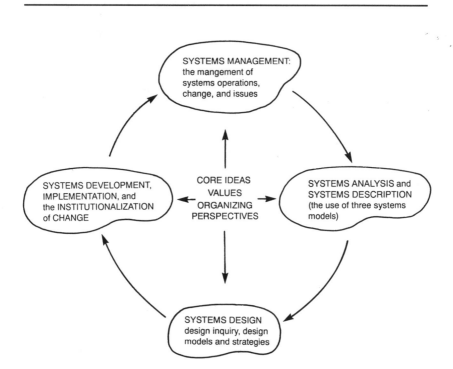

The figure shows how systems design "fits into" the overall context of organizational inquiry. The core ideas guide thinking about the substance of the inquiry. The four domains are in recursive relationship. The inquiry system depicted by the model is not yet manifested in the "mainstream" thinking and practice of the educational community. Nor is this kind of comprehensive inquiry yet part of our educational professional development programs. The lack of such programs and the lack of the use of the type of inquiry described here are shortcomings that offer a partial explanation for the inadequacy of the recent educational reform movement.

REFLECTIONS

In working in the vineyards of educational reform, it is singularly important that we make explicit to ourselves and others in our educational community the worldview and the frame of thinking that undergird the assumptions we are making about education, its societal function, its place in societal development, the way we view change, and the approaches we are using in bringing about change and reform.

In this chapter, I introduced an example of a frame of thinking. What I developed above, however, is just that, an example. The thinking portrayed in the example has worked well for me. I have found the three perspectives (the evolutionary, the design, and the system perspectives) to be internally consistent. Design is the intellectual technology for creating new images and designs for education that could be compatible with the images of the society that have recently emerged. The systems perspective is grounded in the new scientific paradigm of the emerging era of our society.

Chapter Three

CREATING IMAGES OF FUTURE EDUCATIONAL SYSTEMS

"Images of humankind which are dominant in a culture are of fundamental importance, because they underlie the ways in which the society shapes its institutions, educates its young, and goes about whatever it perceives its business to be."   (Markley and Harman)

INTRODUCTION

Changes in societal images are of particular importance today. Our society is now undergoing a transformation which is more profound, more intensive, and more dynamic than at any time in our history. This transformation is shaping—and is guided by—a societal image which is vastly different from the image of the industrial era. But our educational systems are still grounded in that earlier image. Discussing this predicament in Chapter One, we recognized that the use of the outdated image has created an ever-widening gap between the society and its educational systems. Unfortunately, this gap has yet to be recognized by the educational reform movement. The various improvement/restructuring efforts and recommendations still focus on the existing system which is based on the image and design of a bygone era. The reform movement has created the perception that we are faced with a "crisis of performance" in our schools, a crisis that places the "nation at risk." The insight we have gained from the first two chapters, however, suggests that the real source of the current crisis is a "crisis of perception"; it is an "image crisis."

The task of the previous chapters was to point out the peril of the continued use of the old image. It was suggested that the key challenge of the day is to bring about a perceptual shift, a paradigm shift in our "mindset." The challenge is to develop a "new way of thinking" about education and its societal function, and create a new image of education. In this chapter, we begin to describe the process by which such an image might be created. In the first part, we discuss the role of "image" in societal development and in the transformation of the society and highlight the significance of image-creation in education. In the second part, a framework is introduced which enables designers in our educational communities to create images of their very own, images that will guide them in the design of their new system.

I. THE NOTION AND ROLE OF IMAGE
IN SOCIETAL DEVELOPMENT

> *"The image not only makes society, society continually remakes the image."*
> (Kenneth E. Boulding)

Whenever we wish to study the notion of image, many of us go to Boulding's classic booklet: *The Image* (Boulding, 1956). Boulding's first proposition is that BEHAVIOR DEPENDS ON THE IMAGE. The behavior of designers of educational systems depends on the image they have about the societal function of education. That image will guide them in their design.

Boulding's second proposition is that our experiences provide us with messages which produce changes in our image. A majority of the messages do not bring about change. There are some, however, which call for adjustments or which lead to a clarification of what has been vague before. (This type of change in the image of education is the order of the day in the current reform movement.) However, when a message hits the nucleus of the image, "the whole thing changes in a quite radical way" (*ibid.*, p. 8). Images are resistant to change. Thus we often reject a message that challenges our prevailing image. If the message persists, we begin to have doubts. (Recently emerging insights in the educational community have led to questioning our currently used image.) "Then one day we receive a message which overthrows our previous image and we revise it completely" (*ibid.*, p. 9). The ambition of this work is to BE such a message.

Our images are rich and complex. Boulding classified their dimensions as spatial, temporal, relational, personal (the picture of the individual in the midst of the universe of his environment), value/valuation, and affectional/emotional. Modifiers of the image are conscious/unconscious/subconscious, certain/uncertain, clear/vague, having or not having "outside reality," and private or shared/public (*ibid.*, pp. 47 & 48). The prevailing image of education is not characterized on the dimensions described here. In fact it is rarely made explicit. In the recent reform literature the notion of the image of education is not considered, even though it is the image of the human being and humankind that guides our thinking and action. It is on account of this oversight that in this work the concept of image and its creation are placed up front in the design of educational systems. In creating a new image of education, designers will develop core ideas and core values about education and its societal functions that represent the kind of dimensions described above.

Our concern here is primarily the public image, the image that "makes" our contemporary society, the image that at the same time is shaped by the emerging and transforming society. It is important for us to understand the dynamics of this mutual shaping, inasmuch as the same will apply in creating a new image of education. That image IS shaped by the societal image, and the societal image IS shaped by education. Earlier we named this dynamic recursive shaping as co-evolution. This notion may sound at least novel, possibly even strange, to many in education who believe that the key function of education is the transmission of the message of the past. In most educational settings we travel toward the future by looking in the rearview mirror.

"The basic bond of any society, culture, subculture or organization is a PUBLIC IMAGE, that is, an image the essential characteristics of which are shared by the individuals participating in the group" (*ibid.*, p. 64). Much of the society's activity is concerned with the development and protection of its public image. In designing future systems of education, it will be up to the designers in communities everywhere to understand what the unfolding societal image is, what it means to them, and how a new image of education can be developed that both enfolds that image and shapes it.

A public image is invariably recorded in a transcript, which becomes both its referent and its manifestation. The method of constructing the transcript is the very method by which the emerging new image can be created. This transcript is what we called earlier the "cognitive map." The image (the cognitive map) is very much alive. It is confirmed, reconfirmed, questioned, modified, extended. It may be rejected and completely re-created. Its growth or remaking depends on our value structure and its change. This value structure guides the direction of its future development. Thus, in its developmental process "the factual and valuational images are inextricably entwined" (*ibid.*, p. 174). We shall see this entwinement manifested as we stipulate the core ideas and values that will be identified, selected, and integrated into the new image of education. These core values and ideas of the image constitute an inseparable (into its parts) system, an internally consistent and coherent whole. In a dynamically changing and transforming society, the image is shaped as a process of its continually ongoing (re)organization. Thus, the creation of the image is also ever ongoing. Consequently, the design of the system that represents the image is also continuous. The conventional social-planning approach of "we shall have another plan in five years" does not work anymore.

Markley and Harman (1982) reviewed the history of the relationship between the emergence of societal images and the various societal developmental stages. Their time/stage study shows that if an inherited image is used to guide development when a new stage emerges, it hinders and retards societal development (*ibid.*, p. 5). The continued use of the old image, in fact, will open up a developmental gap and will create more problems than it can solve. Such a gap between the inherited image of education and the newly emerged societal image was proposed earlier as the key predicament in education today. When a new image leads socio-cultural development, it provides direction for change and gives meaning and lends reinforcement to each movement toward the realization of the image. We are now in search of a new image that can guide education into the 21st century. This chapter offers a method of conducting that search.

SOURCES UTILIZED IN CREATING THE IMAGE

There is a variety of sources that designers can use in their quest to create an image of humankind and—based on it—an image of education. Designers will search for both "invariant" elements of an image as well as sources that will yield knowledge and insight that reveal important variants. The sources mentioned below are only EXAMPLES.

The continuously changing socio-cultural images seem to have at their very core an INVARIANT "perennial" image, which Huxley (1945) called the "Perennial Philosophy." This image contains universals that can be found in the traditional lore of various cultures as well as in advanced philosophy and in the primitive and the most advanced forms of religion. The central characteristics of this image include the notions of harmony, balance, and wholeness; the universe of consciousness: individual, collective, cosmic, and the divine; an awareness of the higher Self, the limitlessness of human potential, motivation toward development and creativity; the quest toward the realization of the higher Self; and being directed by higher consciousness that enables our participation in conscious evolution.

Churchman (1982) is concerned with future generations. He is outraged by the conditions that we have created for those generations by unleashing the destructive forces of military, technological, scientific, social, and ecological "pollutants." The key invariant value he identifies is "humanity within," which he considers not only an invariant, but also a sacred one. For him, "this implies a moral law with respect to future generations: we should undertake to design our societies and their environments so that the people of the future will be able to design their lives in ways that express their own humanity" (*ibid.*, p.21). This invariant is directly transferable as a key core idea and value in creating new images of education.

In a recent work (Banathy, 1989), I proposed nine dimensions that constitute an internally consistent and integrated guiding image for human and social development. Such an image should have

- a SOCIAL ACTION dimension, implemented by social justice, and an increase in cooperation and integration of our social systems;

- an ECONOMIC DIMENSION with a focus on economic justice and integrated and indigenous development;

- a MORAL dimension of strengthening self-realization, social, and ecological ethics;

- a WELLNESS dimension that nurtures the physical, mental, and spiritual well-being of the individual and the society;

- an EDUCATIONAL dimension of nurturing the full development of individuals and social groups;

- a SCIENTIFIC dimension mobilized for promoting human and social betterment;

- a TECHNOLOGICAL dimension of placing technology under the guidance of socio-cultural intelligence and human wisdom, and harvesting its potential for the nonviolent resolution of conflicts, and the improvement of the quality of life for all;

- an AESTHETIC dimension in pursuit of beauty, in cultural values, in the arts and humanities, and in the enrichment of the quality of our inner lives;

- a POLITICAL DIMENSION of self-determination, governance for peace development, global cooperation and integration, and for the improvement of human conditions.

The purposeful design of societal systems created from the interaction and integration of the above dimensions would provide a powerful agenda for the self-directed development of human systems.

The above section has provided EXAMPLES—and only examples—of sources and ideas that designers may consider as they establish a knowledge base for the identification of societal guiding images and for the creation of a new image of education. Beyond the knowledge-base sources, the primary source of their image creation will be an exploration of the characteristics of the larger society and the implication of those characteristics for the development of a new image and design for education. The methodology for exploring this source is introduced in the second part of this chapter, pages 47-55.

DYNAMICS AND STRATEGIES

There are two important dynamics that can facilitate the transformation of education that is required today. One is the growing espousal of a new image of humankind. The other is the development of progressive awareness of the unworkability of the industrial paradigm and societal image. The discourse offered heretofore aimed to activate these two dynamics and bring them into the awareness of the educational community. Equally useful to designers is a proposed strategy (Markley and Harman, 1982, pp. 195-199) that can guide the creation and transformation of an image. Applied to our current interest, the strategy suggests (a) promoting awareness of the unavoidability of transforming education, (b) the construction of a societal image that can guide the creation of a new image of education, (c) the fostering of experimentation with and tolerance for the exploration of alternative images, (d) the continual development and encouragement of a heightened awareness of collective/public responsibilities for involvement in both image creation and systems design, (e) the promotion of the exploration of our inner life as a source of inspiration and guidance, (f) the acceptance of control during the period of transformation into the new design, and (g) openness to the evaluation and change of the strategies used.

The creation of a new image of education cannot—and should not—be the prerogative of a "chosen few." The education of future generations is a collective responsibility; none of us can escape it. The creation of a guiding image and a new design for education is also a collective responsibility. It is the collective responsibility of people and social groups in each and every community. The strategies outlined above, or some others selected, are to guide the community's involvement. Such involvement may be initiated by a nucleus group, but it should reach into an ever-widening circle of the collective community.

II. A FRAMEWORK FOR CREATING A NEW IMAGE

> *"You see things as they are and ask: WHY? But I dream things that never were and ask: WHY NOT?"*   (George Bernard Shaw)

Staying within the frame of reference of the existing system and focusing on its problems hinders the RE-IMAGING of education. It presents a barrier to going beyond the boundaries of the system, exploring what is desired, creating a new image, and realizing that image by design. Re-visioning and creating a new image of education first and foremost require the breaking of old frames of reference about educational renewal and creating new frames of thinking. Rephrasing Bernard Shaw: rather than asking lots of questions about what is wrong with our existing system—which has been our main occupation in the course of the last decade—we should dream of kinds of education that never were and make the dream come true by design.

The new perspective that has emerged in the course of the present discourse holds that the educational community should do more than merely react to specific problems as they arise. It is not even enough to anticipate emerging trends and speculate about changing conditions in the community and the society. DESIGN IS FUTURE CREATING AND NOT FUTURE GUESSING. In education it means taking responsibility for designing systems of education that enable and empower future generations to direct their own lives and shape their own destiny.

In times of rapid changes and massive societal transformations we should DO more than maintain the status-quo and we should BE more than interpreters of what has been. We should take an active and creating role in societal development. After all, it is the education that we provide that defines the future by engendering and nurturing the beliefs, the values, the competence, and the behavior of future generations.

Image creation should be guided by questions that probe into the very essence of education: the relevance of its purposes, the learning content it offers and the way it offers it, its relationship to the society and, consequently, the designation of its societal functions, and the viability of its organizational forms and arrangements. The FRAMEWORK FOR CREATING IMAGES, introduced next, enables us to formulate SOME of those questions. It leads us to engage in the purposeful exploration of the boundaries of future systems of education. It helps us to consider new images that can be created, based on which new systems can be designed. At the same time, the use of the framework will dramatize the difference between current approaches to educational improvement and the systems design approach that enables us to create a new image and a new design.

DESCRIPTION OF THE FRAMEWORK

A framework for thinking about new educational images and exploring and creating options for their design is depicted in Figure 3.1 and is described in the rest of this chapter. The framework is constructed of three dimensions upon which we can project sets of core ideas and values of a new image. These three dimensions in their interaction constitute the context in which image options can be explored, and within which the selected core ideas and values can be synthesized. In the sections that follow I will (A) identify the dimensions of the framework, (B) characterize its potential uses, and (C) elaborate the constituents of each of the three dimensions.

A. THE DIMENSIONS OF THE FRAMEWORK

The dimensions of the framework and their constituents are described next.

1. The Dimension of the FOCUS OF THE INQUIRY.

The designation of the focus of the inquiry is the most salient dimension of the framework. It leads us to ask the following question: In the hierarchy of the systems complex of education, WHICH SYSTEM LEVEL IS IN FOCUS: the learning experience, instruction, administration, or governance? Or to ask it another way: Which level is designated as the PRIMARY LEVEL around which to design and build the entire systems complex?

2. The Dimension of Establishing Boundaries and Defining the SCOPE OF THE INQUIRY.

This dimension has four options. (a) The boundaries and the scope of the design inquiry can be limited by the boundaries of the existing system. (b) They can be broadened to consider certain issues in the environment. (c) They can be extended to include the entire com-

FIGURE 3.1. THE FRAMEWORK

Patterns That Connect:
Relationships Between
Educational Systems and
Other Organizations and Agencies

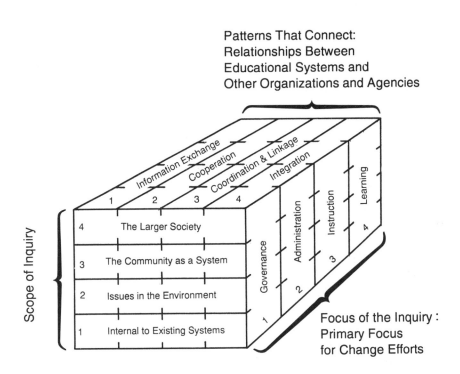

munity as the domain of design. (d) Finally, with the broadest scope and within the most extended boundaries, they may mark the larger society as the space of design.

3. The Dimension of PATTERNS THAT CONNECT.

Four types of interactions patterns may be considered as patterns that may connect the educational system with other societal systems that can offer situations and opportunities for learning and human development. These are (a) information exchange between the system and its environment, (b) cooperation with external systems, (c) coordination, or (d) integration with other societal systems in the community and beyond.

B. THE USES OF THE FRAMEWORK

The framework enables us to accomplish the following:

- Portray the image of the existing system as a "base-line" against which to design or from which to depart.

- Map the overall context within which to explore and create new images of education.

- Consider and create various alternatives to the existing image of education, by creating alternative images.

- Formulate criteria by which to select from the alternatives. (Criteria are formulated by considering the advantages and disadvantages of choices made of available options offered by the three dimensions and their constituents.)

- Select from the various alternatives the most promising alternative and describe it as the new image. Map the selected image into the framework. By so doing, we also define the boundaries of the system we intend to design.

C. A DESCRIPTION OF THE CONSTITUENTS OF THE THREE DIMENSIONS

The constituents of the three dimensions are described below in a way that makes transparent their implications for the creation of images.

1. The Constituents of the Dimension of the FOCUS OF THE INQUIRY and the PRIMACY OF SYSTEMS LEVEL are the learning experience, instruction, administration, and governance.

- If the LEARNING-EXPERIENCE LEVEL is in focus, the learner is designated as the key entity and occupies the nucleus of the systems complex of education. The primary system function is the facilitation of learning. The primary system level is the learning-experience level, around which, in response to which, and in support of which we design the other systems of the complex: the systems of instruction, administration, and governance. A learning-experience focused arrangement is rarely manifested today.

- If the INSTRUCTIONAL LEVEL is in focus, administration and governance are to provide policies and resources for its support. The instructional system defines the content and method of instruction, and students are called upon to respond to it.

This approach is the typical arrangement in higher educational institutions. Some recent restructuring efforts in public schools have proposed a realignment of instructional leadership, by shifting instructional authority to groups of teachers.

- If the ADMINISTRATION LEVEL is in focus it sets the goals of instruction, defines the instructional content and method, and provides directives for the use of resources. Governance sets broad policies and is called upon to secure needed resources. This arrangement is the most frequent in our public schools today.

- The GOVERNANCE LEVEL is in focus when the purpose of education is indoctrination and enculturation. Top decision makers (in the government or in religious institutions) define policies and regulations, and mandate uniform curriculum and instruction.

2. The Constituents of the Dimension of THE SCOPE OF THE INQUIRY. The order of the description of the constituents of the scope of inquiry indicates a move from a (very) limited scope and narrow boundaries toward an ever broader, widening, and extended scope and, consequently, enlarged boundaries.

- If the scope of inquiry is limited to the EXISTING SYSTEM of education, the inquiry stays within the boundaries of the current system and may explore issues surrounding management, organizational communication, instructional effectiveness, staff development, school climate, etc. This narrow scope is typical of current reform, with the goal of making the existing system more efficient or more effective.

- At the next level we broaden the scope and make some changes at the margin of the existing system, and extend the inquiry in order to CONSIDER ISSUES IN THE ENVIRONMENT to which education might respond. For example, the inquiry might focus on such problems as dropouts, drug abuse, teenage pregnancy, students at risk, economic competitiveness, etc.

- Next, the scope and the boundary of inquiry might be further extended into the entire COMMUNITY as the space of systems design. The involvement of a wide variety of societal systems, organizations, and agencies is explored that might provide resources, arrangements, and territories for learning.

- In the broadest scope, we extend our inquiry into the LARGER SOCIETY and re-vision education and guide the design inquiry based on our understanding of the evolving major societal changes and transformations. We seek not only to respond to these massive changes and transformations, but also to create a new image of education by asserting that education has a special and unique responsibility today to participate in shaping societal development.

3. The Constituents of the Dimension of PATTERNS OF INTER-ACTION. This dimension contemplates and maps various patterns of interaction between the educational system and other systems in the society.

- INFORMATION EXCHANGE implies the least amount of interaction. It projects exchange between the school and the community, by providing information to the community about the school and gathering information about the community for use by the school. Information might be developed about resources in the community that could supplement instruction. This pattern of interaction is the most frequent today.

- COOPERATION implies a pattern of interaction between the school and other societal institutions and agencies for the purpose of attending to complementary goals or sharing some resources. Participants in cooperative arrangements still maintain their autonomy but may enter into mutually advantageous relationships.

- COORDINATION implies inter-organizational linkage, and shared ownership of an educational enterprise which is mutually beneficial to the participants. It also implies giving up some autonomy and indicates longer-lasting commitments. Formal organizational arrangements are created for the accomplishment of shared goals of education and human development. In some isolated instances we have created programs that have engaged in this type of interaction (e.g., Experience-Based Career Education Program).

- INTEGRATION is the most intensive and the highest level of inter-organizational arrangement of creating systemic relationships. If integration were to be considered, the entity that we now call school might become a component of a community-wide system of learning and human development. Such a system would be designed from the integration of systems of the public and private sectors, community organizations, and various agencies that have the potential to offer resources and arrangements for learning and human development. Participating systems would integrate a portion of their resources and services into a new entity that would assume the responsibility for designing and carrying out the societal function of education and human development. As of today, we have not seen an example of such a community-wide integrated system.

IMPLICATIONS OF THE USE OF THE FRAMEWORK

Some generalizations can be made of the implications of the use of the framework, including the following:

- If the inquiry space is drawn on the framework so that the intent is to stay within the current boundaries of the system, then we cannot speak of creating an image and design different from those which now exist. We may be concerned with the improvement of the system, but not with the design of a new system.

- If the inquiry space is drawn so that an option or options are chosen that move out from the existing system to a different level of constituent(s) of one (or more) of the dimensions, then we are changing the boundaries of the system, and consequently we are engaging in the creation of a new image, and based on it, in the design of a new system.

- The further we move from the existing level of practice on any one—or more—of the levels of the constituents of the various dimensions, we create a need for an increasingly more extensive knowledge base for the image. We also extend the time frame and resources needed for design, increase the amount of design experimentation and testing, and invite more intensive involvement and participation of people in the system as well as the various clients and stakeholders of the system.

AN EXAMPLE OF SELECTING AN OPTION

Given the three-dimensional framework and the available choices offered by the constituents of the dimensions (as displayed in Figure 3.1), a variety of option configurations can be stipulated that define the image of a new educational system that we wish to design. Which one of the options we select will depend upon our worldview and our view of the society, coupled with our perspectives on the societal functions of education, and our core ideas and values about education and human development. An example is briefly outlined next.

A. A POSSIBLE OPTION, MAPPED IN THE FRAMEWORK

The EXAMPLE introduced here is grounded in an appreciation of the major societal transformation described in the first two chapters, and its implications for education as I understand them. In developing this particular option as an example of the use of the framework, the following choices have been made:

- On the dimension of FOCUS OF THE INQUIRY, the learning-experience level has been designated as the primary systems level around which the systems complex of education is built. Consequently, we shall require a much broader learning resources base than the current educational system utilizes.

- On the dimension of boundary and SCOPE OF INQUIRY, the overall societal context is the choice with the involvement of all societal systems that are relevant to education and that can offer resources for learning and human development.

- On the dimension of PATTERNS OF INTERACTION between the educational system and systems in its environment, coordination that moves toward the ideal of integration will apply.

B. IMAGE ELEMENTS OF THE OPTION

Given the above choices, their INTERACTIVE consideration leads me to propose a VERY LIMITED set of CORE IDEAS that are the key elements of my EXAMPLE—and only an example—of a possible new image.

- The image reflects focus on the learning-experience level with arrangements made in the environment of the learner by which the learner is enabled to fully realize his or her potential as an individual and as a participating and productive member of the society.

- Integrate the functions of nurturing learning and human development as synthesized components of a comprehensive educational system.

- The content of learning embraces all domains of human existence, including the socio-cultural, ethical, moral, spiritual, physical/mental well-being, economic/occupational, political, scientific/technological, and the aesthetic.

- Use a variety of learning approaches: self-directed, other-directed, individually supported group learning, cooperative team learning, and social and organizational learning.

- Use the large reservoir of learning resources and arrangements available throughout the community and the society by which to support and nurture learning and human development.

- Provide resources and arrangements for the lifelong learning and human development of all members of the community.

- Involve and integrate all those societal systems that cannot only offer resources, arrangements, and territories for learning but also are dedicated to human and societal development. Systems involved may include various social service agencies; systems aimed at the development of the physical, mental, and spiritual health of people; and the whole range of private, public, volunteer, and community agencies that will become partners in carrying out the societal functions of education and human development.

The "broad-stroke" picture painted above could represent findings of the first spiral of a multi-spiral process of creating an image. The first spiral may involve the exploration of many possible image configurations that can be created with the use of the framework. We might eliminate some based on the criteria we devised and go for a second spiral which explores fewer images but in more detail. Then, we can go for a third spiral that would explore in much more depth several images, until we develop confidence in selecting the most promising and most satisfying image.

REFLECTIONS

In this chapter I introduced the notion of IMAGE and its relevance to the design of education and presented a framework for the creation of new images of education. I suggested that the framework is useful for considering various image options. The framework enables us to draw some tentative boundaries of a system we aspire to design and implement. The ideas developed are also applicable for exploring the current system. The example provided for using the framework has demonstrated in a very introductory sense the creation of an image option. In the chapters that follow, the use of the framework is demonstrated in some detail.

PART TWO

EXPLORING
ALTERNATIVE IMAGES

A JOURNEY TO CREATE
THE IMAGE: THE SEEDS
OF THE FUTURE

"Journey toward the twenty-first century, the seeds of which already are planted and the ideas already are incubating," is "an odyssey and adventure..."   (John Sculley)

Part Two introduces strategies for creating an IMAGE that will guide the DESIGN of the future system of education. The framework introduced in Chapter Three provides the infrastructure of the journey. Using the framework designers will be able to consider design options and establish the boundaries of the inquiry.

In Chapter Four, a framework is introduced for the selection of the scope of inquiry. As an example, an approach is introduced by which the characteristics of the emerging society can be understood and their educational implications explored. Chapter Five offers a strategy for selecting the focus of systems design. Chapter Six explores the interaction among and the potential integration of all those sectors of the community that can offer arrangements and resources for learning and human development

The core values and core ideas that will emerge from the three chapters are organized in an IMAGE. An example of an image is presented in Chapter Seven.

Chapter Four

SELECTING THE SCOPE
OF THE INQUIRY

CHARACTERISTICS OF THE EMERGING SOCIETY
AND THEIR IMPLICATIONS FOR THE CREATION OF A
NEW IMAGE OF EDUCATION

History has accelerated, and "it will be the human mind that will notice this acceleration, give it a name, and transform those words into deeds."
(Vaclav Havel)

INTRODUCTION

Part Two of this book sets forth the application of the framework introduced in Chapter Three. Keeping faith with design thinking, we should start the creation of the image with the consideration and selection of the "scope of inquiry," which defines the larger CONTEXT of the future system of education and works back from it. In Chapter Two we discussed the vast acceleration of societal evolution and recognized that this acceleration has created a condition of continuing emergence and transformation that has made it difficult to "give a name" to what is emerging. In this chapter, a framework is offered that designers of educational systems might use to envision what is unfolding and "give a name to it." In Chapter Three, it was proposed that what we have to give a name to is the new "image" of the society. The educational implications of that image will be one of the bases for identifying core values and ideas—seeds of the future—that designers will use to forge a new design of education, and give a name to IT. Other core ideas and values will emerge from an exploration of the two additional dimensions of the framework, the focus of the inquiry and interaction with other societal systems.

In the first section of this chapter, the "scope of inquiry" dimension is discussed and the implications of what scope to consider are explored. In line with design thinking, the most inclusive scope, the overall societal context, is used to develop an example. A framework will be offered that designers can use to explore and understand the characteristics of the emerging new society. Examples of those characteristics are presented. Next, the educational implications of those characteristics are discussed, again only as examples. This discussion will lead to the consideration of the societal functions of education, and the formulation of sets of core ideas and values. These are offered as examples of what designers might define based on their exploration of the educational implications of the characteristics of emerged societal features. In systems design, these core ideas and values are considered "seeds of the future" and will constitute the key components of the new image of education. In conclusion, these core elements are presented.

I. THE DIMENSION OF THE SCOPE OF INQUIRY

Chapter Three presented the framework for exploring design options and drawing the boundaries of the design space. The scope of inquiry dimension offers four alternatives: staying within the existing system, exploring changes at the margin, selecting the community as the context of design, or extending the exploration into the larger society and painting the largest possible picture of education within the largest possible context. If the premises presented in Part One are accepted, then designers will be most likely to choose the larger society as their scope of inquiry. Accordingly, that scope is applied here for developing an example. It is emphasized, however, that this selection is just one of the options. Depending on the designers' perspectives, modes of thinking, and commitments, they might elect a different scope. Rationale for selecting the broadest scope is introduced next.

RATIONALE FOR SELECTING A BROAD SCOPE

In Chapter Two we embarked on a historical journey through societal evolution and explored the recently emerged evolutionary stage and transformation. We discovered the existence of a two pronged evolutionary gap. The first is a gap between our highly advanced technological intelligence and our socio-cultural intelligence and wisdom, which lag far behind and hinder our capability to give direction to technological developments. Only by closing this gap can we render a ripening wisdom that could address such multiple perils as (1) the arms race that is still gobbling up our scientific, financial, material, technological, and human resources; (2) the destruction of our natural resources by fouling our air, eroding the earth, and poisoning our soil and our water; and, (3) most significantly, the wasting of our human resources due to starvation and disease, and the wasting of mental and spiritual potential due to the lack of adequate systems of learning and human development. Only through collective human wisdom can we acquire the power to resolve these issues and harness technology's potential for the benefit of all mankind.

The second gap is equally perilous. In this age of global interdependency, our collective consciousness is still locked within national and racial boundaries. The fate of humankind depends upon our attaining global consciousness and forging a global system of the human community. Astrophysicist Eric Chaisson (1988, p. 472) suggests that "As the dominant species on planet Earth we must develop a global culture. We need to identify and embrace a form of planetary ethics that will guide our attitude and behavior toward what is good for ALL humankind. In short, humans must begin to acknowledge that we are first and foremost citizens of a planet, only secondarily of nationally sovereign countries with ever changing boundaries."

The exploration of these two predicaments has led us to recognize the conditions which must be present for the gaps to be closed. The nature of these conditions is such that they can be attained only by the acquisition of new kinds of competencies: new sets of sensitivities, knowledge, understanding, ways of thinking, skills, and dispositions (discussed in this chapter). Only their attainment will empower us individually and collectively to give direction to societal evolution by design. Thus, from this exploration has emerged a new and unique role for education, that of spearheading societal evolution. The requirement of closing the evolutionary gaps provides the initial rationale for selecting a broad, societal-based scope of inquiry for systems design.

The second component of the rationale comes from recognition of another gap, the gap between societal evolution and the evolution of education. The earlier discussion helped us to recognize a major pitfall plaguing current reform efforts. The genesis of this pitfall is to be found in the present practice of reform programs that limit the focus of inquiry to the existing system and proceed with improvements from within. This approach narrows the horizon of the inquiry and keeps it within the boundaries of the current system. Extrapolating from what now exists leads to "technical fixes" and improvements at the margin. An inside focus fails to capture the larger societal picture, which should be the source of informing the transformation of education in a transforming society.

In sharp contrast to the inside-focused approach, the scope of inquiry considered here represents a major shift in thinking about educational reform. The perspectives to be gained by a broad-scoped inquiry will produce rich new insights into the role of education in societal development and will indicate new kinds of competencies required in our current society. These perspectives are developed in this chapter as follows:

- Through an exploration of the CHARACTERISTICS of the EMERGENT FEATURES of our society.

- Through the examination of the EDUCATIONAL IMPLICA-TIONS of those characteristics that enable designers to:

  - (re-)formulate the SOCIETAL FUNCTIONS of educa-tion and explore implications for a NEW LEARNING AGENDA and

  - define CORE VALUES and CORE IDEAS that will make up the new image.

These strategies constitute the frontal set of systems design of education.

II. EXPLORING THE CHARACTERISTICS OF EMERGENT SOCIETAL FEATURES

This exploration will help us to gain insight into the kind of society that is now unfolding and which will constitute the overall context of education today and for years to come. The discussion that follows only hints at the process of this exploration. The examples provided as potential outcomes are merely indications of what insights and understanding might emerge if a comprehensive investigation is pursued. Such scrutiny will require significant investment in time and effort. Designers should determine the kinds of questions asked, establish the knowledge base required for those questions, and for-mulate their findings. Given the above caution and disclaimer, the general features of current major societal transformations are explored next, followed by a characterization of emerged specific societal features that mark the ongoing societal development.

GENERAL FEATURES OF SOCIETAL TRANSFORMATIONS

In seeking to understand the general features of societal transformations, first the work of some earlier scholars is examined. Reviewing previous transformations of Western civilization, Lewis Mumford (1956) noted that every transformation has rested on new metaphysical and ideological foundations and deep stirrings and intuitions, projecting a new picture of the cosmos and the nature of man. He proposed that today we stand on the brink of a new age, an age of renewal and self-transformation. A new world culture will bring about a fresh release of spiritual energy that will unveil new possibilities. Who can set bounds on man's emergence to his highest powers? he asks. Sorokin (1941), summarizing the crisis of our age, suggested that during the industrial age we went so far in the dominance of "sensate" values that we must swing back to a better balance between the inner-directed and outer-directed values. This involves change at the deepest level of our basic beliefs, a change in the DOMINANT PARADIGM. Toynbee (1947) also spoke of a possible transfiguration of the society into respiritualization.

More recent authors, such as Roszak (1977), Toffler (1980), Ferguson (1980), Curtis (1982), Capra (1982), Morgan (1986), Sculley (1987), Gleick (1987), and Naisbitt & Aburdene (1990), discuss different aspects of the common theme of massive and rapid changes in all aspects of our lives and characterize the transformation of the society. They suggest that this transformation surpasses all the earlier revolutionary changes in speed and intensity.

In GLOBAL MIND CHANGE, Willis Harman (1988) suggests that the problem situations and global dilemmas we face today will find their satisfactory resolution only through change in the dominant paradigm. Such a paradigm can emerge from a "search for wholeness, search for community and relationships, search for identity, search for meaning, and sense of empowerment" (*ibid.*, p. 118). It is suggested that these five elements are also dominant aspects of a new image of education.

CHARACTERISTICS OF EMERGED SOCIETAL FEATURES

Characteristics are explored here in two sections. First a set of key markers is introduced, presented in contrast with key markers of the industrial society. The stage is then set for the elaboration of emerged societal features, organized in salient categories, such as socio-cultural, socio-technical, socio-economic, scientific, and organizational.

A. KEY MARKERS IN CONTRAST

The system of societal characteristics introduced here is a construct, based on already emerged and still emerging features that are operating factors and forces effecting societal change and transformation. "Naming" this construct is a difficult task in that it has many dimensions. That is why we have so many different "labels" now in vogue. Depending on the orientation of the "namer," the current age has been called post-industrial, postmodern, the atomic or space age, the age of development, the information age, the knowledge age, the systems age, the age of design, the third wave, and sometimes the new age. Probably all these labels—and their sum—are on target. We still strive to "name" it. My own hopeful label for our emerging era is: the age of human wisdom. Chaisson (1987, p. 9) noted that today we are standing at the threshold of a future epoch that only we can bring about. "Indeed, if we act wisely, quite beyond merely intelligently, then an epoch of something resembling 'ethical evolution' should emerge as the next great evolutionary leap forward." What a challenge for education to nurture an ethical evolution and human wisdom!

The most comprehensive description of emergent features can be found in Daniel Bell's book (1976). He uses the label "post-industrial." A focus on PROCESSING with the use of intellectual technology distinguishes the post-industrial era from the industrial, which focused on FABRICATING with the use of machine technology, and from the pre-industrial period, which was primarily EXTRACTIVE. Bell's designation as "post" also indicates the TRANSITORY nature of our era. We continue to move toward a new society that we have yet to "name." Many of the characteristics introduced in the next section are discussed by Bell.

General characteristics that mark emerged societal features are displayed in Table 4.1. The categories include purpose and mode, power base, dominant paradigm, technologies, principal commodity, and the context of social consciousness. The characteristics of the current era are juxtaposed to those of the industrial age, in order to show contrast and, most significantly, discontinuity between the two periods. Even a cursory comparison shows that the characteristics of the current era cannot be derived and could not have been predicted from those of the industrial age. That is the very reason why we speak

TABLE 4.1. GENERAL CHARACTERISTICS

	INDUSTRIAL AGE	THE CURRENT ERA
PURPOSE AND MODE	PROCESSES ORGANIZED AROUND ENERGY FOR MATERIAL PRODUCTION	PROCESSES ORGANIZED AROUND INTELLECTUAL TECHNOLOGY FOR INFORMATION AND KNOWLEDGE DEVELOPMENT
POWER BASE	EXTENSION OF OUR PHYSICAL POWERS BY MACHINES	EXTENSION OF OUR COGNITIVE POWERS BY CYBERNETICS-SYSTEMS TECHNOLOGY (HI-TECH)
DOMINANT PARADIGM	NEWTONIAN CLASSICAL SCIENCE, DETERMINISTIC, REDUCTIONIST, SINGLE CAUSALITY, ORGANIZED SIMPLICITY	CYBERNETIC/SYSTEMS SCIENCE EMERGENCE, MUTUAL CAUSALITY, DYNAMIC COMPLEXITY, ECOLOGICAL ORIENTATION
TECHNOLOGIES	INVENTING, MANUFACTURING, FABRICATING, HEATING, ENGINEERING	GATHERING/ORGANIZING/ STORING INFORMATION, COMMUNICATING, NETWORKING, AND SYSTEM PLANNING AND DESIGN
PRINCIPAL COMMODITY	ENERGY, RAW AND PROCESSED MATERIALS, MACHINES, AND MANUFACTURED PRODUCTS	THEORETICAL KNOWLEDGE AND INFORMATION USED TO SUPPORT INNOVATION, DESIGN, POLICY FORMULATION, AND SERVICES
SOCIAL CONSCIOUSNESS	NATIONAL AND STATE	EMERGING GLOBAL CONSCIOUSNESS

of societal transformation and, consequently, the transformation of education.

Even a quick review of the information presented in the table will help us to realize how much of what we teach today reflects the characteristics of the industrial era. This will become more apparent as we elaborate the emerged features of the current era.

Stepping back from the specific features of the changed landscape depicted in the table, we can see a major shift from producing goods to generating information and knowledge. We see change in the modes of knowledge, from "empiricism and trial and error tinkering to theory and the codification of theoretical knowledge for directing innovation and the formulation of policy" (Bell, 1976, p. 487). The last item is directly relevant to our focus on directing educational reform and change by systems design.

Bell (*ibid.*, pp. XVI-XVIII) identified a set of currently emerged characteristics, including the centrality of theoretical knowledge, the creation of new intellectual technologies, the spread of the knowledge class, a change in the character of work, the central role of science, and the rise of cooperative strategy. All of these have major implications for education.

B. CHARACTERISTICS OF MAJOR DOMAINS OF TRANSFORMATION

The future is not what it used to be.

The purpose of exploring the characteristics of the current era is to understand their implications for education. The question that leads our investigation is: What are those characteristics of the emerged societal features that can guide us in creating a new image of education? The characteristics are examined in five domains: the socio-cultural, the socio-technical, the socio-economic, the scientific, and the organizational. The exploration of these domains will help us to gain new insights into the societal role of education, the kind of human being and social arrangements to be nurtured, and values that can guide societal development. This exploration will also define the most beneficial kind of learning and show directions we should consider in organizing systems for learning and human development.

1. Socio-Cultural Characteristics

Socio-cultural characteristics shape the unfolding appreciative system of the society and mark the emerging new image of human and societal quality. Examples of these characteristics are:

- The ethical dimension, which has three components: (a) self-realization ethics, which place the highest value on the development of the individual's potential; (b) social ethics, which strive to attain economic and social justice; and (c) ecological ethics, which emphasize the total community of life, and harmony between man and nature.

- The full development and nurturing of socio-cultural intelligence and human wisdom that will enable us to guide scientific and technological developments and advancement.

- The attainment of global consciousness and a world view that complements national consciousness and aims at the integration of all societal systems into a planetary alliance, while valuing, respecting, and nurturing cultural diversities.

- The search for balance and coordination of the various existential systems in which we live; including the social, the cultural, the economic, the intellectual, the scientific, the technological, the physical/mental/spiritual, the aesthetic, and the socio-political.

- The reconciliation of oppositions of the body-mind-spirit, autonomy and responsibility, cooperation-competition; and the search for a holistic perspective on life.

- The emergence of participatory democracy in a more knowledgeable and more active society, in which change is often initiated from below.

- The emergence of a communal society in which people are to be empowered with reconstructive, critical, and creative capabilities which enable them to overcome anxiety, a feeling of powerlessness, and alienation. They forge a common framework of values that can guide societal development.

- The dominance of integrative power in the distributions of the three "faces of power" (Boulding, 1989)—the destructive/threat, the productive/exchange, and the integrative/love. Integrative power "involves the capacity to build organizations, to create families and groups, to inspire loyalty, to bind people together, to develop legitimacy" (*ibid.*, p. 25).

The examples introduced above depict some of the characteristics of our socio-cultural existential system. Designers who wish to explore the larger societal picture will consider these kinds and many others, in order to define core ideas and core values that can guide them in creating new images of education.

2. Socio-Technical Characteristics

The "post-industrial" designation refers primarily to the socio-technical emergent features of the era. Bell (1976) selected this term to "underline a major axial principle, that of an intellectual technology." The post-industrial schema, he says, "refers to the socio-technical dimension of a society" (*ibid.*, pp. IX & X). Examples of key characteristics discussed by Bell follow.

- The strategic role of theoretical knowledge as the new basis of technological developments. Socio-technology is shaped by intellectual technology.

- Information and knowledge as social products. While industrial commodities are produced in discrete individual units, are bought as products, and are possessed by a buyer, information and knowledge—the key products of our age—can be shared by all. Their costs, values, and use are very different from those of industrial products.

- A focus on processing. While industrial technology focused on mechanical production, using energy and machine technology, the new technology is focusing on processing. With the new technology, the theory and practice of information and knowledge processing become dominant features, applying telecommunications and computers.

- The emergence of the "sociologizing" mode. While the industrial era focused on "economizing" as a distinctive feature of life, meaning the best allocation of scarce resources among competing ends, with the market mechanism as the arbiter of allocation, Bell suggests that in contrast, a "sociologizing" mode is focusing on an explicit conception of public interest, based on the idea of social and economic justice.

- A coming to understand the multiple consequences of technological applications, which are often manifested in potentially perilous effects upon sectors of the society and the environment.

- Digital information technologies: telecommunications, such as voice telephone, radio, television, facsimile; computer-based information networks make up the new infrastructure of the socio-technical society. This infrastructure is added now to the transportation and power-transmission infrastructures.

As designers contemplate the above socio-technical characteristics, they will most likely recognize the significant educational implications of both intellectual technology and the process focus of our age. Those characteristics have special meaning for what is learned, how it is learned, and how we should organize for learning and human development.

3. Socio-Economic Characteristics

The socio-economic domain is another component of the recently emerged era. The exploration of its characteristics is particularly significant in the current climate in which economic competitiveness is one of the key issues. It is rather unfortunate that the prevailing consideration of this issue is still grounded in the thinking and practices of the industrial society. Some examples of emerged characteristics are described next.

- Now that information and knowledge are the prominent features of the new economy, we recognize that their economics are not the same as those of material goods. The labor theory of value which dominated the industrial age is now replaced by the knowledge theory of value (Bell, 1976). Emphasis has shifted from goods to services. Services rendered in the form of transportation, utilities, finance, and commerce are surpassed by human services of health, education, social services, professional and technical services, research, evaluation, management services, etc.

- The switch from manual to cognitive activities created "discontinuity," with far-reaching social, cultural, economic, and political implications. Consequently, the ever-increasing "knowledge class" brought about a major shift in occupational distribution in which the scientific, professional, semi-professional, and technical fields now dominate.

- While in earlier times work was experienced in the context of nature (pre-industrial), and in the industrial age with machines, today workers have to learn how to work with each other (Bell, *ibid*). Maintaining relationships becomes the primary purpose of all social systems (Vickers, 1983).

- In the industrial society standards of living were marked by the quantity of goods possessed, while in today's society the quality of life is measured by "the services and amenities—health, education, recreation, and the arts—which are now deemed desirable and possible for everyone" (Bell, 1976, p. 127). It is the inner quality of life which is most important.

- The economics of marketing individual goods were dominated by competitive strategy. Today, as information and knowledge become the strategic resource of the society, a new economic strategy—cooperation—is required to increase the production, dissemination, and utilization of knowledge.

A review of the examples of emergent socio-economic characteristics described above indicates that each item has educational implications. Designers must identify these implications and others, because an understanding of emerged societal characteristics is a significant design task.

4. Characteristics of Scientific Inquiry

The scientific orientation that has emerged in the course of the last forty years has forged a new image and a new paradigm of disciplined inquiry. Some of the characteristics of this orientation are offered here as examples.

- Complementarity of the traditional scientific paradigm and the cybernetics/systems paradigm; the complementarity of analysis and synthesis, and reductionism and emergence. The emerged intellectual technology includes systems analysis, systems inquiry, systems design and development, and systems modeling.

- Selection of methodology that fits the system of interest and the situation; absence of dichotomy between the observer, the observed, and the context of observation; recognition of mutual causality, free will, intention, and purpose.

- An understanding of the "counter intuitive" nature of complex systems. Such systems involve too many variables for them to be seen simultaneously. Intuitive judgments seek immediate cause-and-effect relations which usually hold true only for simple and restricted systems. In complex systems, causes are mutually effected and deeply hidden.

- Participation in decision-oriented disciplined inquiry, which involves the client, the user, the decision maker, and those affected by the outcome of the inquiry.

- The critical element is process, which has brought about the integration of science and technology so that the problems and methods of science are also the problems and methods of technology.

- The employment of design inquiry in the context of human activity systems as "user-designers" assume a central role. Invention, the main activity of the industrial era, is replaced now by the knowledge and intellectual technology-based disciplined inquiry of systems design.

- Purpose, meaning, and ethical/moral considerations have a guiding role in disciplined inquiry. There is a search to establish a grand alliance of science, philosophy, and religion.

What is implied in the examples above is a need to entertain a whole new orientation in providing experiences in learning intellectual skills and methods of inquiry. At the same time, the type of understanding that will emerge from an exploration of the emergent characteristics of this domain will also guide designers in their own disciplined inquiry.

5. Organizational Characteristics

In describing examples of organizational characteristics, it will be useful again to contrast them with the characteristics of the industrial age (Huber, 1986).

- The amount, the variety, and the availability of knowledge —as well as its absolute growth—are significantly higher than in the previous era. Coping with this "knowledge explosion" requires organizations to effect a two-pronged, marked increase in (a) specialization and diversification and (b) integration and generalization.

- Complexity—as a property of organizations and their systemic interaction—is increasing. The more discrete the components of the environment, the greater the complexity of the system, requiring an increase in the amount of information the organization must process in considering actions and new designs in order to enhance environmental expectations and systemic effectiveness.

- In the current era, both the level of external and internal turbulence and uncertainty and their absolute growth have become significantly greater than in the previous era. The higher the turbulence and uncertainty, the higher the premium placed on organizational flexibility, the ability to learn as an organization, and to engage in continuous organizational design/redesign.

- Increase in the rate of change—a characteristic of the current era—increases the pressure on the organization to process information rapidly, distribute it to a larger number of groups, and transform it into organizational knowledge.

An understanding of the kinds of characteristics implied by the examples above will provide a knowledge base as designers contemplate requisite organizational characteristics of new educational systems.

*   *   *

Before we leave the review of emerged societal characteristics, it is appropriate to contemplate Bell's poetic thoughts in the concluding paragraphs of his book as a bridge to exploring the educational implications of those characteristics.

"For most of human history, REALITY WAS NATURE, and in poetry and imagination men sought to relate the self to the natural world. Then REALITY BECAME TECHNICS, tools and things made by man yet given an independent existence outside himself, a reified world. Now REALITY IS PRIMARILY THE SOCIAL WORLD— neither nature nor things, only men—experienced through reciprocal consciousness, a form of imagination to be realized as a social construction." "But what does not vanish is the duplex nature of man himself:

- The murderous aggression, from primal impulse, to tear apart and destroy; and

- The search for order, in art and in life, as the bending of will to harmonious shape.

"It is this ineradicable tension which defines the social world and which permits a view of Utopia that is perhaps more realistic than the here-and-now millennium on earth that modern man has sought. Utopia has always been conceived as a design of harmony and perfection in the relations between men. In the wisdom of the ancients, Utopia was a fruitful impossibility, a conception of the desirable which man should always strive to attain but which, in the nature of things, could not be achieved" (Bell, 1976, pp. 488-489).

Bell's observations lead us into considering the notion of ideal design. In designing new systems of learning and human development, nothing less than the ideal will mobilize our communities, nothing less than the ideal inspires creativity and imagination, nothing less than the ideal challenges the effort and commitment needed to pursue it through systems design. It is only the envisioning of an ideal educational image that will have the power to pull education into the 21st century.

The concept of the ideal systems design is at the very center of current design thinking and practice. It is this concept that is applied here. The ideal is out in front of us on the horizon and will be the guiding image toward which designers will move as they create their systems of learning and human development in which the ideal will come to life.

III. EXPLORING THE EDUCATIONAL IMPLICATIONS OF SOCIETAL CHARACTERISTICS

As we move on to consider strategies for exploring implications, the key question that designers will ask is: How can we capture from an understanding of emerged societal characteristics those features that will have implications for the societal function of education, for the kinds of learning indicated, and for the organization of education? From these implications ideas and values will emerge from which the new image can be created. The sections that follow introduce strategies for answering these questions and provide some examples as possible representations of the designers' explorations. Figure 4.1 portrays the exploration task of designers.

MARKING RELEVANT CHARACTERISTICS

The next task of designers is to review the knowledge base they created in the six domains pictured in Figure 4.1 and mark those

FIGURE 4.1. EXPLORING IMPLICATIONS

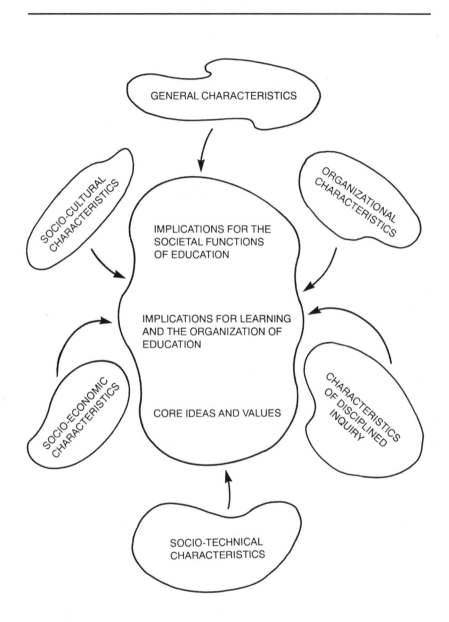

characteristics that have educational implications. In the process they will make judgments as to the degree of relevance of the items they have marked. Such marking will help them to judge the significance of implication of each and every item. Next they turn to considering the items in the center of the figure by asking such questions as : What are those characteristics that have implications for the societal function of education? What are those functions? What new capabilities are called for and, consequently, what new learnings should we provide? What are implications for how to organize new systems of learning and human development? From a synthesis of answers to these questions will emerge sets of core values and core ideas that will provide input to creating a new image of education.

A. EMERGING SOCIETAL FUNCTIONS OF EDUCATION

What follows are examples of societal functions that might emerge from an exploration of the educational implications of characteristics designers marked as significant. The relevance of each example introduced next should be challenged by designers.

Societal functions are of two kinds: those that are representing relationships between the society and education, and those related to learning and human development. The first three examples below represent the relational functions, the rest are relevant to learning and human development.

- ESTABLISHING CO-EVOLUTIONARY RELATIONSHIPS. The societal function of education is shifting from the interpretation of the past to an understanding of the evolution of the society and education's new role in the form of co-evolution with and mutual shaping of the society and even spearheading societal development.

- FORGING NEW KINDS OF RELATIONSHIPS WITH OTHER SOCIETAL SYSTEMS. To enable a balanced co-evolution, education should break out from its current isolation and create functional and mutually helpful and supportive relationships with other societal systems, primarily with those which also have functions of—or can make contributions to—nurturing learning and human development.

- FORGING RELATIONSHIPS WITH EDUCATIONAL SYSTEMS OF THE GLOBAL COMMUNITY. In discussing the existence of an evolutionary gap between national and global consciousness we called for the development of global awareness and consciousness as a major educational function. A fruitful way to attain this function is by establishing and nurturing relationships with educational systems of other countries and envisioning and implementing an agenda for global societal learning.

*   *   *

- NURTURING HUMAN POTENTIAL. Of all the resources on earth, the most valuable and the most wasted is the uniqueness of individuals and their collective societies. The function of education is to enable individuals and their societies to BECOME what they have the potential and aspiration to become.

- ENSURING THE FREEDOM AND RIGHT TO LEARN AND THE RIGHT TO KNOW. These should be among the most valued rights that a society can offer its members. Only if these rights are recognized can we expect the individual and society to achieve full self-development and self-determination. It is by learning that we acquire competence in managing our own lives and participating in the design of our systems. It is by free access to all relevant knowledge that we adequately inform our design.

- ADVANCING HUMAN QUALITY AND WISDOM. In the current stage of societal development the most significant contribution to enhancing societal evolution and enabling a better future for all is the advancement of human quality and wisdom and the development of socio-cultural intelligence that will guide science and technology and allow us to make wise choices and decisions individually and collectively.

- IMPROVING THE HUMAN CONDITION. Education is a force, second to none, for improving the human condition. It encourages and enables individuals and their systems to become the best they can become. The full development of our inner quality enriches our own lives, the lives of the systems to which we belong, and the life of the society.

It is a consideration of the examples described above—and others that designers formulate—that guides design.

B. AN EMERGING LEARNING AGENDA: THE "NEW WINE"

Earlier, the metaphor of "new wine in new wineskin" was introduced. The "new wine" in the context of our discussion stands for "new thinking" and "new learnings." In the previous chapters we recognized that in the context of overall societal development, major perceptual shifts and dramatic changes have evolved during the last decades, touching on all aspects of human affairs. Exploring the educational implications of these shifts and changes, we found that much of the learning we offer today is still grounded in the perceptions and practices of the bygone industrial age. In order to free education from the bondage of the past, a MAJOR SHIFT HAS TO TAKE PLACE not only in the way we perceive the role and function of education but also in the learning experiences we should offer. Designers should formulate a new learning agenda that enables the development and nurturing of those competences and qualities that are required of all of us individually and collectively. Here are some examples of the new agenda:

1. A Shift to Higher Order Learning Content

In general, the substance of learning provided can be classified as data, information, knowledge, understanding, and wisdom. These five constitute a hierarchy and convey a sense of increasing complexity and utility. The higher order embeds and makes use of all others below it. The learner acquires data, information, and knowledge by sensory perception and cognitive internalization. Understanding and wisdom, on the other hand, require experiential use of what has been acquired. According to an estimate, the distribution of the five types today is something like 40% data, 30% information, and 20% knowledge, leaving about 10% to understanding and wisdom.

In order to be able to close the gap between technological and socio-cultural intelligence, a major shift toward attaining more understanding and human wisdom is required. We should create learning that enhances critical thinking, the understanding of the self, the systems and the environments in which we live, and the situations we experience. We can nurture wisdom by creating learning resources and arrangements by which to relate knowledge acquired and understanding gained to pragmatic, moral, ethical, and affective issues. We can then apply wisdom in making judgments, managing problem situations, making decisions, and living out our lives enriched by our growing wisdom.

2. Developing Competence Called For in the Technological Age

In Chapter Two, we described the massive shift from the mechanistic industrial age to the post-industrial cybernetics age manifested in the trend away from "product" to "function" and "process." Biotechnology, laser technology, microelectronics, knowledge processing, robotics, and computer-driven design are just a few examples of new technologies that have the capacity to permeate all sectors of the society. These technologies require enormous changes in the kind of competence required to work and live today.

The systems of this new world are not of the "off shelf" type, characteristic of the industrial age. They have to be learned, experienced, mastered, and controlled. Their use calls for the capacity to insert new ideas into flexible systems. They require educated, sophisticated, open-minded, and creative people, able to cope with and direct new technologies. In turn, these requirements call for a new learning agenda, that focuses on learning PROCESS. It means, for example, learning the processes of knowledge production and utilization and the nurturing of innovation and creativity (Hutchins, 1990). Above all it means learning how to learn, an area to which we now only pay lip service.

3. Learning to Manage and Shape Change

Another new area of learning is called for by the ever-intensifying and dynamic changes that we confront. This implies a shift from what is called "maintenance learning" to "anticipatory and innovative learning" (Botkin, 1979). Maintenance learning involves the acquisition of fixed outlooks, methods and rules for dealing with known events and recurring situations. It promotes already existing ways of life and systemic arrangements. Maintenance learning is indispensable for the functioning of the society. But in times of turbulence, rapid change, and discontinuity—characteristics of our current era—such learning has to be complemented by another type: innovative/anticipatory or evolutionary learning, which is even more essential at the current stage of societal development (Banathy, 1987). Innovative learning enables us to develop the capability to face new and unexpected situations, and to shift from reactive adaptation to change to its purposeful direction and management. Such learning engages and nurtures our creative potential as we learn to envision alternative images of future systems, evaluate those alternatives, and realize the selected image by design. Learning how to conduct systems design becomes an essential part of the new learning agenda.

4. Acquiring Competence in Cooperation

In our current educational practices, competition is promoted and rewarded. Today, however, there is a new thrust in societal development toward cooperation. The educational implications of this thrust call for the nurturing of cooperation as a mode and method of learning (Johnson & Johnson, 1982) as well as the development of competence in cooperative interpersonal and group interactions (Banathy & Johnson, 1977). By acquiring ways of thinking, skills, and dispositions that promote cooperative behavior, we increase our capacity for entering into ever-extending human relationships, while concurrently developing competence in managing and resolving conflicts in a non-violent manner.

5. Competence in Systems Thinking and Action

The ever-increasing complexity and changing dynamics of our systems call for competence by which we can understand and manage complexity, cope with ambiguity and uncertainty, and grasp the connectedness and interdependence of the systems of which we are part. The acquisition of competence called for here requires learning to think systemically and applying systems thinking by learning to use systems approaches and methods. Through systems learning, we develop capability to relate functionally to the societal systems in which we are nested, attain a systems view of the world, and ultimately learn to appreciate the oneness of humanity and ascend to global consciousness.

The five domains of the new learning agenda are intrinsically interconnected. In their synergic interaction and interdependence they begin to exemplify a new system of learning programs: the new wine of the emerging new system of education. Learners will find learning in these five domains to be directly relevant to their concerns and useful in situations they confront in their daily lives. The five domains described here are only examples. Given the value system of the designing community and their aspirations for the future, other learnings should be identified and integrated into those provided here.

C. ORGANIZATIONAL IMPLICATIONS

This exploration constitutes the next task in systems design. Designers should review emerged organizational characteristics in order to identify their implications for organizing the system they design. A sample set of implications is described next.

Educational organizations should learn to:

- Interact with constantly changing (multiple) environments and coordinate with many other systems in their environment.

- Cope with constant change, uncertainty, and ambiguity and maintain their viability by co-evolving with their environment, by changing and transforming themselves and their environment.

- Live and deal creatively with change and welcome—and not just tolerate—complex and ambiguous situations.

- Become organizational learning systems, capable of differentiating between situations where maintaining the organization by adjustments and corrections is appropriate (single-loop learning) and those where changing and redesigning are called for (double-loop learning) (Argyris, 1982).

- Seek and find new purposes, carve out new niches in the environment, and develop increased capacity for self-reference, self-representation, self-correction, self-direction, self-organization, and self-renewal.

- Recognize that the continuing knowledge explosion requires a two-pronged increase in specialization and diversification AND integration and generalization.

- Increase the amount of information they can process, process it rapidly, distribute it to a larger number of groups and people, and transform the information into organizational knowledge.

The above examples of organizational capacities and learning are indicative (but not exhaustive) of the kinds of organizational learnings in which educational systems need to engage in order to become viable organizations with the capacity to coevolve with the larger society.

D. CORE VALUES AND CORE IDEAS

The first major task of the systems design of education is to forge an image that will guide the design of the system. This image is formed from core ideas and core values that designers have and which they develop as they explore the three dimensions of the framework introduced in Chapter Three. In this chapter we demonstrate how core values and ideas might emerge from an understanding of the educational implications of the characteristics of emerged societal features. In this closing portion of the chapter, sets of core values and core ideas are presented as examples.

1. Examples of Core Values

- There are two absolute values: the individual and the global system of humanity. (Arrangements of human activity systems between these two are socio-cultural inventions that should serve both. Systems of learning and human development are such arrangements.)

- The most valuable resources on earth are the uniqueness and the unique potential residing in the individual, in the family, and in our various societal systems.

- Among the highest-order values of human rights are the freedom and right to learn.

- The attainment of inner quality of life and its enrichment should be central in life's aspirations.

- High value should be placed on ethical, moral, and spiritual development and cultural diversity, while we aspire to articulate and live universal values.

- The increasing significance of maintaining interpersonal and social relationships as a key value in societal life, coupled with the value placed on cooperation.

- Of the three powers that govern societal life (Boulding, 1989), namely, threat (political/military), exchange (economic), and social (integrative), highest value is placed on integrative power.

- Among all the societal functions provided to individuals and collectively to the society, the nurturing of learning and human development is of the highest value.

The above set reflects my interpretation of values. Designers should develop their own set. In systems design it is imperative for designers to state their values explicitly and publicly. Values influence the choices and decisions made in the course of design.

2. Examples of Core Ideas

- Learning and human development are to be intrinsically inter-meshed and should not be (institutionally) separated. Thus, the content and the experience of learning and human development should be integrated.

- Systems of learning and human development are those agencies of the society that should nurture the physical, social, cultural, intellectual, emotional, spiritual, aesthetic, ethical, and moral development of individuals and groups.

- There are no limits to learning, and learning and human development never end.

- Systems of learning and human development are to provide arrangements, opportunities, and resources by which to nurture the uniqueness and develop the unique potential of the individual.

- The content of learning and human development should include knowledge, understanding, ways of thinking, skills, dispositions, and values.

- Societal evolution and characteristics of the current stage of evolution are primary sources in determining the content of learning and human development.

- There must be provisions made for learning competence that will empower individuals and societal groups to give direction to their evolution by design.

- Systems of learning and human development are evolutionary systems: they are to co-evolve with the larger society as well as spearhead societal evolution.

- Systems of learning and human development should develop the organizational capacity and human capability to engage in continuous organizational learning and design.

The core ideas and core values proposed above are examples, and are potential components of a larger set that will emerge as designers explore the focus of design inquiry and the scope of the learning territory. Core values influence core ideas. The core sets should be internally consistent. Furthermore, the value and idea sets should represent the consensus of all those involved in the design of a particular educational system.

REFLECTIONS

In this chapter, strategies for selecting the scope of design inquiry were introduced and examples were presented that demonstrated potential outcomes of the use of strategies. Of the alternatives offered by the framework the largest scope was selected as the one which is appropriate when there is a mismatch between the society and the education provided for the society. Characteristics of emerged societal features were examined and their implications for education explored. This exploration led to the formulation of examples of the societal functions of education, new learnings to be provided, and new organizational features to be attained. In conclusion, core ideas and core values were set forth as examples that can become components of a new image of new systems of learning and human development.

Chapter Five

THE FOCUS OF THE INQUIRY

"The human future can be sought nowhere else but within ourselves. What is needed is for all of us to learn how to stir up our dormant potential and use it from now on purposefully and intelligently."

(Aurelio Peccei)

INTRODUCTION

In Chapter Three a framework was introduced that designers can use to explore design options and draw the boundaries of their inquiry. Now, in Part Two the use of the framework is demonstrated. In the previous chapter the framework was applied in contemplating the scope of the inquiry. In this chapter the framework offers designers the opportunity to make what is considered to be the most crucial choice in design, the choice of the focus of the inquiry, the choice of the level around which to design the system. The framework offers four choices: the institutional, administrative, instructional, or learning-experience level.

In the first part of the chapter, the implications of selecting one of these levels are examined and, as a demonstration of a choice, the learning-experience level will be selected. This choice is compatible with the discussion presented in Part One and with the core ideas and values generated in Chapter Four. In the second part, a learning-focused educational system is characterized. Next, the practices of the current instructional focus are contrasted with the practices of a learning-focused program. In conclusion, core ideas and core values are generated.

I. A CHARACTERIZATION OF FOUR OPTIONS

The formalized manifestation of education is a systems complex operating at several levels. These levels and systems organized at these levels will be characterized first. Then, the rationale for considering a particular level as a primary level will be examined. This examination serves two purposes. First, it helps us to understand the significance of the difference between the current organization of education and organization around the learning-experience level. Second, it builds a bridge to the exploration of focus at the learning-experience level. This exploration will lead us in the second section of this part to the contemplation of systems of learning and human development which implement the primacy of the learning-experience level. The following is an adaptation of an earlier writing (Banathy, 1987).

THE SYSTEMS COMPLEX OF EDUCATION

The systems complex of education is portrayed here by pursuing a set of interrelated inquiries. The set includes the following elements:

- Clarify the levels at which the systems of education are organized and describe the systems operating at those levels.

- Designate the primary systems level in the hierarchy.

- Clarify the key systems entities around which the various systems are built.

- Specify the purposes of these systems.

- Specify the input and output of the systems.

- Designate control and decision-making authority at the various levels.

- Display the relationships among the various systems, and

- Define the degree to which the systems are closed/open.

There are four elements in the set above which are normative and are central to our present exploration. These are the issue of the designation of the primary systems level, the selection of the key entity, the defined purpose, and the degree to which the system is closed or open. Any change in these leads to a change in the very nature of the educational enterprise. Furthermore, as we shall see, these elements are interrelated and have a systemic effect on all the other elements.

In the current practice, the systems complex of education is organized at four levels. At the INSTITUTIONAL LEVEL the society interfaces and interacts with the administration of schools. The system at the ADMINISTRATIVE LEVEL implements decisions made at the institutional level, and manages resources that support the instructional level. The system at the INSTRUCTIONAL LEVEL attends to the functions of educating students. The LEARNING-EXPERIENCE LEVEL has recently come to the fore with the potential to become a full partner in the systems hierarchy of education.

The designation of the PRIMARY SYSTEMS LEVEL is probably the least understood aspect today, even though such designation is most crucial. Depending on which of the levels is selected as primary, several distinctively different "models" of education emerge, discussed in the next section.

The second significant point of inquiry is to designate clearly the KEY SYSTEMS ENTITY around which each of the systems is built. Often we fail to state explicitly who or what the key entity is, or else we view entities as being interchangeable among the various systems. Such lack of specificity has led to confusion and has hindered an understanding of problem situations in current reform efforts.

The four systems are to be characterized further by specifying their PURPOSE, their INPUT, and their OUTPUT. Here we should understand the relationship between purpose, input, and output. It has become clear to us, for example, that we cannot designate "attained learning" as a direct output at the instructional level, but only at the learning-experience level. The matter of who CONTROLS and who DECIDES at various systems levels must be made clear. The nature of RELATIONSHIPS among the various systems that constitute the systems complex of education is determined by the designation of the primary level and by the nature of intersystems relationships, which can be either subordinate, centralized, or egalitarian.

The degree of OPENNESS or CLOSEDNESS is another critical normative dimension. Contrary to the current rhetoric, the thrust in education has been toward isolating the school from its environment. This tendency has become a major source of the evolutionary gap between the society and education, as we saw it earlier. It has become a source of inefficiency, discontent, and dissatisfaction with the school and, consequently, it resulted in loss of support.

The elements of inquiry described above will be used next to characterize the four major models of organizational arrangements of education.

THE FOUR CONTRASTING MODELS

Depending on which level is selected as the primary one, four distinctively different organizational models of education can be identified. A display and discussion of these models, their underlying rationale, and their contrasting features will help us to see the LEARNER SYSTEMS in proper perspective and to recognize the necessity of organizing education around the learning-experience level. The characteristics of each model are described in a standard outline form.

A. THE INSTITUTIONAL LEVEL AS THE PRIMARY LEVEL

Organizing the educational systems COMPLEX around the institutional level (Model A) is the organizational construct (a) in societies where educational authority is centralized (e.g., a national system of education); (b) in cases where education is defined as part of a larger organization, such as a church; and (c) in traditional societies where the only or primary purpose of education is enculturation in the tradition of the society.

Model "A": Institutional Focus

THE GOVERNANCE LEVEL

Purpose: To enculturate, indoctrinate children and youth

Key Entity: National, societal, or organizational goals

Primary Decision-Maker: The educational authority: minister of education, religious or tribal authority

Input: Social definitions of needs and values, financial resources, laws, constraints, etc.

Output: Educational goals, organizational schemes, policies, standards, methods of operation, budgets

THE ADMINISTRATIVE LEVEL

Purpose: To establish regulations by which to implement input and account for resources

Key Entity: Information received as input and resources allocated to the system

Primary Decision-Maker: Educational administrators

Input: The output of the institutional level

Output: Guidelines, directives, doctrines, curriculum specifications, course materials, evaluation programs

THE INSTRUCTIONAL LEVEL

Purpose: To provide instruction as defined by the administration

Key Entity: The prescribed curriculum

Primary Decision-Maker: Department chairman, principal

Input: System output from the administrative level

Output: Specification of instructional arrangements, specification of instructional resources, organization of teaching staff

THE LEARNING-EXPERIENCE LEVEL (Classes of students)

Purpose: To respond to instruction

Key Entity: Instruction

Primary Decision-Maker: Teacher

Input: The output of the instructional level: instructional materials, aids, lesson plans, and tests

Output: Students passing courses, earning grades

Model "A" implies a system of education that is rather closed toward the learner in that decisions are being made far removed from him/her. The system complex is regulated by top decision-makers who affirm the purpose of enculturating and indoctrinating children and youth. The system is "top-down," "rigidly controlled," almost mechanistic (a reference to the five system types discussed in Chapter Two). Model "A" represents a uniform curriculum and instruction.

B. THE ADMINISTRATIVE LEVEL AS THE PRIMARY LEVEL

Public education in the U.S. is organized around the administrative level. This way of organizing the educational systems complex is displayed next as Model "B."

Model "B": Administrative Focus

THE GOVERNANCE LEVEL

   Purpose: To enculturate, educate children and youth

   Key Entity: Societal goals, community expectations

   Primary Decision-Maker: Board of Education or similar authority

   Input: Information on educational needs, community values, financial resources available to education, and constraints that limit operations

   Output: Stated educational goals, policies, organizational schemes, budgets, facilities

THE ADMINISTRATIVE LEVEL

   Purpose: The management of the operational system of education

   Key Entity: Information received as input and resources allocated to the system

   Primary Decision-Maker: Educational administrators

   Input: The output of the institutional level and information on the needs of the instructional level

   Output: Specification of educational programs, standards, materials, rules, and regulations

THE INSTRUCTIONAL LEVEL

   Purpose: To provide instruction in line with defined educational goals

   Key Entity: The prescribed curriculum

   Primary Decision-Maker: Department chairman, principal

   Input: The output of the administrative level, resources, facilities, and students

   Output: Specification of instructional experiences, instructional arrangements, scheduling, organization of teachers, staff, and students

THE LEARNING-EXPERIENCE LEVEL (Classes of Students)

Purpose: To respond to instruction

Key Entity: Instruction

Primary Decision-Maker: Teacher

Input: The output of the instructional level: lesson plans, materials, aids, tests

Output: Students passing courses, earning grades, advancement to next grade

Model "B" indicates a system that is more open than the one described as Model "A." It is more open to the immediate environment in which the school is embedded. But decision making is still quite removed from the learning-experience level. Model "B" can be characterized as a "deterministic" or bureaucratic system. This model allows for sharing in decision making between the two top levels of the hierarchy.

C. THE INSTRUCTIONAL LEVEL AS THE PRIMARY LEVEL

Organization of the educational systems complex around the instructional level can be found in education contexts where instructional systems approaches, aided by instructional technology, are used, and recently in "restructured" arrangements whereby a group of teachers is given authority/responsibility/resources to organize and conduct instructional programs.

Model "C" : Focus on Instruction

THE GOVERNANCE LEVEL

Purpose: To provide facilities and resources in support of the operating systems

Key Entity: Needs, requirements of the environment and their operating systems

Primary Decision-Maker: Managers, policymakers, boards

Input: Educational needs and community values, resource requirements of the instructional system, financial resources available

Output: General educational goals, allocation of resources in support of operating the instructional system, and policies regulating the use of resources

THE ADMINISTRATIVE LEVEL

Purpose: Given policies and resources, support the instructional level

Key Entity: Information relevant to educational expectations/requirements, institutional policies, and instructional system needs

Primary Decision-Maker: Administrators, school principals

Input: The output of the institutional level and requirements of the instructional system level

Output: Policies regulating the use of resources and specifying educational requirements

THE INSTRUCTIONAL LEVEL

Purpose: To provide instruction to students

Key Entity: Instructional goals and objectives

Primary Decision-Maker: Instructional manager, teacher team leader

Input: The output of the administrative level, instructional objectives, staff, facilities, students

Output: Instructional arrangements, instructional delivery systems, learning resources

THE LEARNING-EXPERIENCE LEVEL

Purpose: To optimize instructional arrangements

Key Entity: Instruction

Primary Decision-Maker: Teachers, teacher groups

Input: The output of the instructional level and implementation plans geared to specific instructional arrangements

Output: Students who can perform on specified instructional objectives

This model implies a system which is more open than those described previously—open to both external and internal influences. This system type can be defined as "purposive." Primary educational decisions are made at the middle level of the systems hierarchy, closer to the learner. Consequently, within a specific school, a variety of instructional systems and arrangements may be operationalized. Any given instructional system, however, is relatively closed in that it is designed against predetermined instructional objectives.

D. THE LEARNING-EXPERIENCE LEVEL AS THE PRIMARY LEVEL

We have had only limited experience with organizing education around the learning-experience level. The ancient tutorial approach of "sitting on the log," and some more recent innovative and alternative educational programs hint at the nature and potential of this type of program.

Model "D": Focus on Learning

THE GOVERNANCE LEVEL

> Purpose: To facilitate the availability of resources in support of the learning-experience level

> Key Entity: Societal expectations and the requirements of the instructional/learning system(s)

> Primary Decision-Maker: Educational policymakers and representatives of various societal-based resource systems

> Input: Society's educational needs and values, and requirements of the instructional/learning systems; financial resources and constraints

> Output: General educational goals, allocations of resources available to the instructional/learning system

THE ADMINISTRATIVE LEVEL

> Purpose: To formalize information about requirements for resources that facilitate learning and negotiate the use of those resources

> Key Entity: Instructional/learning resources, educational facilities

Primary Decision-Maker: Managers and administrators for financial and learning-resource acquisition and resource management

Input: The output of the governance level and the institutional learner levels.

Output: Policies regulating the involvement of various societal systems and the use of society's educational resources and overall educational requirements

THE INSTRUCTIONAL LEVEL

Purpose: To provide resources and arrangements that facilitate learning

Key Entity: Learner needs, objectives

Primary Decision-Maker: Managers of the learning resources and providers of those resources

Input: The output of the administrative level; information about learners' procedures, learners' requirements

Output: Information about the curriculum framework; instructional/learning resources and arrangements; organized, readily available resources

THE LEARNING-EXPERIENCE LEVEL (individual learners)

Purpose: To master learning tasks, to become competent

Key Entity: Information about desired learning outcomes

Primary Decision-Maker: Learners and learning-resource managers

Input: The output of the instructional level, learners' needs and objectives, specific plans for making use of instructional/learning resources

Output: Learning tasks mastered, progress toward becoming an individually and socially competent person

Model "D" projects systems of learning and human development which are open toward the learner. Broad-based societal sources are available, beyond the current boundaries of the school, that can support learning. Decisions relevant to the educational experience are made jointly by the learning-resources management personnel and by the learners. Thus, this type of system is "purpose-seeking." Furthermore, the boundaries of the learners' systems are extended into the various societal sectors that can provide opportunities, arrangements, and resources for learning.

IMPLICATIONS OF THE USE OF MODELS

The choice of which model to operationalize in a given societal context depends on several factors, some of which follow:

- The SOCIO-POLITICAL CONFIGURATION of the particular society. More open and enlightened societies will tend to move toward Model "D," which focuses on the learning-experience level. More closed, autocratic, and traditional societies have schools that are more uniform and prescriptive, like Model "A."

- The UNITARY VS. PLURALISTIC nature of the society. A pluralistic society will not be likely to support a uniform system of schooling like the one represented by Model "A."

- The PREVAILING CONCEPTION OF LEARNING AND THE LEARNER. If individual differences are recognized, if the learner is judged to be capable of making his or her own decisions, and if the thrust is to fully develop the individual and social potential of the learner, then Model "D" will be the direction toward which the organization of education will move.

Models "A," "B," and "C" are the most familiar to us. The model focused on learning experience, however, is much less known. Even though we often recognize the significance of Model "D," we do not yet have a clear idea of all the implications of a systems complex organized around the learning-experience level.

In the next section learning-focused education supported by the mobilization of societal resources is elaborated.

II. AN INITIAL IDEA OF A LEARNING-EXPERIENCE FOCUSED SYSTEM

In this part, organizing perspectives and requirements are reviewed that have emerged in an exploration of the learning-experience focused model. Then, these perspectives and requirements will guide the projection of a learning-experience focused system.

ORGANIZING PERSPECTIVES
AND SYSTEMS REQUIREMENTS

When contemplating systems built around the learning-experience level, we can be guided by certain organizing perspectives and requirements that include the following:

- The learner is the key entity and occupies the nucleus of the systems complex of education.

- The primary systems function is the facilitation of learning.

- The primary systems level is the learning-experience level, around which a systems complex is built.

- There is a large reservoir of learning resources in the society which can be defined, developed, and made available to support learning.

- Left to his or her own devices, the learner cannot attain easy access to these resources.

- Learning resources need to be identified, developed, and organized, and their availability communicated to and their use arranged for the learner.

- There is a wide array of learning types and models that has to be explored, selected, defined, and operationalized, such as self-directed, other-directed, socially supported, team learning, social learning, organizational learning.

An elaboration of the first five perspectives provides rationale for organizing systems complexes around the learning-experience level. The last two items present requirements that have to be transformed into the design of systems that can support learning and human development.

KEY PROPOSITIONS AND CONDITIONS

A consideration of the implications of the organizational models, and the organizing perspectives and requirements just described lead us to the following propositions:

- Recognize the learning-experience level as the primary level in the systems complex of education.

- Identify a new level—the societal level—that should be included as the fifth level at which education is organized.

- Define, as a major task, the design of systems that connect the learning-experience level with societal systems that have the potential to offer learning resources.

The realization of the above propositions leads to the establishment of some key conditions that designers should consider. These key conditions are described next.

- In addition to the institutional, administrative, instructional, and learning-experience levels, the societal level is recognized and established as an essential systems level of the complex. At this level we have systems with the potential to offer resources, opportunities, and arrangements for learning.

- The systems that operate at the institutional and administrative levels must be reconceptualized as systems that have the function of connecting societal systems offering learning resources, opportunities, and arrangements with systems operating at the learning-experience level.

- Systems at the instructional and learning-experience levels should be integrated and organized for connecting with those systems in the community that offer arrangements and resources that facilitate and support learning and human development.

From the above discussion the idea emerges of a new system operating within widely extended boundaries, drawing upon a much larger resource base than the conventional, school-based education. This idea is represented in Table 5.1.

TABLE 5.1. THE NEW LEVEL SCHEME

SOCIETAL LEVEL RESOURCE SYSTEMS	Various societal systems that have the potential to offer their resources for learning and human development
(Old Administrative Level)	Systems that have the tasks of identifying, developing, accessing, and administering learning resources
(Old Instructional Level)	Systems that provide information about learning resources, opportunities, situations; manage the use of resources and learning
LEARNING EXPERIENCE LEVEL	Learners' systems organized and in need of resources, arrangements, opportunities, and situations
GOVERNANCE LEVEL	Governing the systems complex described above

The notion of the learning-experience focused system complex will be introduced in Chapter Six as one of the rationales for the creation of a broad societal-based system of learning and human development.

III. THE OLD STORY VERSUS THE NEW

In order to demonstrate and dramatize the difference between the current school-based practice of education and the contemplated practice of the societal-based system, the two practices are juxtaposed in Table 5.2 as the "old story" vs. the "new story."

TABLE 5.2. INSTRUCTIONAL VS. LEARNING FOCUS

FOCUS ON INSTRUCTION: THE OLD STORY	FOCUS ON LEARNING: THE NEW STORY
Curriculum goals are established which guide the performance of the instructional staff.	A statement of learning outcomes tells what the learner will be able to do and know. This statement serves as a guide to the learner and to those assisting the learner.
A class of students is given assignments for completion either in school or at home.	Learners are involved in directing their own learning and evaluate their own progress. They participate in the selection of their learning tasks.
The student's age and time spent in school, and course and school grade completed are bases to determine progress and promotion.	The mastery of prerequisite capabilities is the only requirement for starting to work on a new learning task.
Students use textbooks as sources of information and instruction.	A set of alternative resources is available from which to select. Selection is made based on the progress of the learners, their needs, interests, and learning styles.
Subject matter is presented in a single mode through instruction. The teacher presents information to the class, and holds students responsible for completing the assigned work.	Different learning situations and different types of learning arrangements are available, including self-directed learning, guided learning, team learning, tutorial, and the use of technology.

TABLE 5.2.   CONTINUED

FOCUS ON INSTRUCTION: THE OLD STORY	FOCUS ON LEARNING: THE NEW STORY
A group of students sit in a class and listen and respond to the instructional program; the teacher is the actor on the instructional scene.	Learners are involved directly and intensively as actors on the learning stage. The teacher is involved in managing the learning environment.
Members of the class undergo the same experience both qualitatively (same kind of instruction) and quantitatively (same amount of time).	Learners are provided a variety of learning experiences from which to select. Time spent on a learning task may vary with individual students.
Students spend most of their time with 20 to 30 other students under the supervision of a teacher.	Learners are working in settings best suited for the attainment of the specific learning task: on their own, in the learning laboratory, at times in small groups, at times in larger groups.
The progress of the class is evaluated by the teacher.	The progress of learners is determined mainly by self- and group-evaluation and the guidance of the manager of learning. Learners assume increasingly more responsibility for their own learning.
The teacher rewards and admonishes students.	Above all, it is the learner who generates his/her own motivation for learning.
The achievement of students is measured by a prearranged schedule of tests.	The achievement of learners is measured at a time when they have acquired all the relevant capabilities needed for the mastery of learning tasks.

The two characterizations can be summed up as follows:

When instruction is in focus, the teacher is the actor on the instructional scene and the students, as a class, are the audience.

When learning is in focus, the learner is the actor and the teacher becomes the manager of learning resources.

The two characterizations present contrasting practices: the teaching-focused and the learning-focused practice. Figures 5.1 and 5.2 display the contrast.

FIGURE 5.1. TEACHING FOCUS   5.2. LEARNING FOCUS

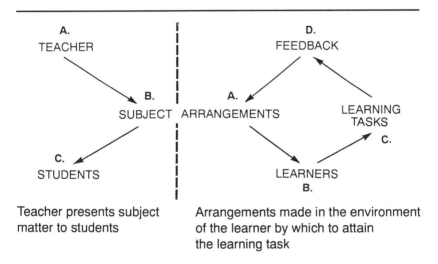

Teacher presents subject matter to students

Arrangements made in the environment of the learner by which to attain the learning task

5.1 WHEN TEACHING IS IN FOCUS, the environment is organized in order to enhance teaching. Teaching aids are used to support instruction. Students are expected to pay attention to the teacher. The size of the student group is usually limited by the size of the instructional space and the teacher's capability to control the group. Thus, when instruction is in focus, the key activity is: Teacher teaches subject matter.

5.2 WHEN LEARNING IS IN FOCUS, arrangements are made in the environment of the learner which communicate the learning task, and learning resources are made available to learners so that they can explore and master the learning tasks. Arrangements may include the selection and organization of content which represents the learning task; selection and organization of learning experiences by which

learners are confronted with the content; management and motivation of the learners; assessment of progress made; selection of components which take part in the arrangements; scheduling, etc. The
key activity in this mode is: Learner masters learning tasks.

Figure 5.1 represents the traditional, conventional instructional
mode, which still dominates in education today. However, whenever
we are seriously interested in helping students attain specific competencies, such as in athletics or team sports, we manage to operate
in a learning—or performance—centered mode.

Figure 5.2 appears to be an emerging pattern demonstrated in
"restructuring" projects or innovative programs. The significance of
instruction is not questioned here at all. The point made is that the
learning task should be the nucleus around which educational experience is to be designed. If learning were truly in focus today, no
one would set up classes with 30 to 40 students, for five to six periods
a day, within a rigidly set time schedule. Neither could one seriously
suggest that this many students can learn the same way during the
same amount of time, or for that matter learn much at all in such a
setting.

IV. CORE VALUES AND CORE IDEAS

Examples of values and ideas that support a learning-focused organization of education are introduced in this closing section of
Chapter Five.

CORE VALUES might include the following:

- The resources of the highest value are the uniqueness and the
  unique potential and creativity of the individual.

- The most profitable use of societal resources—the one which
  produces the highest value—is nurturing learning and human
  development.

- The full development of oneself is the greatest value that one
  can attain.

CORE IDEAS ABOUT THE LEARNER might include the
following:

- The individual has a basic desire to learn, to seek knowledge
  and understanding, and to become competent.

- The individual is capable of initiating, directing, and assuming increasingly more responsibility for learning.

- The individual's development is best facilitated if his or her uniqueness is recognized, respected, and nurtured.

- The individual's motivation is the most powerful facilitator of learning.

- The most potent satisfiers to the learner are discovering something new, gaining new insights, and acquiring new skills.

- Self-confidence develops in the learner as a result of successful exploration, mastery of learning tasks, and using the competence attained in real-life situations that are meaningful to the learner.

CORE IDEAS ABOUT LEARNING AND HUMAN DEVELOPMENT might include the following:

- Learners should assume the central position in education.

- Learning can flourish only in a climate in which caring relationships are created, and support and trust flow both ways between those who learn and those who foster learning. Nurturing builds confidence and encourages exploration; it creates openness for creativity and continuous learning and development.

- There are differences among learners, and these exist on many dimensions. Their acknowledgment and a respect for differences are essential in creating a climate for learning.

- Learning is enhanced when the learner becomes an active participant in planning and conducting arrangements for learning and evaluating learning attained.

The core ideas and values presented above will be considered in Chapter Seven, where a new image of education will be created and set forth as an example.

REFLECTIONS

The main contribution of this chapter to understanding the process of systems design was to highlight the crucial choice that designers will have to make as they consider the FOCUS of the INQUIRY. The four options of focus were described and their implications explored. Reflecting the "new thinking" discussed in Part One and the choice of scope of inquiry developed in Chapter Four, the learning-experience level was selected here as an example. Characteristics of learning-focused education were described and an initial and tentative description of a learning-focused system was presented. To further clarify the nature of learning-focused education, it was contrasted with the practices of instructional-focused systems. In conclusion, core values and core ideas that underlie the notion of learning-focused education were introduced.

Chapter Six

ORGANIZING SOCIETY'S RESOURCES FOR LEARNING

"Imagination is more important than knowledge."   (Albert Einstein)

INTRODUCTION

In Part Two a framework has been used that enables designers: (1) to explore design options, (2) to establish the boundaries of the design inquiry, and (3) generate core ideas and values which will constitute input to the creation of the IMAGE of the future system of learning and human development. In Chapter Four the scope of the inquiry was considered and in Chapter Five its focus was explored. In this chapter the four options of the third dimension—the dimension of the "patterns that connect"—provide the context within which designers make choices and determine connecting/integrating relationships and interactions between education as a system and other systems in the larger context of the community and the society. They will draw boundaries around the territory of learning and human development. Working with this dimension truly challenges the designers' creativity and imagination.

The framework displays four choices with respect to the types of interacting patterns that may connect educational systems with other societal systems that offer situations, resources, and opportunities for learning and human development. These are:

- INFORMATION EXCHANGE between the educational system and other societal systems.

- COOPERATION with other systems that enhances the carrying out of the societal function of education.

- COORDINATION that weaves education and other social and human service systems into interorganizational arrangements in order to provide coordinated services, and

- INTEGRATION of all social and human service systems into a community-based systems complex of education and human development.

Recent reform efforts have not gone beyond cooperation. Adjustments have been recommended and made at the margin by addressing specific social issues, such as students at risk, the disadvantaged, the disabled, the drug issue, teenage pregnancy, etc. But meaningful coordination and integration with other societal systems have not occurred. In this chapter the intent is to explore the COORDINATION and INTEGRATION alternatives and introduce examples of what would happen if the relationship and interaction between education and other societal systems were established and an extended learning territory were created and mapped out.

In the first part, a rationale is developed for a broad-based system that extends the boundaries of education into the community. The second part characterizes a societal-based system of learning and human development. In the third part, the model of such a system is presented as an example. In closing, the concept of a learning society is set forth and core values and ideas are proposed.

I. RATIONALE FOR CREATING A BROAD-BASED SYSTEM

A rationale for a broad-based system emerged from a consideration of the scope and the focus of the inquiry developed in the two previous chapters. From an exploration of the educational implications of the characteristics of the recent societal transformation, several core ideas called for the integration of the content and the societal context of learning and human development. Consequently, we envision the creation of a coordinated/integrative relationship between the educational function and other social and human service functions offered by a variety of social systems. In exploring a learning experience-focused education in Chapter Five, it was recognized that once we shift from an instructional focus to a learning experience focused education, we shall require a substantially extended scope and depth of learning resources that can be accessed only if we expand the learning territory into other societal systems. At the end of the chapter, an initial image of a societal-based system of learning and human development was presented.

The rationale for a broad-based conceptualization of education is supported by numerous observers and analysts in the fields of education and other human services. The "Nation at Risk" document suggested that education in the 21st century will fail if it continues to be limited to a single institution as it is today. Still, most recent reform efforts have maintained a narrow view of education and have ignored the interdependent nature of the workplace, schools, social service systems, and community institutions. The broader view of individual and collective competence that emerged from the previous chapters, as well as several current sources we reviewed in Part One, calls into question the capacity and capability of the existing system to carry out the educational functions required today.

There is an increasing recognition of the need for a broader-based arrangement for education and human development. Heath and McLaughlin (1987) reviewed current societal realities and suggested that the educational functions have been fundamentally altered, and that calls for a change in perspectives. They propose that a "broader view of the strategies and institutions necessary to social competence is required," and they draw attention to the learner as actor "in a larger societal system and to the institutional networks and resources present in that larger environment." They further suggest that "We can think of the school in a new way, as a nexus of institutions within this environment" (*ibid.*, p. 578). Other writers redefine the role of schooling from that of "deliverer" of educational services to "broker" of multiple services required for learning and human development (Hobbs, 1979; Smith & London, 1981; Zigler & Weiss, 1985).

Going beyond education and viewing all social and human development service functions, Schorr (1988) proposes that it is "within our reach" to create an integration of those services. She points out that as a rule in the human services field, "complex intertwined problems are sliced into manageable but trivial parts.... Evaluators assess the impact of narrowly defined services and miss powerful effects of a broad combination of interventions. Successes achieved by health centers, schools, and family service agencies have characteristics which form patterns that are rarely perceived" (*ibid.*, XVII-XVIII). Presenting compelling evidence of many success stories, she identifies the common patterns that indicate that those services are integrated, comprehensive, intensive, and flexible; are coherent, easy to use, and continuous; and adapt or circumvent traditional and bureaucratic limitations.

The brief review presented above is an indication of a major shift in perspective that has emerged from a realization of the changed landscape of the society. In the rest of the chapter, this new perspective and the new thinking introduced in Chapter Two form the conceptual texture from which the proposition for a new kind of system of learning and human development emerges.

II. THE SOCIETY AS THE LEARNING TERRITORY: A REINFORCEMENT OF THE RATIONALE

Education is more than schooling. The development of children and youth and the continuing development of adults are intertwined with opportunities available in all facets of life. Beyond the boundaries of the school, formal and informal resources and opportunities are offered or are available in a great variety of settings and ways: in the home; through various media; in peer, neighborhood, civic, and religious groups; through the community; through youth and cultural agencies; in the world of work and leisure, and in many everyday situations. These learning resources and opportunities have been fragmented and separated from each other, and have not yet been organized into a comprehensive and integrated system of learning and human development. It is one of the central postulates of a societal-based view that the linkage, coordination, and integration of these systems, through purposefully focused design, may generate benefits for learning and human development, well beyond what the fragmented use of those systems could produce (Banathy, 1980).

A powerful potential resides in the notion of an alliance of all societal sectors that can offer resources and arrangements for learning and human development. If formally constituted, such an alliance could identify, integrate, and energize the many systems in society that possess the vast reservoir of resources and opportunities needed today for the full development of the individual and the society. Based on the learning-focused image, introduced earlier, the proposition is that we can and should design a system of comprehensive social and human services for the nurturing and enhancing of human and societal potential.

In the broadest sense, education as a societal system is a collective integration of human activity systems that embrace all arrangements, resources, and opportunities that enable the learning and development of children and youth, and the continuous learning and development of adults through life. Viewed in such a broad sense, there are a large number of formal and informal societal systems, agencies, institutions, and societal sectors that—in addition to their own assigned functions—may also address the educational function. Let's take a look at these.

- The systems that are closest to the individual are informal in nature. These are the family, peer and friendship groups, the neighborhood, and others with whom the individual is in frequent and close contact. We call these PRIMARY SOCIAL GROUPS. They nurture individual and social development and have much to contribute to learning.

- There are a variety of FORMAL EDUCATIONAL systems, having the function and responsibility to offer instruction. (As we shall see later, however, their function is not coordinated with other systems of the society described here.)

- Next, social and youth organizations, religious institutions and various community, civic, and cultural groups—which we call COMMUNITY AGENCIES—offer a wide range of educational resources. Furthermore, several health and social service agencies are devoted to attending to HUMAN DEVELOPMENT FUNCTIONS.

- Another domain offering several sources of information and knowledge is COMMUNICATION SYSTEMS. These are the news media, TV and radio broadcasting, libraries, museums, and the many forms of art and science groups and exhibits. All these have the potential, and many even have the purpose, of offering opportunities and resources for learning.

- The OCCUPATIONAL AND WORK SYSTEMS are powerful domains that offer educational resources and opportunities by the very nature of their purpose and function. Beyond these, there is another large domain which includes life situations, social events, and recreational and leisure activities that may contribute to learning and human development. These could be called AD HOC LEARNING RESOURCES SYSTEMS.

All the above project an ever-expanding context of carrying out the societal functions of education and imply an ever-broadening resource potential for learning and human development (Banathy, 1980). Figure 6.1 displays an image of this broad-based potential,

FIGURE 6.1. SYSTEMS THAT CAN SERVE LEARNING

The learning territory

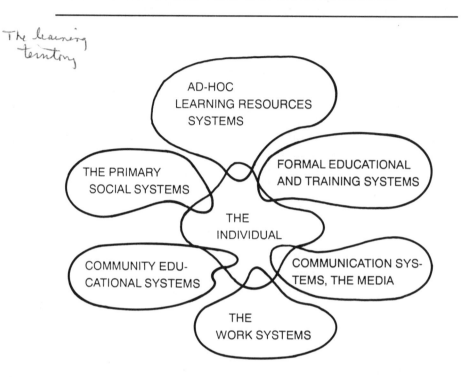

which, however, has yet to be understood, yet to be explored, and yet to be engaged by our formal educational institutions.

The systems portrayed in Figure 6.1 make up the broad resource base of an emerging systems complex of learning and human development. The function of this expanded systems complex is to explore, identify, develop, and integrate all resources and opportunities available in the society that can nurture learning and human development.

In the context of the proposition made above, at this point designers may consider two alternatives. One would place the educational functions in focus and look for other systems in the community and the larger society with which to coordinate in order to engage resources and opportunities for learning and human development. This option would encompass the wide range of involvement that was defined as the relationships dimension of the framework and implement the COORDINATING option. A more ambitious undertaking would enlarge the range of involvement into the INTEGRATION of all societal systems that are involved in social and human services.

In this chapter, the COORDINATING option is developed as an example, with the view that such can be a step toward the design and development of an INTEGRATED societal system of learning and human and social development. The inquiry introduced next explores the COORDINATING option. It intends to lead to an initial formulation of a coordinated system. This inquiry might include such questions as:

- What resources are or might be available in the various societal/community systems that can facilitate learning and human development?

- What arrangements could be made to discover and map out those resources?

- What are ways by which we can interrelate and integrate the various resource systems?

- What are the specific functions that the various resource systems can perform in offering resources and opportunities for learning?

- How can the resources offered by the various resource systems best be positioned for the use of the learner?

- What system can best integrate and manage those resources?

- How could the system be designed, developed, implemented, and maintained?

The system—the functions of which begin to take shape here —is referred to from here on as the New System. In the section that follows, as a contrast to the emerging idea of the New System, I shall review the current practice of carrying out the educational function.

A CHARACTERIZATION OF THE CURRENT SYSTEM

Today, schooling formalizes and claims the educational function as its autonomous domain (Banathy, 1980). Through all the years that schools have existed as institutions, the autonomous position has had an upper hand and succeeded in keeping schooling within well-defined boundaries that have isolated and separated what is within the system from what is outside it.

The physical boundaries mark the educational plant. Socio-cultural boundaries tell us what—and what kind of—people constitute the human population of the school and the values that people have about education. Legal boundaries refer to the laws and rules that regulate education. Geopolitical and economic boundaries define the geographic and political domains, the economic setting, and the financial support base. People who constitute the school—staff and the learners—become part of the school when they enter its doors. Resources that are used for teaching are housed within the school's boundaries. Occasional excursions into the environment are looked upon as extracurricular or supplementary. The school as instituted today is a rather closed system. The "breaks" in its boundaries are well guarded and protect its autonomy. Those who guard this autonomy feel that opening up the school to substantive involvement with other sectors of the society will disturb its "homeostasis," create complexity and "noise," and hinder program control.

In spite of this tendency for closure, some attempts have been made recently to create more openness. Whenever we have looked at education as a societal function in a broader sense, it usually has resulted in efforts to reach out into the environment in two possible ways. A more modest approach has attempted to relate the subject matter presented in school to real life, thereby allowing, even enabling, students to extend the application of their learning beyond the confines of the school. This approach at times has been coupled with bringing into the classroom representatives or representations from the outside. A more dynamic interaction with the environment has emerged, for example, through the career education movement, in the form of cooperation between the school and the various public and private sectors of the society.

An examination of the current system in the context of the four alternatives (information exchange, cooperation, coordination, integration) noted in this chapter, leads to the following characterization. The current system operates basically in the information exchange mode. Some efforts have been made in some settings to establish a cooperative relationship with other systems that can contribute to the educational function. The current configuration of schooling represents an autonomous social system having an instructional focus.

THE DESCRIPTION OF A "NEW SYSTEM"

In the course of considering and working with the ideas and propositions presented in the previous chapters, our journey toward

the systems design of education has led us into a clearer understanding of the societal function of education in the current age. It
has created a more focused image of the kinds of systems of learning
and human development that are required today; systems that have
the capacity to nurture the full development of individuals and engender in them the will, the competence, and the wisdom to give
direction to their life and participate in giving direction to the evolution of the systems to which they belong. The focus of our inquiry at
this point of our journey is guided by two questions: What systems can
be created that will have the capacity to fulfill the kind of educational
functions envisioned here? and What kind of thinking and strategies
can we propose that are adequate to the task of designing those
systems?

In the previous section, the society and the community within the
society were defined as the new territory for learning and human
development. This broad-based view guided us to look beyond the
existing boundaries of the school and seek to map out a widely
extended space for a New System that has a new set of functions and
components to carry out those functions. This system is to be designed
with the involvement of all those systems that can offer territories for
learning and human development, including various types of social
service systems, systems serving the physical, mental, and spiritual
health of people, and a whole range of public and private organizations and volunteer agencies. The key issue becomes how to connect
the learning-experience systems of learners with other systems that
can offer learning territories and resources for learning. With a
learning experience focus—as discussed in Chapter Five—the various
subsystems of the current educational system have to be drastically
redefined as to their functions. This "re-functioning" brings into focus
the idea of the total "transformation" of education. It implies the
"self-transcendence" of the current state, and its reorganization at a
higher level of complexity, namely, reorganizing education at the
societal level.

NEW BOUNDARIES, NEW TERRITORIES, NEW RESOURCES

In contrast with the current educational system, which operates
within tightly drawn boundaries, we envision a greatly expanded space
and boundaries for the New System. Even though legal, geopolitical
and financial support boundaries can be rather well defined, it appears that, at least initially, it will be somewhat difficult to delineate
some of the other boundaries. In many respects we may not be able

to clearly mark what is within the system and what is outside it. The New System will extend into domains that today are not considered part of the school. Two questions help us to establish new boundaries: What do we mean by territories for learning? and What do we mean by resources for learning?

A LEARNING TERRITORY is a location which can be specifically identified in terms of a site or sites at which people and other resources can provide direct support to learners in their learning experiences. The purpose to be served by a prearranged use of various territories is to (a) offer direct experiences in attaining learning tasks, (b) make learning relevant to the learner, (c) enable the learner to apply what is being learned in real life situations, (d) provide a context for learning that fits the learner's interests, abilities, and aspirations, and (e) bring learners in contact with people who not only are helpful, but who also might serve as role models. Learning territories are located in organizations and in a variety of systems and groups that have not been involved in educational functions. Therefore, a major task in designing the new system is the mapping out, enlisting, developing, and maintaining of learning territories.

LEARNING RESOURCES are of many kinds. Resources for learning are people: teachers, managers of learning, tutors, mentors, fellow students, learning teams, parents, and guides to the use of learning resources. Resources include texts, learning modules, other types of print materials, media publications and productions, software, interactive audio and video tapes and discs, hypertext, demonstrations and laboratory devices, exhibits, resource books, and any other types of materials and facilities that are designed or selected to support or provide for individual and group learning. Learning materials are constantly reviewed, modified if needed, improved, and extended in scope and detail in order to meet learners' requirements. They are catalogued, indexed, and housed at the learning resource center, at various designated locations functioning as learning territories, and in the learner's home. The key consideration is always accessibility and usefulness to learners. As we explore potential resource territories, we shall grasp and learn to appreciate the immensity of the universe of learning resources that can be tapped. The specific functions by which learning resources are acquired, developed, maintained, and used are described in the next section.

For the time being, let us replace the idea of boundaries as lines that can be drawn, that clearly define a space, with the notion of open and expanding learning resource territories that we can access in a planned way in order to identify, select, and organize resources for learning. Some territories will be more accessible, better developed and organized, and more facilitative of learning than others. The notion of "mapping" comes in handy here. Mapping may be continuously pursued so that larger and better learning resource territories and opportunities can be identified and incorporated. As new educational requirements emerge, new territories and new resources will have to be developed. Conversely, as new territories open up in the course of the continuous societal development, new learning resources can be identified in those new territories for the learners' use.

III. A TENTATIVE MODEL OF THE NEW SYSTEM

In a learning experience-focused system, the LEARNERS' SYSTEM is the key entity around which the system is built. It is supported by a great variety of learning resources. The use of those resources is planned and arranged by the RESOURCES, INFORMATION, PLANNING, AND ARRANGEMENT SYSTEM. Certain laws and policies that govern the arrangements and resources needed to carry out the educational function are attended by the GOVERNANCE SYSTEM, which also acquires and provides financial support to the system complex portrayed here. THE RESOURCE ACQUISITION AND CONTROL SYSTEM has the responsibility to acquire the learning resources, secure the learning territories, and coordinate with all those systems in the community that make available those resources. These systems make up the LEARNING TERRITORIES AND RESOURCES SYSTEMS. Thus, we can speak of a systems complex consisting of five integrated systems. This complex is pictured next in Figure 6.2.

Elaborating the general definition of the systems complex introduced above, the five component systems are characterized next by describing (a) the goal of the particular system, (b) its main functions, (c) its key entities, (d) its relationship with other systems, and (e) the position of the system within the systems complex.

The GOVERNANCE SYSTEM (A) is organized in a given community.

- Its overall GOAL is to ensure that each and every member of the community has easy and organized access to resources that nurture learning and human development.

FIGURE 6.2. THE NEW SYSTEMS COMPLEX

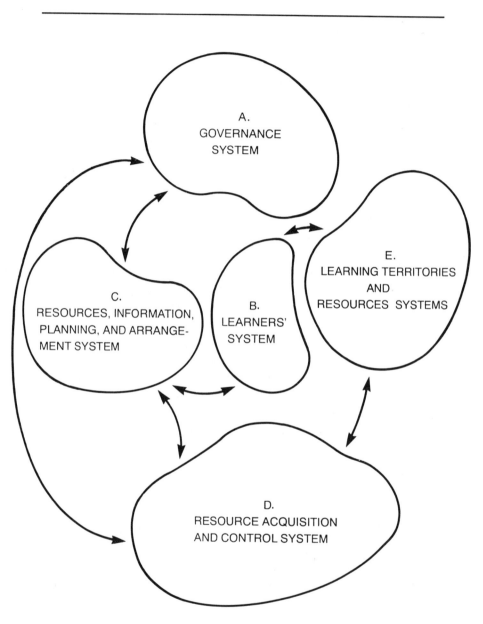

- The main FUNCTIONS of governance are to (a) establish and maintain institutional arrangements for the development, allocation, and use of learning resources available in the community, (b) create the financial and political bases needed to support those arrangements, (c) formulate policies that govern those arrangements and the use of financial resources, (d) monitor and manage the systems of the systems complex, and (e) interact with the community and the larger society.

- The KEY ENTITIES of this system are (a) institutionalized arrangements, (b) policies, (c) financial resources, and (d) the people in the system.

- A dynamic RELATIONSHIP exists between the Governance System (A) and all other systems of the complex. This relationship is direct with the Resource Acquisition and Control System (D) and the Resources, Information, Planning, and Arrangement System (C). These two systems receive their financial support and guidance directly from Governance. Governance provides guidance and support to the Learners' System through System (C), and to the Learning Territories and Resource Systems (E) through System (D).

- The POSITION of Governance (A) is one level removed from the Learners' System. But whatever it does is targeted to serve and support the learning experience.

THE LEARNERS' SYSTEM (B)

- The GOAL of the learner is to acquire knowledge, understanding, and competence; develop attitudes, values, and sensitivities; and through all these develop his/her full potential.

- The central FUNCTION of the Learners' System is to facilitate and enable learning and nurture the development of the learner. Component functions include (a) setting goals and preparing for learning, (b) planning and designing the learning program in cooperation with System (C), (c) engaging in the use of learning resources, (d) mastering learning tasks, and (e) participating in evaluating the mastery of tasks.

- The KEY ENTITY of the Learners' System, as well as the entire systems complex, is the learner.

- The RELATIONSHIP between the Learners' System (B) and the Resources, Information, Planning, and Arrangement System (C), and the Learning Territories and Resources Systems (E) is direct in the mode of continuing interaction. These systems are integrated and cannot be separated.

- The POSITION of the Learners' System is central in the systems complex. Other systems are coordinated with it and serve it.

LEARNING RESOURCES, INFORMATION, PLANNING, AND ARRANGEMENT SYSTEM (C)

- The GOAL of this system is to respond to the learner's requirements and facilitate learning by the arrangement of the use of resources, opportunities, and situations that are available in the Learning Territories and Resources Systems (E).

- The main FUNCTIONS of the system are to (a) develop a curriculum plan and instructional/learning arrangements and approaches that have the potential to assist the learner; (b) identify, plan, and arrange the use of resources that have the potential to provide for the learner's mastery of learning tasks; (c) display information to the learner about (a) and (b) and assist the learner in the use of resources; (d) monitor the learner's use of resources; and (e) advise the learner and provide information on progress made.

- The KEY ENTITIES of this system are (a) information and guidance provided to the learner and (b) the manager(s) of this system.

- The RELATIONSHIP of this system with the Learners' System (B), the Resource Acquisition and Control System (D), and the Governance System (A) is direct and continuous interaction. Relationship with the Learning Territories and Resources Systems (E) is maintained through the Resource Acquisition and Control System (D).

- The POSITION of this system is central between the Learners' System (B), the Learning Resources Acquisition System (D), and Governance (A).

THE RESOURCE ACQUISITION AND CONTROL
SYSTEM (D)

This system interfaces with the various societal systems that have the potential to provide learning resources and opportunities.

- Its GOALS are (a) to arrange for the identification and operational use of learning resources and (b) to oversee adherence to policies that govern the use of those resources.

- The main FUNCTIONS of this system are to (a) register learning resources requirements coming from system (C); (b) continuously explore, map, and develop resources and resource territories; (c) ensure the availability of resources for use by learners; (d) monitor the use of resources; (e) manage the use of resources; and (f) maintain communication/relationship with the resources systems.

- The KEY ENTITIES of this system are (a) learning territories and resources, (b) policies and regulations governing the use of resources, and (c) the managers of this system.

- The RELATIONSHIP of this system to Governance (A), to the Learning Territories and Resources Systems (E), and to the Resources Information, Planning, and Arrangement System (C) is direct and continuous representation, interaction, and coordination.

- The POSITION of this system is central between the Learning Territories and Resources Systems (E) and the Resources Information, Planning, and Arrangement System (C).

THE LEARNING TERRITORIES AND RESOURCES
SYSTEMS (E)

These systems are the most salient partners of the learner in the New System. As systems of potential learning resources, they include people, materials, arrangements, situations, and opportunities for learning and human development.

- The GOAL of these systems is to provide means and methods by which to facilitate learning and human development.

- The main FUNCTION is to display, maintain, and provide access to the learning resources.

- The KEY ENTITIES of these systems include (a) the resources they offer, and (b) the arrangements through which the resources are provided.

- The RELATIONSHIP of these systems is direct and accommodating to the Learners' System (B) and coordinated with the Resource Acquisition and Control System (D).

In Appendix C an example is presented of a community-wide resource-based educational system.

IV. THE IDEA OF A LEARNING SOCIETY

The concept of the societal learning system introduced in this chapter has its roots far back in history in the Greek idea of PAIDEIA. In the Athenian society, all institutions functioned to promote learning in its broadest possible definition. Hutchins (1968) elaborated the same idea as the "Learning Society," a society in which learning, fulfillment, and becoming truly human are the primary goals. In the Athenian culture, educational arrangements became the organizing framework of the society. "Paideia was education looked upon as lifelong transformation of the human personality, in which every aspect of life plays a part" (Harman, 1988, p. 147). Paideia aimed at the attainment of the wholeness of the human being. This notion was developed earlier in Part One, suggesting that education should embrace all domains of the human existential experience, including the cultural, social, ethical, physical, mental, spiritual, economic, scientific and technological, aesthetic and political (Banathy, 1989).

CORE IDEAS AND VALUES

- The core idea that has emerged in this chapter can be best represented by the notion of creating a system that will organize society's resources for societal learning, thus creating a LEARNING SOCIETY. Others relevant to the creation of a new image include the following:

- Learning should be valued as the means by which we can become truly human and reach our full potential.

- Arrangements for learning and human development should be intrinsically intermeshed and mutually supportive.

- We have available a large yet untapped resource base for learning and human development, residing in many systems of the community and the larger society.

- The power and the potential of social and human services will dramatically increase by the integration of the various systems that provide for those services and by the design of a comprehensive system of learning and human development.

The core ideas and values described above are presented as examples of a possibly much larger set that designers might consider. The set described here will provide input into the new image of education introduced in the next chapter.

REFLECTIONS

In this chapter we explored options that designers will consider as they explore various possible patterns that may connect the educational function of the society with other social and human service functions. The option selected as an example projected the creation of a system which links up various social service systems with educational systems into an interorganizational coordinated arrangement and makes use of society's resources for learning and human development. This arrangement is a major step toward the creation of a LEARNING SOCIETY.

Chapter Seven

CREATING THE IMAGE: AN EXAMPLE

"A young nation is confronted with a challenge for which it finds a successful response. It then grows and prospers. But as time passes the nature of the challenge changes. And if a nation continues to make the same once successful response for the new challenge, it inevitably suffers a decline and eventual failure." (Arnold Toynbee)

INTRODUCTION

Systems design creates a normative description, a representation or model of a future system. This creation is grounded in the designers' vision, ideas, and aspirations regarding what that future system should be. In Part Two a framework was introduced for considering design options and drawing the boundaries of the design inquiry. Strategies were outlined and examples presented for the use of the framework. Examples included sets of core values and core ideas to be used in creating the image. Once the designers finish using the framework and clarify collectively their core values and core ideas, they are ready to move on toward the creation of their image of the new systems of learning and human development. In the course of their design work, designers have by now realized—as has been said in the present work repeatedly—that the existing system of education is based on a very outdated image. The quotation from Toynbee makes this point elegantly. At the end of the twentieth century, we face a new challenge of a new era. This challenge requires a new educational response. It requires a new image and a new system of education, very different from what we now have. In this chapter an approach for creating this new image is described. The approach has three component strategies:

- Creating a VISION, the grand ideal, with its underlying value system (which is to be generated from the CORE VALUES).

- Synthesizing the CORE IDEAS into systems that elaborate the vision and guide the creation of the image.

- Creating the IMAGE based on the vision, on the core values and core ideas, and proceeding with the design of the system that will bring the image into reality.

In Chapter Seven a description is provided of the approach described above and an example of an image is presented.

I. CREATING A VISION

"Where there is no vision, the people perish."   (*Proverbs, XXIX. 18.*)

"Vision" is defined in the dictionary (Webster, 1979) as an act or power of seeing, an act or power of imagination, a revelation, an object of imagination, an unusual discernment or foresight. All of the above are relevant to what designers are called upon to do at this point. The manifestation of their vision may take a variety of forms. It can be presented as a metaphor, as an event foreseen, as a visual representation, or as a linguistic description. The issue that designers face now is how best to present the GRAND IDEA, the IDEAL of the society that education serves as well as the grand idea of the future system of education. This "vision-quest" will engage imagination and creativity, and create excitement and inspiration. The quest is both individual and shared. Examples follow.

EXAMPLES

- The grand idea of PAIDEIA, the LEARNING SOCIETY, seems to be a vision of a society in which learning, fulfillment, and becoming truly human are the primary goals.

We can represent the shift in vision from the old to the new in a variety of ways.

- In the shift from the "me generation" to the "learning society," two visual images are offered. Looking in the mirror each morning, the "me generation" reads on labels pasted on the mirror: How much money will I make today? How much fun will I have? Shifting to a scene of the nineties, to the "learning society," the labels say: What will I learn today? What can I do to help?

- A visual description of an ASSEMBLY LINE using outdated machinery and producing more rejects than good products is a visual metaphor for the old vision. A CREATIVE ARTISTS' STUDIO in which everyone is excited by learning to create and creating uniqueness is a vision of a new system of learning and human development.

- The old vision is expressed by "Learning to make a living" and the new vision by "Learning to make a life."

- The invariant PERENNIAL VISION of the limitlessness of human potential and the quest for the realization of higher self through ongoing learning and human development is another representation.

- A 1995 decision of the US Supreme Court case, designated as "Rejected vs. the State of California," will say that "The individual has the right not only to be educated but to realize his or her full potential by the educational experiences provided."

- We can share with Harman (1988, p. 152) a vision of a "global commonwealth in which each of Earth's citizens has a reasonable chance to create through his or her efforts a decent life for self and family; in which men and women live in harmony with the Earth and its creatures, cooperating to create and maintain a wholesome environment for all; in which there is an ecology of different cultures, the diversity of which is appreciated and supported; in which war and flagrant violation of human rights in the name of the state have no legitimacy anywhere, and there is universal support of the rule of law throughout the world; in which throughout the entire human family there is a deep and shared sense of meaning in life itself."

EXAMPLES OF CORE VALUES

It is of utmost importance that designers articulate their individual beliefs and values about education. Values underlie the vision and guide the design inquiry. Designers will articulate their values as they consider design options with the use of the framework introduced earlier. They will also generate value statements in the course of the vision-quest. Once a vision is pictured or described by a designer, that person should also tell the design group the value(s) and belief(s) that support the vision. The outcome of sharing visions will enable designers to forge their collective vision and make it explicit. An example of a core value set follows. It is based on the core values generated in the three previous chapters.

- There are two absolute values: the individual and the global system of humanity. Socio-cultural systems that exist between these two should serve both. Systems of learning and human development are such arrangements.

- Of all the resources on earth, the resources of the highest value are the uniqueness and the unique potential and creativity residing in the individual, in the family, and in our various social systems.

- Among the highest order of values of human rights are the freedom and the right to learn.

- The development of inner quality of life is of the highest value for the individual.

- Developing and maintaining creative and cooperative interpersonal and social relationships are key values in societal life.

- Of all the values provided to individuals and to society collectively, the nurturing of learning and human development is the highest.

The above examples are provided only to indicate the kind of statements that designers are asked to make explicit.

II. DEFINING SETS OF CORE IDEAS

The VISION and the CORE VALUES inspire the creation of the IMAGE, but the CORE IDEAS are the "stuff" of which the image is made. The core ideas that designers generated in the course of using the framework will have to be arranged in sets that enhance the creation of the image and the design of the system. The example idea sets generated in the previous three chapters are arranged here in three sets. The first presents core ideas about the educational function and purpose, the second addresses ideas about the learner, and the third is directly relevant to systems design.

CORE IDEAS ABOUT FUNCTIONS AND PURPOSES

- The creation of a Learning Society is the central core idea; others may include the following:

- Learning should be provided by which the individual and societal systems develop competence and will become empowered to give direction to their own evolution by design.

- Systems of learning and human development should co-evolve with the larger society as well as spearhead societal evolution.

- Educational systems should nurture the entire range of existential experience: the social, cultural, ethical, economic, physical, mental, spiritual, intellectual, aesthetic, and moral domains of the life of the individual and the society.

- The content and experience of learning and human development should be integrated into the stream of educational experience.

- Educational systems should develop the organizational capacity and human capability to engage in continuous organizational learning and design.

- Arrangements, resources, and opportunities should be provided by which to nurture the uniqueness and develop the unique potential of the individual.

CORE IDEAS ABOUT THE LEARNER AND LEARNING

- There are no limits to learning; learning and human development never end.

- The individual has a basic desire to learn, to seek knowledge and understanding, to become competent.

- The individual is capable of initiating, directing, and assuming increasingly more responsibility for learning.

- The individual's development is best facilitated if his or her uniqueness is recognized, respected, and nurtured.

- Inspiration and motivation are the most powerful facilitators of learning.

- The most potent satisfiers to the learner are discovering something new, gaining new insights, and acquiring new skills.

- Self-confidence develops in the learner as a result of mastery of learning tasks, and using what has been learned in real-life situations.

- There are differences among learners existing in many dimensions; acknowledgment of and respect for these differences are essential in offering resources and arrangements and creating a climate for learning.

CORE IDEAS THAT WILL GUIDE DESIGN

- Learners should assume the central position in systems of learning and human development.

- The content of learning should include knowledge, understanding, ways of knowing and thinking, skills, dispositions, sensitivities, and values.

- Characteristics of the transforming society and requirements that emerge from the transformation are the primary sources used in selecting the content of learning and human development.

- Learning can flourish only in a climate in which caring relationships are created and support and trust flow both ways between those who learn and those who foster learning. Nurturing builds confidence and encourages exploration. It offers openness to creativity and continuous learning and human development.

- We have available in the society a large yet untapped resource base for learning and human development, residing in many systems and situations of the community and the larger society.

- The power and the potential of social and human services will dramatically increase by the integration of the various systems that provide for those services and by the design of a comprehensive system of learning and human development.

III. THE CREATION OF A NEW IMAGE

The image created provides us with the first "broad-stroked picture" or "macro-view" of the future system. The image outlines the essential "markers" of the system. These markers may vary, depending on the work accomplished by the designers with the use of the framework, their vision, and the core ideas they generate. The more complete and detailed their work, the more core ideas will be defined, and the clearer the vision that was created, the more detailed and clearer will be the image. The following text is ONLY an example of what might emerge as an initial image of a future system of learning and human development.

AN EXAMPLE OF AN IMAGE

The example presented here is grounded in the core ideas and values and in the vision introduced in the preceding section of this chapter. For demonstration purposes seven "markers" are selected: (a) relationship with the society, (b) relationship with other systems, (c) the overall function, (d) the scope of the educational experience, (e) the key organizational imperative, (f) types of intervention, and (g) resources used. The image is introduced by contrasting it with the image of the existing system. The juxtaposition is probably dramatized in favor of the new image. The statements in the left-hand column present the markers of the image of the new system. The right-hand column represents the image of the existing system of education. It is suggested that the characteristics of the existing system present barriers to the attainment of the new system.

THE IMAGE OF A DESIRED FUTURE SYSTEM	THE IMAGE OF THE EXISTING SYSTEM
Education should reflect and interpret the society as well as shape the society through co-evolutionary interactions, as a future-creating, innovative and open system.	Education is an instrument of cultural and knowledge transmission, focusing on maintaining the existing state and operating in a rather closed system mode.
Education should be coordinated with other social and human service systems, integrating learning and human development.	Education is an autonomous social agency, separated from other societal systems.
Education should provide resources, arrangements, and lifelong experiences for the full development of all individuals and the society.	Education now provides instruction to individuals during their schooling years.

THE IMAGE OF A DESIRED FUTURE SYSTEM	THE IMAGE OF THE EXISTING SYSTEM
Education should embrace all domains of human and societal existence, including the socio-cultural, ethical, moral, economic/occupational, physical/mental/spiritual, political, scientific/technological, and aesthetic.	Education focuses on the basics and preparation for citizenship and employment.
Education should be organized around the learning-experience level; arrangements should be made in the environment of the learner by which to master the learning task.	Education is now organized around the instructional level; arrangements are made that enable teachers to present subject matter to students.
We should use a variety of learning types: self-directed, other-directed, individually supported group learning, cooperative learning, social and organizational learning, all employed to enhance individual and social learning.	Today teacher-class and teacher-student interactions are the primary means of the educational experience.
We should use the large reservoir of learning resources and arrangements available in the society in order to support learning.	The use of educational resources and arrangements is very much confined within the school.

The image of the new system presented above is probably revolutionary, but the move toward it is evolutionary. The image is speculative and serves the purpose of triggering discussion and further exploration. An image should be created by designers as a collective representation of what "should be." Components of the image should be compatible with each other. They should merge into a system of internally consistent "markers."

The image projected above, more than any other argument one could advance, indicates the immensity of the task confronting the society in general, and educational designers in particular. It indicates the requirement of a total transformation of education. At this juncture two questions arise: Do we have the will and the commitment to engage in this major task? and Do we have available to us approaches and methods of disciplined inquiry that are appropriate to carry out the task? While the answer to the second question is a definite YES, meaning that we now know how to conduct systems design, the answer to the first question should be given by the educational community collectively.

REFLECTIONS

Once designers have created an image of a desired future system, they have reached a major milestone in their design journey. Before they move on and engage in the design of the system—based on the image they have created—they might retrace the path they have already traveled and reflect upon their achievements. Such reflection will help them to gain confidence to continue their journey.

PART THREE

DESIGN THINKING AND DESIGN PRACTICE

"The core of purposeful and creative action is design, the active building of relations between man and his world."   (Eric Jantsch)

Having reached that juncture of our journey where we shall focus on the processes and products of design, it helps to review the two previous stages of our journey.

In Part One, first the issue of the improvement or transformation of education was explored. The discussion led to a resolution that a transformation of education by design is unavoidable. Next, it was proposed that transformation should be based on new thinking and new perspectives, and it should be accomplished by a new intellectual technology: systems design. Then, a framework of exploring design options was presented.

In Part Two, the framework, introduced in Part One, was used to explore options related to the scope of design inquiry, its focus, and its inclusiveness. The product of the exploration was a NEW IMAGE which expresses the intent of designers and which will guide design. But—as it was repeatedly said—intention does not yet create a system, only design does.

In Part Three, in Chapter Eight, the notions of thinking about and working with change are discussed, and thinking that leads to change by design is brought into focus. In Chapter Nine, the design journey is mapped out, and strategies for "getting ready for design" are introduced. In the last chapter, the processes and products of design are introduced, and design is placed in the larger context of a comprehensive organizational inquiry.

Chapter Eight

CHANGE BY DESIGN

"While an unchanging dominant majority is perpetually rehearsing its own defeat, fresh challenges are perpetually evoking fresh creative responses from newly recruited minorities, which proclaim their own creative power by rising, each time, to the occasion." (Arnold Toynbee)

INTRODUCTION

Change goes on around us continuously. Its speed and intensity are ever increasing. It may dazzle us or swirl us around. Often it leaves us confused. It always generates uncertainty and ambiguity. Change happens to us. It happens in the systems to which we belong, in other systems that surround us, and in the environment in which we are nested. From these, change flows into our systems. And it flows from our systems into the environment. Change happens at ALL levels of the society: from local to global. Change is universal, ever ongoing, and nowadays it happens ever faster. We may fear change or we may want it; we may go against it or go with it. Often we wish we could participate in it or influence it, even take charge of it. How we relate to change makes all the difference. We can be its victims; and we often are. We can be its spectators; most of the time we are. Or we can give direction to it: we can design it and make it happen. THE CHOICE IS OURS. But having the INTENT to participate in change or direct it is not enough. We should know HOW TO DO IT. We should have the will and acquire the skill to initiate it and design it, and to implement it. If we want to TAKE CHARGE OF OUR FUTURE, if we want to MASTER CHANGE, we should develop COMPETENCE in directing and MANAGING CHANGE. No small tasks...

One of the characteristics of "taking charge of change" is that it is the result of deliberate DESIGN and planning that leads to ACTION by which we can implement and MANAGE change. Such action has to be responsible action. If we initiate change, we have to take responsibility for its management and for its results. Before designers approach the task of designing new systems of learning and human development, they need to understand how they themselves and others in their design community relate to change. The material presented in this chapter offers a set of "mirrors" which allow self-reflective understanding of how one relates to change. Four styles of working with change are described here, which interpret Ackoff's work (1981). Following an exploration of each of the styles, designers should individually and collectively assess whether one—or more— of the "mirrors" reflect their attitude and relation to change. The second part of the chapter introduces sets of distinctions that are aimed at helping to clarify basic concepts about change and design and high-light differences among various forms of inquiry.

i. VARIOUS STYLES OF PERCEIVING AND MANAGING CHANGE

The purpose of this section is twofold: (1) to explore diverse ways we perceive and react to change, and (2) to help participants under-stand the implications of those styles for organizational behavior and outcomes. The four styles introduced here are described in terms of the following dimensions constructed—based on Ackoff's work—in order to enhance comparison, exploration, and self-reflection.

- General attitude toward change

- Dealing with the "arrow of time" (past—present—future)

- General approach to problem and change management

- Perception of the role of science and disciplined inquiry

- Perception of the role of technology

- Organizational mode or model

- Organizational culture and values

- Approach to planning

- Approach to working with problems

- Attractiveness of a specific style

The four styles are labeled as (1) reactive or reactivating, (2) inactive, (3) pre-active, and (4) interactive. The overriding differences among these styles derive from our orientation and attitude toward change. Often we shall find that our own working styles are not reflections of a "pure" form but are a mix of styles. Still, most likely we will be able to detect a "dominant" orientation toward one of the styles. Orientations might shift from time to time, depending on the situation or the preferences people have. And orientations might change once we understand the implications of our orientation. There are strengths and weaknesses in all four styles, and we shall explore these. Still, in this presentation there is a strong preference for the interactive style, which is the most effective style for change by design.

TYPE "A": THE REACTIVATING or RE-ACTIVE STYLE—"BACK TO THE FUTURE"

A. GENERAL ATTITUDE TOWARD CHANGE

In this style the general attitude toward change is derived from a dominant orientation toward "unmaking" changes that have happened. Effort and energy are focused on "swimming against the tide of change" and wishing to return to the shore from which change has pulled us away. We romanticize, for example, about the "good old days" when we had no teachers' unions and no disciplinary problems.

B. DEALING WITH THE ARROW OF TIME

This resistance to change is reinforced by a corresponding "temporal" orientation toward the past, a wish to "turn the arrow around." We seem to drive toward the future by looking into the rear view mirror. Our vision is focused on where we have been instead of where we are going. (Back to basics may be an example here.) We do not realize that the arrow of time is irreversible.

C. GENERAL APPROACH TO PROBLEM AND CHANGE MANAGEMENT

Here a one-directional cause-and-effect view governs our thinking about change. Every problem we face was created by something or someone. Let us find the cause, suppress, or remove it, and the problem will disappear. (But, getting rid of what is not wanted does not give us what is desired.) Dismissing students who have a bad attendance record or are creating disciplinary problems is an example of trying to remove the cause. It may solve the immediate problem facing the school but will create larger problems for the society.

D. PERCEPTION OF THE ROLE OF SCIENCE

Consonant with the reactivating or reactive style, our evaluations and decisions are rooted in the perception that "experience is the best teacher. " Looking for answers posed by organizational problems and issues emanating from environmental changes, we seek guidance from past experiences and history rather than the knowledge base offered by science and the disciplines that are relevant to social and educational systems. Rather than pursuing disciplined inquiry, our mode of operation is based on trial and error, directed and evaluated in terms of past experiences and memories of similar events and occurrences.

E. PERCEPTION OF THE ROLE OF TECHNOLOGY

Having a dominant orientation toward the past and a thrust toward unmaking changes, we consider technology to be the main cause of societal change, and we have little use for it. We rationalize this position by pointing to such past failures of technology applications as the language laboratory cemeteries, failed "TV classes," and currently unused or under-used computers. The fact that we failed to develop appropriate programs/software is not considered in our general dismissal of technology.

F. ORGANIZATIONAL MODE OR MODEL

Corresponding to the past and experience-focused orientation of the reactivist style, we have the tendency to rely on old, "well-proven" and familiar organizational forms and, as a rule, operate according to authoritarian and paternalistic hierarchical organizational models. This mode is compatible with the rigidly controlled systems type discussed in Chapter Two. In education it creates large bureaucratic structures housed in a central office. Directives come from the top, where goals and objectives are defined and modes of operation prescribed and described in operational manuals. At lower levels freedom of choice is limited. At most we allow for choices in methods and tools. The current structure of the organization is protected—often at all cost. Change is discouraged and innovation stifled.

G. ORGANIZATIONAL CULTURE AND VALUES

The values are those of the past. Those in authority tend to be nostalgic about the past and often romanticize about "what we had" and "the way we were." Inherent in the top-down organizational and authoritarian mode is the presence of at least two different organizational cultures: (1) the culture of the management, the well-stated "official culture," and (2) the employee culture, which is usually not articulated "officially." (In education teachers' unions articulate this culture.)

H. APPROACH TO PLANNING

In this style, planning begins at the top. The superintendent tells his/her associates to develop an annual plan in four months. The associates tell the next level to submit their plans in three months. Department chairs and principals have two months for their planning. Teachers have one month. Planning proceeds at the lowest level by listing current deficiencies and proposing projects to remove their causes. Costs and benefits are estimated project by project or program by program, and priorities are established. Selection is made and submitted assuming the availability of more resources than we actually expect to receive. This selection is sent to the immediate superior. The superior adjusts/edits the submissions, aggregates them, adds a "fudge" factor, and passes the output to the next level. This process continues until it reaches the top level, where final selection and aggregation are carried out, thus completing the analytical process.

I. APPROACH TO WORKING WITH PROBLEMS

Those of us who operate in the reactive mode tend to deal with problems separately and not systemically. Approaching each one in a piecemeal fashion, we fail to see their vital interconnections, how one problem impinges on another, and thus we miss the essential properties of the whole. This approach is based on three misguided perspectives. One—already mentioned—is the assumption that we can find and remove the "cause" of a specific problem and thus "solve" it. The second is our belief that if we get rid of what we do not want, we will have what we want. The third is failure to realize that a "solution" to a problem usually will have both intentional and unintentional effects. This narrow view of solutions may create new and even more severe problems. During the early phase of the recent reform movement, this problem-solving approach dominated.

J. ATTRACTIVENESS

Ackoff (1981) suggests that a reactive orientation has three main attractions. First, it maintains a "sense of history" from which some things can be learned. Not everything that occurs is new (and we add to this that not everything that is new is necessarily good). Second, this orientation also embodies a desire for continuity and seeks to avoid abrupt, disruptive, and often poorly understood changes. Finally, by preserving tradition and staying on familiar ground, we might maintain a feeling of security and stability. This feeling of stability, however, often may prove to be false. What we fail to realize is that "the ground beneath us might be crumbling."

TYPE "B": THE INACTIVE STYLE—
"DON'T ROCK THE BOAT"

A. GENERAL ATTITUDE TOWARD CHANGE

The general attitude toward change is derived from a dominant orientation toward maintaining the organization in its existing state and, therefore, resisting change. The label "inactive," however, is misleading. A great deal of energy and effort is spent on keeping things as they are and preventing change from happening. The operating principle is "preserving stability." It takes a lot of work to keep things from changing.

B. DEALING WITH THE ARROW OF TIME

Inactivists want to stop the arrow of time and remain in the present. "Things may not be the best today, but they are good enough or as good as can be reasonably expected." In any event, most change is temporary or "illusory." If nothing (new) is done, little or nothing (new) will happen, and things will stay as they are. And that is what we want. We want the future to be what the present is.

C. GENERAL APPROACH TO PROBLEM AND CHANGE MANAGEMENT

As a rule, inactivists delay reacting to (external) changes or problems until a crisis arises, until their stability or survival is threatened. Thus, they practice "brinkmanship" and post-crisis management. They try to "get by" with making marginal adjustments; thus they do the least that is required. Whatever they do is aimed at returning to "equilibrium." They attempt to alleviate or remove whatever is interfering with the current status quo. They often say that "the best way to solve a problem is not to consider it a problem." For example, in the school environment, faced with complaints, management will "ride out" the problem situation, anticipating that people will get tired of complaining.

D. PERCEPTION OF THE ROLE OF SCIENCE

Oriented toward maintaining the status quo, management relies on an understanding and grasp of current events rather than past experience or scientific findings. They articulate whatever they can muster as rationale in support of the current state rather than engage in disciplined inquiry. An awareness of what is going on today and why, and connections with those in power are of paramount importance. In the school environment this behavior is referred to as a "reasoned pragmatic" approach.

E. PERCEPTION OF THE ROLE OF TECHNOLOGY

Having a dominant orientation toward the present, preserving the status quo, and avoiding or preventing changes, we are reluctant to bring in new technology, even fearful of its effects. We do not want technology to cause or force change upon us. What we have now is good enough. Surely, "we don't even use well what we now have." In education, if we bring in new technology, we assign to it the support of ongoing programs.

F. ORGANIZATIONAL MODE OR MODEL

Given the desire to keep things just as they are, our operational mode is basically bureaucratic, and we rely on red tape as our indispensable instrument to slow things down and avoid change. Our organizational model is the "committee model." Study groups, task forces, and commissions are formed and re-formed in an endless process of gathering facts (the facts are never all in), passing on information from one group to the other, revising positions and recommendations, and persisting in this process until there is no reason anymore to make a decision or introduce changes.

G. ORGANIZATIONAL CULTURE AND VALUES

Organizations with a dominantly inactive style are preoccupied with conventions, customs, rules, and correct behavior. "Conformity is valued more than creativity." Loyalty to the organization and its management is most important and highly rewarded. Conforming to the status quo is the way to avoid troubling ambiguity and uncertainty that change would bring about.

H. APPROACH TO PLANNING

In view of our desire to avoid change, our planning focuses on maintaining the current state and keeping things from happening. If recommendations are produced by our various committees and study groups in time for action—and if those cannot be ignored—they are accepted, but we offer insufficient resources and management support for their implementation so that their failure is virtually assured. (This reminds me how educational R&D projects have been handled in the course of the last three decades.) Not providing adequate resources for change is often justified in publicly supported organizations—such as public education—on the grounds that we cannot get additional support for doing something new and untried. A predisposition toward this type of attitude often prevents serious consideration of change.

I. APPROACH TO WORKING WITH PROBLEMS

The inactive style of problem and change management is supported by an articulate group of political and social scientists, according to the doctrine of "disjointed incrementalism." As with the reactive style, this doctrine calls for treating each problem separately, disjointedly, rather than as a system of problems, and thereby doing as little as possible. This strategy is also called "muddling through," a process which can usually be extended long enough so that the specific problem that initiated it changes sufficiently to make the "solution" outdated. This reminds us of recent educational reform efforts that follow an incremental piecemeal approach.

J. ATTRACTIVENESS

Ackoff suggests that the inactive style is practiced if the perception is that (1) there are situations in which doing nothing is better than doing anything, (2) some problems will fade away if left alone, (3) if one acts cautiously one seldom makes mistakes of catastrophic proportion. (When inactive organizations die, they die slowly.)

TYPE "C": THE PREACTIVIST STYLE—
"RIDING THE TIDE"—"GETTING ON THE BANDWAGON"

A. GENERAL ATTITUDE TOWARD CHANGE

In the preactivist style we seek to anticipate change and prepare for the opportunities that it brings. Since we believe that change is brought about by external forces, we should do all we can to guess where it leads and ride its tide so that we can get wherever it is going before anyone else. Preactivism is the dominant style today in the corporate environment.

B. DEALING WITH THE ARROW OF TIME

This eagerness for change looks toward the future. As preactivists we are not willing to return to the past or settle for things as they are in the present. We are convinced that the future will be better than the present or the past. We are impatient with the present and want to expedite our moving into the future. We are not willing to settle for doing well enough. We want to attain the best possible, we have a drive to "optimize."

C. GENERAL APPROACH TO PROBLEM AND CHANGE MANAGEMENT

Believing that the future will be very different from the past, preactivists place little reliance on experience; we rely on FORECASTS of the future. We are more concerned about missing an opportunity than about making errors. Errors of commission are less costly and easier to adjust than errors of omission. The fear of "cost-regret" is our operative word. Change management is management to ADJUST to change. The best way to do this is by finding out from experts possibilities for the future and being prepared to meet them, in whatever form the future comes.

D. PERCEPTION OF THE ROLE OF SCIENCE

Since the key to moving into the future is our ability to foresee it, we rely on and promote the "science of prediction." We can prepare effectively for the future only if it is predicted accurately. Thus, we put a great deal of effort into exploring forecasting. We augment forecasts by such "science-based" methods as linear programming, predictive computer models, operations research methods, program planning and budgeting, and risk analysis.

E. PERCEPTION OF THE ROLE OF TECHNOLOGY

As preactivists we agree on one thing with the reactivists, namely, that technology is the principal cause of change. But unlike the reactivists, we believe that change is good, and therefore we embrace and promote technology. We appreciate technology's potential and power and we wish to make it available to us. We believe that the future of technology best represents the future. Thus, "when the future comes we will be ready for it." We treat the latest technology and each new technique as a potential panacea. We "demonstrate" our advanced status by the number of computers we have in the classroom. Never mind how we use them.

F. ORGANIZATIONAL MODE OR MODEL

As preactivists our organizations are "purposive," meaning that our purpose is clearly defined. We structure ourselves as "ends-autocratic," such as making profit in the corporation. We are, however, "means-democratic" or "means-permissive," having freedom to select means and methods of operation. We operate in a management-by-objectives mode. Being means-permissive we are often decentralized and informal. The latest approaches in the reform movement are often of this type, reflected in reorganization and realignment of responsibilities.

G. ORGANIZATIONAL CULTURE AND VALUES

Corresponding to our organizational mode, we value inventiveness rather than conformity, and we like to be the first to try new things. We value growth, want to become bigger, to capture the "largest share of recognition," to be "number one."

H. APPROACH TO PLANNING

In the preactive mode our planning relies on predicting the future and preparing for it. It also involves taking steps to minimize or avoid future threats as well as exploit future opportunities. Planning proceeds from the top down. Future environmental conditions are forecasted by our professional planning staff, based on which goals and objectives and broad strategy for our entire organization are formulated. The output of this process is passed on to the next lower level, where appropriate lower-level plans and strategies are prepared. This process is repeated at each successive lower level. Given several or many possible futures, we prepare a plan and strategy for each: we call this contingency planning.

I. APPROACH TO WORKING WITH PROBLEMS

Our future orientation leads us to shift emerging problems to the future. We seek their solution or resolution by developing new techniques or technologies. We believe there are few problems that technology cannot solve. Therefore, the more we are on the cutting edge of technology, the fewer problems we shall have and, if we have them, the more readily we can solve them. "Technology-fix" is the name of the game.

J. ATTRACTIVENESS

Its close association with modern science and technology accounts for much of preactivism's great appeal as well as its prestige. Accepting and advocating change, preactivists appear to take a progressive stance at the frontiers of the future. Their preoccupation with the future gives the impression that they have it well in hand.

TYPE "D": THE INTERACTIVE STYLE—
"STEERING THE KAYAK DOWN THE RAPIDS"—
THE DESIGN RESPONSE TO WORKING WITH CHANGE

A. GENERAL ATTITUDE TOWARD CHANGE

The interactivist style is based on a desire to give direction to change rather than : (1) disregarding it or trying to "unmake it" as the reactivists wish to do, (2) being its victims as the inactivists are, or (3) becoming its spectators as the preactivists are. As interactivists we believe that it is in our power to steer our system down the rapids of change toward a desired future that we ourselves can envision and bring about, provided we learn how to do it and have the willingness to do the steering. In changing education by design, our actions are guided by our vision and image of future educational systems.

B. DEALING WITH THE ARROW OF TIME

Interactivists accept the irreversibility of the arrow of time. We consider the past and present as the context from which we can move into the future, connect our present interactively with the past and future, and make our existence internally consistent through time.

We do not desire to return to a previous state as the reactivists wish, and will not settle for things as they are as the inactivists do. Finally, we do not blindly accept projections about the future as do the preactivists, who believe that the future is largely out of our control and we should rely on the forecasting of experts. As interactivists, we believe that the future depends more on what we do between now and then than it does on what has happened until now.

C. GENERAL APPROACH TO PROBLEM AND CHANGE MANAGEMENT

The interactivist's general approach toward change is consistent with the attitude and temporal orientations described above. While the preactivist contemplates the future with a search for "what COULD BE," the interactivist focuses on "what OUGHT TO BE." The key to the interactivist's approach is design: the design of a desirable future, the one that "ought to be," and the creation of ways to bring it about.

While the preactivist's main concern is acceptance and adaptation to forecasted futures which may evolve independently from us, we interactivists believe in co-evolution with our changing environment and interact with and influence our environmental context. The inactivist tries to hold a fixed position in a moving tide. The reactivist tries to swim against it. The preactivist tries to ride with the leading edge of the tide—wherever it leads. We interactivists are not content to be swept along by the current of change; instead, we set our own course, creating a guiding image, a vision of the future, and steer resolutely toward it.

D. PERCEPTION OF THE ROLE OF SCIENCE

In creating our image of the future and describing the desired future state of our system, we interactivists engage in the disciplined inquiry of design. This inquiry is disciplined in that it is based on the science of design and applies systems approaches and methodologies to (1) explore and understand the environment; (2) formulate purposes we wish to attain; (3) create, explore, and select alternatives appropriate to the stated purposes; (4) describe the design of the future system; and (5) implement and manage the selected design. Furthermore, the interactivist develops a knowledge base for design that draws upon findings of the various social and behavioral sciences that apply.

E. PERCEPTION OF THE ROLE OF TECHNOLOGY

Corresponding to the science-based orientation described above, the interactivist applies intellectual technology as means of creating an image of the future and bringing it about. Unlike the reactivist who views technology as one of the main causes of problems, and unlike the preactivist who considers technology as the solution, we interactivists believe that the effects and value of technology depend upon what use we make of it.

F. ORGANIZATIONAL MODE OR MODEL

In accordance with our future-shaping interactive style, our organizational mode integrates the various system levels and systems operating at those levels through continuous interaction. The reactivists operate according to an authoritarian and paternalistic hierarchical style. The inactivists work in a bureaucratic, red tape-driven, decision-avoidance mode. The preactivists follow an ends-autocratic and means-democratic decentralized mode. We interactivists manage change and engage in a continuous organizational learning and regenerating design. The model of this operational mode is an interlocking and overlapping system of management and design boards. Each board includes representation from three contiguous organizational levels and ensures information flow in both directions. Such an arrangement has the capacity to best harvest the creative potential and capability of all who are part of the system (Ackoff, 1981).

G. ORGANIZATIONAL CULTURE AND VALUES

Inactivists are willing to settle for doing well enough: to "satisfy." Preactivists want to do as well as possible: to "optimize" within a future presented to them. We interactivists "idealize." We believe that humans are more than end-seeking creatures; we are ideal-seeking. We want to do better in the future than the best we are capable of doing now. Therefore we focus on continuous design over time. Our objective is to maximize our ability to learn to develop and to become the best we can possibly be. We pursue the ideal, knowing that we cannot ever attain it. It is the quest that gives us the reward and makes us truly human.

H. APPROACH TO PLANNING

The interactive concept of planning implies two major operations: designing the desired future and planning for ways and means for its attainment. In the reactivist style, plans devised at the top become the context for plans below. The inactivist's planning focuses on trying to maintain the status quo. The preactivist attempts to acquire the expert's prediction of the future and plans to be prepared for it. We interactivists work out and design our own desired future, display it, and plan interactively within our own system and with other systems in our environment to bring it about.

I. APPROACH TO WORKING WITH PROBLEMS

The reactivists deal with problems in a piecemeal fashion, trying to find and then remove the cause of a particular problem. The inactivists have a somewhat similar approach as they treat problems separately and disjointedly, doing as little as possible by muddling through. Preactivists believe that most problems can be fixed by new technologies, thus they are constantly searching for new technologies and then for problems to which they apply. We interactivists believe that we fail most often because of an inability to define and face the right problems rather than because of an inability to solve the problems we face.

Ackoff (1981) suggests that to deal interactively with any problem situation, two things are required. We must determine what the situation has in common with other situations that we have previously experienced. This tells us which part of our available knowledge is relevant. Science enables us to do this. Second, we must also know how the situation we face is unique and requires knowledge which is not yet available. The arts and humanities enable us to do this. In addition to science, the arts and humanities reveal the questions yet to be answered and the values yet to be obtained. They jointly provide answers to those questions and offer ways of pursuing those values.

J. ATTRACTIVENESS

Obviously, the presentation above is based on a bias for the interactive style. We are proponents of this style of managing change and pursuing organizational purposes because we believe that it provides the best chance we have for coping effectively with the knowledge explosion, accelerating societal and technological change, increasing organizational complexity, and environmental turbulence and uncertainty. This style enables us to shape our future rather than to become victims of changes around us. Furthermore, the interactive mode is the only mode of the four that explicitly attempts to harness individual and collective creativity and aspirations, while addressing itself to increasing individual, organizational, and societal development and improving the quality of life. For all the above reasons and others that have already been discussed, it is strongly believed that the systems design approach offers the most promising form of disciplined inquiry for educational reform.

II. DEFINITIONS BY DISTINCTIONS

In the closing section of this chapter, a set of distinctions is introduced that clarifies various forms of organizational inquiry. These distinctions juxtapose design and design-related approaches with other forms of inquiry. Distinctions are made between (1) systemic change and piecemeal change, (2) single-looped and double-looped inquiry, (3) the single-trek and dual-trek approach, (4) planning and design, and (5) designing for the future and designing the future.

SYSTEMIC VS. PIECEMEAL CHANGE

SYSTEMIC CHANGE is based on a systems view of an organization, and it is guided by the principle that any change in a part of the system affects the whole system, and any change in the whole affects all of its parts. Second, the system is more than the sum of its parts, more by the interaction among the parts and the emergent effects produced by the interaction. Third, change occurs by purposeful design. Fourth, a systemic change—even the smallest one—is contemplated in view of the relationship between the system and its environment.

PIECEMEAL CHANGE allows tinkering with or changing parts in an effort to improve the system. Change is not "mapped" into the whole system. Changing parts happens without consideration of its effect on the relationships that operate among parts and between the system and its environment. On account of this "non-systemic" nature of piecemeal change, change is usually short-lived because it was not accomplished with the involvement of other parts and lacks their cooperation.

SINGLE-LOOPED VS. DOUBLE-LOOPED ORGANIZATIONAL INQUIRY

In a SINGLE-LOOPED mode, the organization takes actions, detects error, programs correction, and implements action again. This mode of inquiry is a closed single-loop process. The thrust is to maintain the system on its previously set course in a "steady as it goes" mode. It aims to reduce any deviation from the set course: "don't rock the boat."

In a DOUBLE-LOOPED mode, the organization opens up the loop. It moves out from its boundaries and looks back on itself in the context of the environment and reexamines (1) its guiding perspectives, (2) purposes, and (3) methods and modes of operation, and is prepared to make changes in all of those aspects. Double-looped inquiry often leads to redesign. The most articulate description of these modes can be found in Argyris' work (1982).

There are many instances when a single-looped mode is appropriate. In time of dynamic changes and transformations, however, a double-looped approach is called for.

THE SINGLE-TREK VS. DUAL-TREK APPROACH

If systems design is accomplished in the context of an existing system, we cannot abandon the system as it exists and deal only with the redesign effort. We need to attend to the "here and now" concerns that enable the existing system to improve its effectiveness and efficiency. Thus, we engage in a dual-trek organizational inquiry. The two treks will not be isolated but will become sources of mutual support, information and knowledge base development, and motivation. If this strategy is followed, eventually the two treks will meet.

PLANNING VS. DESIGN

This distinction can be best demonstrated in a juxtaposed presentation.

PLANNING	DESIGN
works out from the existing system	works back from an ideal image
prescribes goals/objectives	explores values, aspirations, and expectations
sets forth specific steps to take within a time scheme	devises and describes the SYSTEM that has the potential to realize the aspirations
proceeds in a linear fashion	works in a spiral and recursive fashion
establishes an overall time frame (3-5 years) at the end of which another planning cycle starts	is continuous and becomes the approach to organizational change and renewal

Planning proceeds once we describe the system that we have designed and plan its development and implementation.

DESIGNING FOR THE FUTURE VS. DESIGNING THE FUTURE

DESIGNING FOR THE FUTURE is based on the assumption that somehow we know what the future will be. This assumption is based either on an extrapolative projection of so-called "current trends" or on scenarios created by futurists. Designers thus take either the extrapolated definition or the one created by the futurists and design for it.

By DESIGNING THE FUTURE we take responsibility for its creation. This notion is based on the belief that we can take charge of our future, and we have the power to engage in systems design, enlightened by an understanding of the characteristics and requirements of the environment and inspired by our own aspirations and expectations.

REFLECTIONS

In Part Three we continue the design journey. In this chapter we have devoted time to understanding how people work with change and what change styles are used by them, and we have developed an appreciation of the interactive style as the style that is best suited to systems design. We have also learned to make some distinctions that have furthered our understanding of design.

Chapter Nine

THE DESIGN JOURNEY

Where we are going there are no roads.

INTRODUCTION

Educational reformers who have elected to take the design path marked by this work have traveled, up to this point, the frontal terrain of systems design. They have explored reasons for design, contemplated design ways of thinking, and considered the kind of system they might design. More specifically, they have:

- Explored the existing state of education and recent reform efforts, and developed a rationale for systems design.

- Recognized the need for new ways of thinking about education and familiarized themselves with three interrelated components of a new mind set: evolutionary, systems, and design thinking.

- Engaged in front-end design work with the use of a framework which enabled them to select the scope of design inquiry and its focus, and contemplate patterns of interaction between education and other societal systems.

- Initiated a vision-quest, articulated their core values and core ideas, and, based on all the above, formulated an image of the future system.

- Contemplated their way of thinking about and their approach to working with change, and considered an interactive approach that enables people to give direction to change by design.

All the above having been accomplished, in this chapter the continuation of the design journey is mapped out, a comprehensive definition of systems design is offered, and strategies of getting ready to conduct systems design are outlined.

I. A MAP OF THE DESIGN JOURNEY

Design is a journey of creation. "Journey" is defined (Webster, 1979) as "travel or passage from one place to another." It is not aimless wandering. For a journey to lead to "another place," we need to confront such questions as: Where are we now? Where do we want to go? What route should we take to get there? To answer these questions we need to consult a map. If we have traveled to the "other place" before, and know the route well, this map may already be imprinted in our mind. If not, we need a map that represents the terrain of our proposed journey in such detail that we can easily select the route and navigate to the designated place we wish to go.

Design is a journey toward a desired future state which we define for ourselves and want to realize. Engaging in design, we ask questions similar to those we might ask when planning any journey, namely: Where are we now? What is our present state? Why do we want to take the design journey? Where do we want to go? What is the future state we wish to attain? What route should we take? And, what do we have to do to design the desired future state?

If we have made previous design journeys, the MAP OF HOW TO GO ABOUT DESIGN may be imprinted in our mind. If not, we need a map that is a descriptive and explanatory representation of the design inquiry. It is an instrumental map: an instrument of disciplined creation, an instrument that shows the territory of design and the paths we should travel to accomplish the design. The map introduces visual images of design inquiry. It intends to orient designers toward their journey and the narrative provides guidance to activities that enable them to design the future system they wish to create.

The map does not tell us what to accomplish. It shows us only what is involved in designing a system. What we make of the experience is up to us. The design map is described here in the functional context of education. Judging from the current literature and the various studies and reports on educational reform, the educational community is not familiar with and is not practicing systems design; "there are no roads marked out" yet for a design journey in the field of education. Neither schools of education nor educational professional development programs offer curricula in systems design. The material presented in this book aims to make a contribution to educational reform by introducing systems design as a disciplined inquiry and by marking the road thereof.

MAPPING THE TERRAIN OF DEPARTURE

The front-end part of the map—shown as the left-hand circle of Figure 9.1—represents the "space" of initial exploration. In this space we examine and describe the current state of our educational system and its environments, the community and the larger society. From an understanding of the educational implications of these explorations, we might generate an intent to engage in design. Next, we formulate core ideas and articulate values that will guide design inquiry and create an image of the desired future state of education (where do we wish to go?). Finally we engage in activities that will help us to "get

FIGURE 9.1. MAPPING THE FRONTAL SPACE

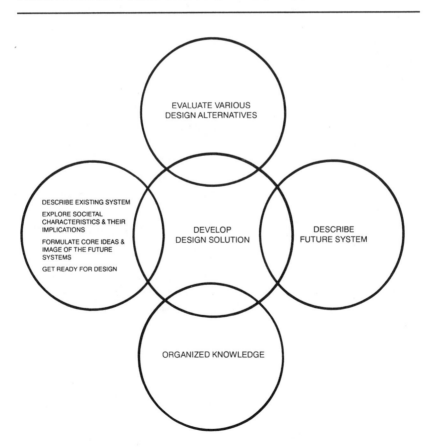

ready" for the design journey. The experiences we gain in the exploration space help us to develop information and knowledge we can use
in the course of design and formulate perspectives and ideas that will
guide us in our journey. Figure 9.1 depicts these activities as the frontal
space of the design journey. In addition to the frontal space, marked
by the left-hand circle, there are four more circles, representing the
four major spaces or terrains of the design journey. At this point I
insert major labels in these circles. I will map and explain them in turn
in the rest of this section.

MAPPING THE TERRAIN OF THE DESTINATION

Here we map out the space of our destination, the space in which
we shall display the outcome of design, a description of the future
system we wish to create. At the front-end stage of the journey we
already created an IMAGE of the desired future system. That image
was the first expression of our intent and aspiration. But INTENT
AND ASPIRATION DO NOT CREATE A SYSTEM, ONLY DESIGN
DOES. And this is exactly what design is about. Design produces a
detailed systems description which, when developed, will realize the
image. The outcome of design will be displayed in the space of the
future system. In this space we shall describe in detail a comprehensive
representation or model of the new educational system. We shall also
display there the environmental systems in which the future system is
nested. The environmental systems are not given. Their design and
description are an essential function of design inquiry. The system we
create will depend upon the support of these systems. The specifications of what support is required and the design of the interaction
between the future system and its environmental support systems are
crucial design tasks.

In Figure 9.2 the map is redrawn and labels are placed in the space
of destination, in the space of the future system. Whatever will be
displayed there is produced in the three circles in the middle of the
figure, representing the three spaces of the design journey between
the frontal space and destination. It is in these three spaces that we
shall formulate the mission and purpose, the specifications, the functions, the content, the context, and the structure of the future system.
(See Figure 9.2.)

FIGURE 9.2. MAPPING THE SPACE OF DESTINATION

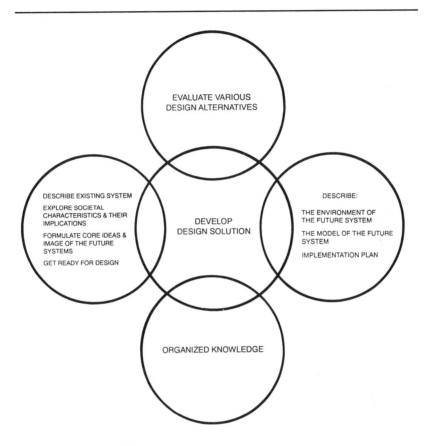

EVALUATE VARIOUS
DESIGN ALTERNATIVES

DESCRIBE EXISTING SYSTEM

EXPLORE SOCIETAL
CHARACTERISTICS & THEIR
IMPLICATIONS

FORMULATE CORE IDEAS &
IMAGE OF THE FUTURE
SYSTEMS

GET READY FOR DESIGN

DEVELOP
DESIGN SOLUTION

DESCRIBE:

THE ENVIRONMENT OF
THE FUTURE SYSTEM

THE MODEL OF THE FUTURE
SYSTEM

IMPLEMENTATION PLAN

ORGANIZED KNOWLEDGE

MAPPING THE JOURNEY BETWEEN
THE START AND THE END

Two questions drive the journey between the beginning and the
end: What route should we take? and What do we have to do to
accomplish the purpose of our journey, the design of a new system?
There is a large terrain between the beginning and the end which we
shall navigate. It is this terrain on which no roads are yet marked out
by the educational community. We are marking such a road now. This
road marking and navigation require the hard work of disciplined
inquiry and the exciting adventure of creating. The interaction and
integration of these two constitute systems design.

As we have already seen in the previous figures, this terrain is
mapped as three partially overlapping spaces. The largest of these—in

the center of the map—is labeled "DEVELOP DESIGN SOLUTION." This space overlaps with those labeled "ORGANIZED KNOWLEDGE" and "EVALUATE ALTERNATIVES." In the rest of this chapter, I will define the activities accomplished in these three spaces of design and describe the route of the design journey that cuts across them.

The design space that occupies the center of the map represents the most significant terrain of the journey. Here activities are carried out that will eventually produce the design solution and lead to the development and display of the comprehensive description of the new educational system. It is this space in which we conceptualize and create potential alternatives of the future system by traveling through four spirals.

During the FIRST SPIRAL, activities focus on the formulation of the core definition of the system to be designed, its mission and purpose. This definition interprets the SOCIETAL FUNCTIONS already identified and the IMAGE of the future system which we have created. During the SECOND SPIRAL, we elaborate and transform the core definition into systems specifications by asking such questions as: Who is the client? What services should be provided? and to whom, when, and how? What responsibilities should be specified to whom? Who is the owner of the system? etc. Design during the THIRD SPIRAL focuses on the question: What functions have to be carried out by the system in order to attain the mission and purpose and meet the requirements of the specifications? The key design imperative of "function first" is implemented here. The identification and systemic arrangement of the functions identified will represent the first description or model of the future system. It represents an interactive and integrated design of all the functions that have to be carried out by the system. The FOURTH SPIRAL represents the design of the systems that will manage the functions and the organization that has the capacity and human capability to carry out the functions and, thus, fulfill the mission. A description of these systems, coupled with the systems model of functions, provides us with the comprehensive normative model of the new system. The last task is to prepare a plan for the implementation of the design.

In the course of our journey through the four spirals of developing the design solution, at each decision point we shall consider alternatives. In the language of the journey we ask the question: Which of the alternatives is the best—the most promising—to lead us to our destination?

The map in Figure 9.3 shows that our journey cuts through the boundaries of the various spaces as we extend our travel to Organized Knowledge and Design Evaluation. If the design solution process would NOT reach into these two spaces, our design would be pure speculation. It would not qualify as disciplined inquiry. At best it would be an invention. In the next two sections I will map these two spaces of our journey.

FIGURE 9.3. MAPPING THE DESIGN SOLUTION SPACE

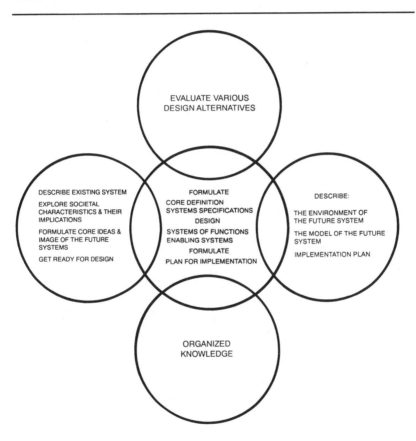

MAPPING THE SPACE OF THE KNOWLEDGE BASE

This space on the map of our design journey represents activities that include the collection, analysis, synthesis, and display of design-relevant information and knowledge. Disciplined inquiry has to be knowledge based. As we travel the four spirals of design solution, we constantly draw upon and use the knowledge base. The territory of organized knowledge maps four domains: (a) knowledge we generated as we explored the characteristics of the larger society and their implications for education; (b) findings of the exploration of design options; (c) the core values and ideas, the vision, and the image that guide our design; (d) knowledge about design and how to conduct it. The application of knowledge in design is discussed in the closing part of this section. Figure 9.4 displays the mapping of the space of organized knowledge.

FIGURE 9.4. THE MAP OF ORGANIZED KNOWLEDGE

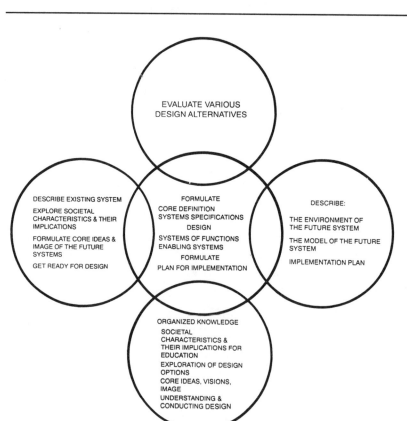

MAPPING THE TERRITORY OF DESIGN EVALUATION

We travel into this territory in order to experiment with various design solution alternatives and test and evaluate those alternatives. This part of our journey is a journey of "assurance," as such evaluation mitigates errors in "perceiving the real world" in portraying our design solution. It builds confidence in the design we create. As we develop alternatives we shall experiment with and test them in order to select the most promising: the one which will make the best contribution to our design. Figure 9.5 completes the mapping of our design journey.

FIGURE 9.5. COMPLETING THE MAP

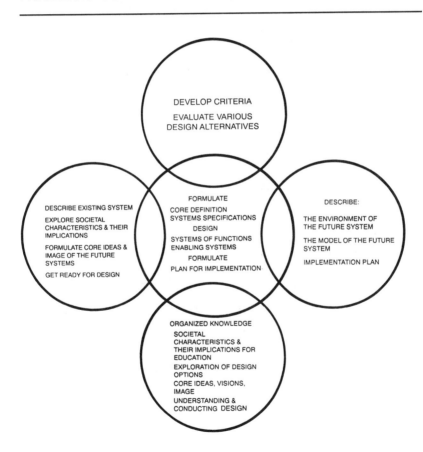

THE DYNAMICS OF THE JOURNEY

The image that has emerged from the description of the design journey and a review of the map depicting the journey clearly show that the route is not linear, it is not a straight line. Even beyond the fact that we are constantly crossing into the knowledge base and design experimentation as we pursue our design inquiry and gain new insights, we return to the formulations articulated in the front-end of our journey and might revise and reshape our stated purposes, aspirations, and images. We ask recursive questions: How does what we formulated earlier shape what we do now? and How does what we formulate now change the purpose, the vision, and the images we shaped earlier? The same is true as we journey into the knowledge base in the course of traveling through the four spirals of the design solution. The questions we formulate in the design solution space become ever more informed and the answers ever more enlightening as we consult organized knowledge. Often those questions will require the acquisition and analysis of new knowledge; thus, our knowledge base is enlarged. Traveling into design experimentation, we reality-test our emerging design solutions and gain knowledge that further informs our design.

Design is an ongoing journey of creation. In organizations that are "alive" and want to co-evolve with their environment, design never ends. If education wants to remain viable in our constantly changing environment and become socially responsive to society, then the journey of creation—the journey of design—will always continue, and it will lead us to design systems that will be ever more capable of nurturing learning and human development.

II. A DEFINITION OF DESIGN

In an age when the speed, intensity, and complexity of change increase constantly and exponentially, our ability to shape change rather than being its victims depends upon (a) the availability of theories and methods of disciplined inquiry that enable us to give direction to our systems by design, and (b) the acquisition of competence in the use of models, approaches, methods, and tools which empower us to participate in the design of our systems.

Herbert Simon in his book THE SCIENCE OF THE ARTIFICIAL (1969) made an important distinction between the natural and behavioral sciences and the science of design. Natural and behavioral sciences describe what things are and how they work. They form theories and make predictions based on those theories. Organized in compartmentalized and differentiated domains, such as the physical, biological, behavioral, and social sciences, inquiry in these disciplines is oriented toward knowledge production, and their salient intellectual process is analysis. They are concerned with WHAT IS. On the other hand, fields such as engineering, medicine, law, architecture, management, government, business and industrial production, education and social services, etc., are concerned with constructing and reconstructing systems, creating them or shaping them according to stated purposes and expectations, and coordinating them with their environment. They are concerned with WHAT SHOULD BE. They are in the business of design. Design inquiry is decision-oriented. It uses knowledge developed in the various disciplines. Its salient intellectual process is synthesis. Therefore, the tasks encountered by practitioners of these professions invite ways of thinking and methods of practice that are markedly different from those in use in the various scientific disciplines.

Human activity systems, organized at various levels of a society, from the family on up to global systems, can give direction to their evolution and shape their future by engaging in systems design. They can enhance their continuing development and effectiveness by purposeful design. Design is a creative, decision oriented, disciplined inquiry that aims to accomplish the following:

- Diagnose and describe the design problem situation.

- Clarify the reason for engaging in design.

- Establish the boundaries of the design inquiry.

- Formulate core ideas, values, and an image of the future system that will guide the design.

- Define expectations, aspirations, purposes, and requirements of the system to be designed.

- Create and evaluate alternative representations of the future system.

- Establish criteria by which to evaluate alternatives.

- Using the criteria, select the most promising alternative.

- Describe the future system, and

- Plan for the development of the system, based on its description.

Of the set of design tasks outlined above, at this juncture we have completed the description of the first four. Before we describe the rest, in Chapter Ten, a brief review of what has been accomplished is in order.

The decision to engage in the systems design of education was formulated based on an exploration and understanding of unfolding societal developments, the major changes that have happened in the course of the last several decades. This exploration has helped us to gain insight into the larger picture of our transforming society, which constitutes the overall context of education. This exploration has shown that the societal characteristics of the current age are markedly different from—and are discontinuous with—those of the industrial age, in which our educational systems remain rooted. The major shift toward what we often call the Post-Industrial Information Society is manifested in massive changes in general societal characteristics, in socio-cultural, socio-technical, socio-economic, and scientific characteristics, and in organizational characteristics. These characteristics reflect major transformations in all aspects of our lives, a total change of our societal environmental landscape. Such a transformation requires radical changes in the "whats," "hows," "when," and "where" of education. This calls for nothing less than a massive transformation— or metamorphosis—of our educational systems.

An understanding of the implications of the changed societal landscape has helped us (a) to redefine the societal functions of education, (b) to select the focus of design inquiry, (c) to formulate core ideas and values that will guide design, and (d) to create an image of new systems of learning and human development. The image will have the power to direct purposeful systems design and development. It is conceived as an evolutionary image in the sense that it should enable the continuing reshaping of education and the continuous co-evolution of education and the society. The image expresses our aspirations and intentions. But "Intentions are fairly easy to perceive, but frequently do not come about and are not fulfilled. Design is hard to perceive. But it is design and not intention that creates the future" (Boulding, 1985, p. 212). An expression of intention is the beginning of the creation of the system. We now have the difficult task of transforming the image we have created into a design of the future system. To engage in design requires a certain degree of readiness. It requires organizational capacity and human capability and competence. In the last section of this chapter, the tasks of "getting ready" for design are described.

III. GETTING READY FOR SYSTEMS DESIGN

Getting ready for systems design requires (a) an understanding of what design is and how it is carried out, (b) the development of design capability in user-designers, (c) organizational capacity to carry out design, (d) willingness of the community to support the design effort, and (e) the preparation of a plan for engaging in the design inquiry. As these activities are described, comments will be made as to WHY they are necessary.

UNDERSTANDING SYSTEMS DESIGN

Understanding systems design and recognizing the power it offers for the transformation of education are prerequisites for engaging a community in the design of its educational and human development services. This understanding and realization cannot be limited to a few. It has to be generated across the community and reach policy makers, leaders of the public and private sectors, representatives of the many community groups, professionals across all levels of the educational system and in social service organizations, parents, students, and others having an interest in education and human development. Only such a broad based designing community will be empowered in making significant contributions to the design of its educational and human service systems. Initially, and as a first step toward the development of the design community, an orientation program will create awareness of emerged societal characteristics and the existence of a mismatch between the rapidly changing society and the educational services we currently offer. This program will generate an appreciation for the need to transform education by creating new systems of learning and human development. An understanding of how design can respond to this need, and what design is and how it works, will enable people to explore and reflect upon their personal and collective designing responsibility, and the specific contribution they can make to the redesign effort (Banathy & Jenks, 1990a).

DEVELOPING CAPABILITY AND COMPETENCE IN DESIGN

Understanding design and its value to and usefulness in educational reform is the first step in the process of creating a community of "USER-DESIGNERS." The concept of user-designers was introduced earlier. Systems design in the context of any human system is a future-creating activity. People engage in it based on their vision of what their system should be. They are "think future—act now" kind of people. They don't wait for others to act for them. These USER-

DESIGNERS aim to create a system that will have a "goodness of fit" with their own purposes and expectations as well as those of the larger society. The notion of USER-DESIGNERS is based on the belief that systems design is most successful, it is most viable and productive, and commitments to implementing the design are most binding, when it is directed by the users of the future system rather than by outside experts. It is for this reason that I postulate that competence in systems design is a quality of the highest value. I say this knowing well that this competence is rare today. Unfortunately, the acquisition of competence in systems design is not on the agenda of our educational professional development programs. It is hoped and expected that once we understand the need for and significance of systems design, we will provide programs for developing competence in it.

Attaining individual and collective capability to engage in design involves (a) developing design thinking in preparation for design action, and (b) acquiring competence in the use of approaches, methods, and tools appropriate to designing educational systems. The development of competence will require the preparation or adaptation of learning resources in design for use by the educational community and by educational stakeholders. Fortunately, resources for adaptation are now available.

The two kinds of capabilities noted as (a) and (b) in the above paragraph should be addressed by developing two design learning programs: one that will develop DESIGN LEADERSHIP in the community and another that will develop DESIGN ACTION capability in teams that will carry out design.

A. DEVELOPING DESIGN LEADERSHIP

Participants in this program are leaders of the community, including educational leaders, who may be designated to initiate and manage a community-wide design of systems of learning and human development. The purposes of this program include the following: (a) to develop an awareness and appreciation of the roles and role-related competencies and organizational capacities that are necessary for initiating and conducting a comprehensive systems design of education, (b) to develop competence in providing leadership to and learn to manage such a comprehensive systems design in the community, and (c) to develop awareness of resources that are needed to conduct the design. Learning resources have been already developed for a design leadership program (Banathy & Jenks, 1990b).

B. DEVELOPING DESIGN ACTION TEAMS

This guided program of learning about and conducting comprehensive systems design will build design teams, which will carry out the community-wide design. This program aims to (a) develop design and systems thinking and operational design capability in participants who will take the responsibility to become the "core-group" of the systems design program, (b) learn to use the methods and tools applicable in the design of a comprehensive educational system, (c) learn to design and organize the system (people, procedures, resources, arrangements, etc.) that will carry out the design, and (d) learn how to generate in the community an understanding and appreciation of design inquiry as a way to approach comprehensive educational renewal.

In addition to the program described above, advanced training in design is proposed by which individuals would acquire capability in GUIDING AND FACILITATING OTHERS IN DESIGN LEARNING and applications. This program could be offered to personnel in training organizations, professional educators, staff of professional education and public service agencies at higher educational institutions, and most importantly learning to conduct and guide systems design should be the focus of professional development in Educational Technology.

Without having available the kind of multi-level "capability development infrastructure" proposed here, we cannot expect to generate and sustain a local-to-national potential in the systems design of educational and human development services. To create this potential should become the responsibility of educational and social services R&D agencies, professional associations, and universities.

DEVELOPING ORGANIZATIONAL CAPACITY FOR DESIGN

The design of a human activity system such as an educational system requires the development of organizational capacity. In a community which engages in a purposeful design or redesign of its education, a system has to be established which has the organizational capacity and human capability (discussed above) to carry out this process. Throughout this discourse, the notion of USER-DESIGNERS has been emphasized. In the design of educational systems, the implementation of the notion of self-directed design by user-designers means that community representatives and educators organize themselves into a formal design activity system. Such a system is established by constituting interacting design teams at various levels of the systems complex

of the educational and human development services of the community, and organizing design support systems that will provide the
necessary human, material, financial, and facilities support.

GENERATING WILLINGNESS IN THE COMMUNITY TO SUPPORT DESIGN

The development of organizational capacity to carry out design
cannot happen without the explicit commitment of the community
to "underwrite" and support the design activity. Such support cannot
be "legislated." It has to be generated by inviting and encouraging a
genuine involvement of representatives of the community in the
design activity, and providing information to the community initially
on the intended design program, and continuously on progress made
as design unfolds. To sum it up, the design of systems of learning and
human development in a community should be a project BY and FOR
the whole community. Only in this way will the system truly be "owned"
by the community.

PLANNING THE DESIGN INQUIRY

The next major cluster of activities involves the arrangement of
design tasks into an integrated system of inquiry. This cluster follows
the accomplishment of the "getting ready for design" activities
described above. Having accomplished those, user-designers are now
ready to "map out" their design inquiry system, including:

- Formulating ORGANIZING PERSPECTIVES that will guide
  the design inquiry.

- Defining the TYPE of SYSTEM the designers wish to create.

- Establishing CRITERIA (in view of the above) for selecting the
  appropriate design approach, methods, and tools.

- Arranging the selected methods and tools into an internally
  consistent SYSTEM OF INQUIRY, and

- PLANNING the IMPLEMENTATION of the design inquiry
  system.

The five activities identified above will be described in turn.

A. FORMULATING ORGANIZING PERSPECTIVES

The very first task in initiating design inquiry is the formulation of
perspectives that help us to organize our thinking about the inquiry.

By developing these perspectives, we make explicit (a) the values that should guide decisions made about the way we carry out design inquiry, and (b) the notions we have about the nature of design as a human activity and disciplined inquiry. Here examples are presented that indicate the kinds of perspectives designers might formulate.

- The overall strategy of the inquiry should reflect openness; the continuous evolution of images, the revisiting of the vision, the generation of new core ideas about the societal function of education as well as about the inquiry itself.

- The various stages of the inquiry should not be viewed in isolation or as locked in a linear sequence. The inquiry should enhance interaction and recursive and mutually influencing treatment, resulting in an ongoing synthesis and emergence of the design solution. This approach will encourage us to learn to make new distinctions and to gain new insights and, based on these, continuously shape and reshape and elaborate the design solution.

- Another set of perspectives includes the imperatives of participatory design (the notion of user-designers we already discussed), design as the best means to nurture organizational learning, the notion of the power of ideal systems design, readiness for continuing design, and design as a means to serve human betterment and the enrichment of quality of life for all. These perspectives will be discussed in the next chapter.

B. DEFINING THE TYPE OF SYSTEM WE WISH TO DESIGN

A definition of the type of system we wish to design is a necessary prerequisite to selecting the design approach, methods, and tools appropriate to the design of the selected system type. In human activity systems we can differentiate system types based on their characteristics. This notion was already discussed in Chapter Two and Chapter Five. Here a juxtaposition of two types will suffice as an example. An educational system which is controlled by the state or by a religious institution is a rather closed system. It allows limited freedom of selection by people in the system. It discourages diversity and is either rigidly controlled or deterministic. On the other hand, an educational system in which learning is in focus—as discussed in Chapter Five—by definition is an open system. It should allow for selecting learning goals, objectives, methods, and means that best suit the learner. It should, therefore, nurture diversity and distribute control. In fact, it will emphasize motivation rather than control. Using the system-types designation, it becomes either a heuristic or a purpose-seeking system.

C. SELECTING DESIGN METHODS

The specification of the type of system designers wish to create enables the selection of design methods that are appropriate to the type specified. Two kinds of selection criteria should be considered (Banathy, 1988c):

- EXTERNAL CRITERIA should include and probe (a) the general validity of the design method in view of the system type, (b) the soundness of the theoretical base of the methods considered, (c) evidence of testing and evaluation, and (d) evidence of successful applications.

- INTERNAL CRITERIA assess the "goodness of fit" with the particular design effort intended. In considering/selecting design methods, we shall ask such questions as: (a) Do they encourage exploration of alternatives? (b) Do they permit design flexibility and experimentation? (c) Do they provide for continuous feedback and feedforward? and (d) Do they promote continuous synthesis and emergence?

D. ORGANIZING THE DESIGN INQUIRY SYSTEM

The general perspectives and the criteria formulated enable the consideration of various design methods that might be appropriate to our particular design inquiry. Fortunately, today we have available, from the general literature and practice of systems design, a wide range of approaches and methods that can be considered. Once selected, the approach and the methods should be organized and integrated into a design inquiry system. Such organization and integration require the availability of a framework within which to arrange and synthesize what we have selected. In the first part of this chapter, such a framework was introduced as a map of design journey. The framework was created for the very purpose of facilitating the organization of design inquiry.

E. PLANNING THE IMPLEMENTATION OF THE DESIGN INQUIRY

This activity brings together all that we have developed in the course of the various "getting ready" activities described here. It involves (a) the "revisiting" of the design system we have organized in order to take another look and probe its "goodness of fit" with the selected approach/methods/tools, (b) the assessment of our competence in conducting design, (c) the reexamination of organizational capacity to carry out the design inquiry, and (d) the institutionalization and scheduling of the design inquiry, coupled with the allocation of required resources.

REFLECTIONS

In this chapter three additional steps have been taken toward understanding and practicing systems design. First, the "map" of design inquiry was presented. Then, a comprehensive definition of design was introduced. In the last part, activities of "getting ready for design" were described. Now we can take another look at where we are in the course of our design journey. What have we accomplished? What have we yet to accomplish? Our assessment will most likely show that we have developed an understanding and appreciation of systems design as an intellectual technology for use in educational reform. We have reached the threshold of READINESS and state of PREPAREDNESS that are needed to proceed with the rest of the design inquiry. Chapter Ten takes us beyond the threshold and leads us to the completion of the journey.

Chapter Ten

THE PROCESS AND PRODUCTS
OF DESIGN

*"Two roads diverged in a wood—and I—I took the one less traveled
by, and that has made all the difference."*   (Robert Frost)

INTRODUCTION

Systems design is the road that makes the difference. It can make
the difference in educational reform. The design road is the road "less
traveled by" in the educational community, but once it is taken and
followed, it will become a journey to create the future and not just
retrace the past. The educational reform movement is not out of the
woods yet. It stands at a juncture where it can either continue on the
well-traveled road of improvement or select the less-traveled road of
systems design.

The description of the exploration and "get ready" stage of design
having been completed, in this chapter the remaining processes of
design inquiry are introduced and their products characterized. Figure 10.1 lays out the context of this chapter.

First, organizing perspectives are introduced that guide thinking
and decisions about design inquiry, followed by a description of the
processes of FORMULATE, CREATE, and DESCRIBE. In the third
section the products of design are characterized. In the last section,
system development and implementation are dicussed.

I. ORGANIZING PERSPECTIVES

Engaging in design inquiry, designers share their own values and
perspectives about design. Explicitly stated perspectives help them to

FIGURE 10.1. AN OVERVIEW OF THE DESIGN PROCESS

EXPLORE ⟶ FORMULATE ⟶ CREATE ⟶ DESCRIBE

EXISTING SYSTEM	CORE DEFINTION	FUNCTIONS MODEL	ENVIRON-MENT OF FUTURE SYSTEM
	&	&	&
CREATE IMAGE	SPECIFICATIONS	MODEL OF ENABLING SYSTEMS	FUTURE SYSTEM
GET READY			

organize their thinking and action and guide them in their inquiry. The perspectives introduced here are examples of the kinds designers of systems of learning and human development might define as they engage in design work.

COMMITMENT TO PARTICIPATION. Participation of all those who will inhabit the system and/or have a stake in it invites and nurtures creativity in individuals. It makes it possible for them to make a contribution to the creation of the system, and at the same time, it enhances their own continuing development. It enables people to incorporate their individual and collective aspirations and values in the design. Participation also generates consensus in the group and will ensure that people will take part more effectively and with a deeper level of commitment in the implementation of the design. Participation is empowering, and design is empowered by it.

COMMITMENT TO IDEALIZED DESIGN. This means the determination to create the most inspiring and best possible design, one that will act as a magnet and pull us toward its realization. Once the ideal future state of the system is represented by the design, then—and only then—shall we consider constraints and enabling resources in order to attain a feasible, workable, and now implementable design.

The ideal will be "out there" and will inspire our continuing move toward it.

DESIGN IS LEARNING. By learning to design and by engaging in design, we learn as individuals and as an organization. As individuals we improve our understanding of the system and will realize how our performance affects the performance of the whole. As an organization, we learn to reexamine our purposes, perspectives, values, and modes of operation, and develop knowledge and insight based on which we can (re)design our system and make continuous contribution to its life.

DESIGN IS CONTINUOUS. As we move toward the horizon, the horizon is moving ahead of us. Thus, we realize that the ideal model will change. As time goes by, we shall remake the ideal. As we move toward the realization of that ideal, the environment and the situational context in which we operate will change. Based on our commitment to co-evolve with the environment, we shall reexamine and possibly reshape our ideal model. Furthermore, as we pursue something of value—such as the ideal model—the value that we place on it may change as we get closer to it. Our perspectives may also change, suggesting again a new look at both the model and the way we bring it about.

NURTURING HUMAN VALUES AND HUMAN QUALITY. We consider the systems we design to be a human activity system in which human beings are the most valued and are the ones to be served by the system. We consider the system we design to be one in which we collectively seek to attain shared purposes and to define new purposes. We believe that it is our destiny—and it is within our power—to guide our own evolution and the evolution of our system and to give direction to our individual and collective future by design.

II. THE PROCESS OF DESIGNING THE SYSTEM

Once we have gained a good understanding of what design is and completed our planning of the design inquiry, we are ready to engage in the designing or the redesigning of our system. Inasmuch as we wish to create an ideal system, the design inquiry should be constraint-free and operate in the broad space of possibilities. It involves conceptualizing and testing potential alternatives, and selecting the most desirable alternative. The selected design, however, should be technologically feasible to implement. Furthermore, it should be viable in the sense that it is designed to attain the purpose as formulated, and

FIGURE 10.2. THE SPIRALS OF DESIGN

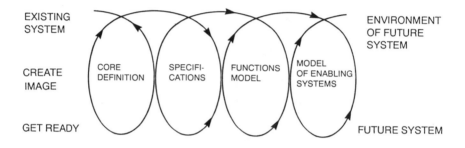

the system designed should be capable of organizational learning and continuous (re)design(Ackoff, 1981).

Design inquiry from here on can be pictured as having four spirals that cross the design solution space, the knowledge base, and the design evaluation space of design inquiry, discussed in Chapter Nine. Inquiry during the FIRST SPIRAL focuses on the formulation of the "core definition" of the system. The SECOND SPIRAL represents the development of specifications for the future system. The THIRD SPIRAL stands for the design of the ideal system of functions. The FOURTH SPIRAL represents the design of systems that provide the organizational capacity and human capability to carry out the functions. Figure 10.2 depicts the four spirals. Sets of questions are formulated for each of the spirals. These questions indicate the substantive program of the inquiry.

Note that the arrows on the spirals point in both directions. This indicates the feedforward and feedback nature of the inquiry. Design work accomplished at any point of the inquiry may have an effect on what already has been done and may lead to a reformulation of earlier resolutions. At the same time, design is also in a feedforward mode as its ongoing inquiry provides bases for making subsequent design decisions. Furthermore, each spiral is made up of a number of decision/choice points at which alternatives are created and considered.

SPIRAL ONE: FORMULATING THE CORE DEFINITION

The spiral which represents the process of formulating the core definition is pictured in Figure 10.3 on the next page.

Here we ask the overall question: WHAT IS THE SYSTEM ABOUT?

More specific questions that guide the inquiry include the following: What are our aspirations regarding the ideal system of learning and human development? What is the mission of the system in serving humanity and the larger society, the community, the learners, people who serve the system, and other stakeholders? What is the shared vision of all these people with respect to the societal function of education and human development? What is the purpose that can give everyone served by the systems and those in the community a sense of clear direction and commitment? A well-structured explanatory synthesis of all answers to these questions will provide us with a comprehensive and very rich core definition of the system to be designed.

In the course of the "front-end" design exploration portrayed in the previous chapters, a great deal of information was developed as designers considered design options, and identified general societal functions of education and human development which were formulated as the educational implications of emerged societal characteristics were considered. They defined core ideas and core values, and created an image of the future system. All this information is now placed in the knowledge base and used in formulating the core definition. The richness of this knowledge base is such that designers have all that is necessary from which to synthesize and formulate a comprehensive mission statement and elaborate it as a statement of purposes of the future system.

A. THE MISSION STATEMENT

A MISSION is a very general statement that can endow everyone in the system and in the community with a sense of commitment. It provides guidance to the design inquiry as it becomes its focus and enables the creation of internal cohesiveness and clear identity for the system, and also informs those who are outside the system. Thus, it

FIGURE 10.3. THE CORE DEFINITION SPIRAL

EXPLORE ⟶ FORMULATE ⟶ CREATE ⟶ DESCRIBE

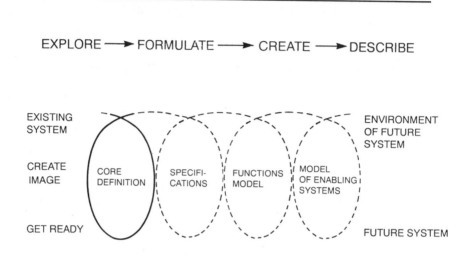

should be both inspiring and informing. Following an expression of the highest level of aspiration, statements of the mission should tell us what the system is going to do for (a) learners and the community, (b) the environment, (c) other systems, (d) its members, and (e) how it sees itself. An example follows. It was generated from examples provided in Part Two. The future system should:

- Become a societal institution that has a global vision of humanity as a whole, and one which makes a purposeful contribution toward human betterment.

- Design, develop, and offer programs and arrangements by which individuals and social groups in the community can attain their fullest potential, enrich their inner quality of life and the quality of their environments, and learn to direct their own life and the life of their systems.

- Develop the community as a LEARNING SOCIETY in which learning, fulfillment, and becoming truly human are collective goals to live by.

- Create a coordinated interorganizational linkage of all social and human service systems in the community in order to offer integrated arrangements and resources for learning and human development that are coherent, easy to use, and continuous.

- Ensure a high quality of working life to its members, encourage and reward cooperation among individuals and groups, and facilitate personal and professional development.

- Become a self-directive and self-organizing system that can learn as an organization and give direction to its continuing development through design, and manage itself by the widest possible participation of its members and the community.

B. A STATEMENT OF PURPOSES

A statement of PURPOSES complements the mission statement as it interprets the IMAGE created in Chapter Seven. The mission statement is a very broad and comprehensive statement, while the statement of purposes focuses more on the design of arrangements for learning and human development. Keep in mind that the image from which purposes are derived was itself a synthesis of the vision and the core ideas and values that emerged from the exploration of design options. The PURPOSES of the future system are to:

- Reflect and interpret the society as well as shape it through co-evolutionary interaction, as a future-creating, innovative, and open system.

- Provide resources, arrangements, and life-long experiences for the full development of all individuals and engender in them the will, the competence, and the wisdom to give direction to their lives and participate in shaping and serving the systems to which they belong.

- Embrace all domains of human and societal existence, including the socio-cultural, ethical, moral, economic/occupational, physical/mental/spiritual, scientific/technological, aesthetic, and political.

- Design and organize the entire system around the learning-experience level; make arrangements in the environment of the learner by which to master learning and human development tasks.

- Make available a wide array of learning types, including self-directed, other-directed, individually supported group learning, cooperative team learning, organizational learning, and learning by the use of technology, all employed to enhance individual and social learning and development.

- Identify, integrate, and energize the many systems in the community that possess resources and opportunities for learning and human development and arrange the easily accessible use of those resources.

The "core" definition of the future system is a composite of the mission and purposes. In formulating the core definition, designers draw on work they have already accomplished and ALWAYS consider ALTERNATIVE formulations which they will test against the core ideas/values and the image.

The examples introduced above are ONLY examples. They have emerged from a particular design option configuration described as an example in Part Two. Selecting a different configuration would result in the production of a different knowledge base for formulating mission and purposes. Even if the same configuration were used, designers operating in a specific environment, which is always unique, would most likely come up with different statements, which is the reason for suggesting that each and every community should design its own system.

SPIRAL TWO: DEVELOPING THE SPECIFICATIONS OF THE SYSTEM

The core definition, formulated as the outcome of spiral one, becomes the basis of developing the specifications of the future system. (See Figure 10.4.)

The inquiry now frames questions the answer to which will lead designers to transform the core definition—the mission statement and statement of purposes—into sets of specifications of the future system. The specifications should be stated in such detail that they can provide a knowledge base adequate to proceed to the next spiral of design, the identification and systemic arrangement of functions that have to be carried out in order to meet the requirements of the specifications and achieve the mission and purposes. A commitment to the ideal systems approach to design suggests that we formulate ideal specifications. The following clusters of questions may guide such formulation:

- Who are the clients of the system? What educational and human developmental services should be offered to them?

FIGURE 10.4. THE SPECIFICATION SPIRAL

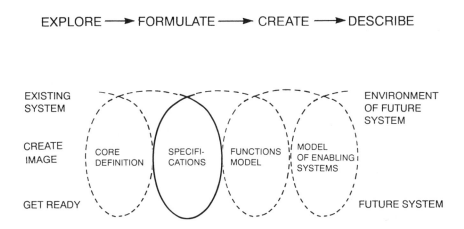

What characteristics should those services have? Where, when, and how should those services be provided?

- Who should "own" the system? How should we distribute ownership? What rights and responsibilities should owners have?

- What kinds of responsibilities should the system have toward its clients, the community, and the larger society? How should these responsibilities be handled?

- How should the educational system relate to the various levels of government? What should be the responsibility of these levels toward the system?

- What kind of relationship should the system have toward the community, community organizations, the private sector, volunteer agencies, and other educational systems and agencies within and beyond the boundaries of the community?

The above clusters of the inquiry are "general" types of examples, the kinds designers would be most likely to ask. There are others that will emerge that are specific to the context of design. In working with those questions, designers should consider all the decisions already made in the course of the inquiry. Within the context and scope of those decisions, they should explore ALTERNATIVES, select the alternative that is most responsive to the core definition, and ensure that there is internal consistency among the elements of the specifications. At this juncture of the design process, no examples are offered, for two reasons. First, the sample questions are self-explanatory and straightforward. Second, by this time decisions have been made by the designers, and a particular example given here would not exemplify.

Answers to questions that lead to specifications are to be synthesized into a comprehensive statement. This statement and the core definition developed earlier constitute SYSTEMS REQUIREMENTS against which we shall design the system.

SPIRAL THREE: DESIGNING THE SYSTEM OF FUNCTIONS

The core definition and systems specifications provide the basis for the consideration and selection of functions that the future system should carry out. Spiral three represents this process as pictured in Figure 10.5.

Spiral three inquiry leads into the design of the first representation or model of the ideal system. Questions pursued in the course of this inquiry probe into setting the boundaries of the system and designing the functions model of the future system.

A. ESTABLISHING THE BOUNDARIES OF THE IDEAL SYSTEM

Boundaries are drawn to mark and set aside a system from its environment. In the course of exploring design options, designers already set boundaries for the design inquiry. Now they are setting the boundaries of the future system, based on the design information that has been developed in the course of the two design spirals. Questions that frame the inquiry include the following:

- Where should we draw the boundaries of our new system so that it will have the organizational capacity, the human capability, and the resources to enable it to achieve the stated mission and purposes and meet the requirements of the specifications?

- What systems of the community should be included within the boundaries that can provide the necessary organizational capacity, collective human capability, and resources required?

- What boundaries mark the SYSTEMIC ENVIRONMENT, the environment with which the future system will constantly inter-

FIGURE 10.5. SPIRAL THREE: DESIGNING THE SYSTEM OF FUNCTIONS

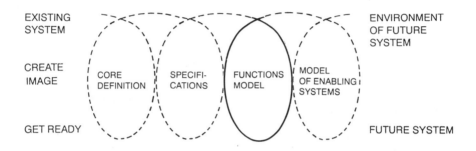

EXPLORE ⟶ FORMULATE ⟶ CREATE ⟶ DESCRIBE

EXISTING SYSTEM   ENVIRONMENT OF FUTURE SYSTEM

CREATE IMAGE   CORE DEFINITION   SPECIFI-CATIONS   FUNCTIONS MODEL   MODEL OF ENABLING SYSTEMS

GET READY   FUTURE SYSTEM

act in order to acquire the various resources needed for the operation of the system?

Earlier, when designers used the framework within which they explored design options, they considered some of the boundary questions. Now they reconsider them in much more detail in view of the core definition and systems specifications.

B. DESIGNING THE FIRST MODEL: THE SYSTEM OF FUNCTIONS

The concepts of model and model building are discussed first, followed by a characterization of building the first model of the future system: the functions model. Then, ways by which the model is evaluated are introduced.

1. Models and Model Building

The product of design inquiry is a representation or MODEL of a future system. The term "model" has several meanings. Underlying them is the notion of a construct or a description that stands for something. Here we are concerned with conceptual models, and among them both deductive and inductive models. A deductive model illustrates the known relationships and characteristics of an existing system. An inductive model is a representation of a system that does not yet exist but is being designed. The deductive model is used to describe the existing state of an educational system. Systems design produces a model of the future educational system. We must represent or model the future system and make the inaccessible accessible so that we can make judgment about the adequacy, relevance, and feasibility of building a desired system. Model building is a most cost-effective and economical mode of disciplined inquiry. It makes it possible to freely speculate about design solution alternatives that can be described and tested in order to arrive at the most promising solution, without a large investment of resources. IT IS MUCH CHEAPER TO DESIGN AND TEST ALTERNATIVE MODELS THAN TO BUILD AND TEST ALTERNATIVE SYSTEMS. Systems design and model building are activities that can save a great deal of money and disappointment to the educational community. Throughout the years we have wasted unknown and untold amounts of resources by not knowing how to design educational systems.

2. Building the Functions Model

A human activity system, such as an educational system, is designed and organized by people in order to attain purposes. These purposes are attained by carrying out functions. Thus, PURPOSES and the FUNCTIONS mark the system. Once the purpose has been determined, the issue becomes: What functions have to be carried out to attain the purpose? And only then: What components have to be involved in what arrangement (the organization) that have the capability to attend to the functions? Thus: "FORM FOLLOWS FUNCTION."

The functions model is "an account of the activities the system must DO in order to BE the system named in the definition" (Checkland, 1981, p. 169). This model is built from VERBS which denote the functions. The relationship of these verbs to each other marks the structure of the model. The model is constructed at several levels of resolution. The key or major activities are organized at a low resolution level and then expanded at a higher level of resolution when the components of each major function are identified. As a result, a systems complex of functions will emerge which will be "pictured" by displaying the functions and connecting them with arrows that represent interdependencies. Questions that drive the identification and systemic arrangement of functions include the following:

- What key functions are to be selected that enable the system to attain its mission, purposes, and expectations as specified in the core definition, satisfy the requirements of the specifications as stated, and provide the services as identified?

- How do these key functions interact, and how do they integrate (at a low resolution) to form a system of functions of the future educational system?

- What are the subfunctions of the key functions displayed at a higher resolution, and how can those be organized into subsystems of the key functions?

- How can designers portray the system complex of functions as an arrangement of the key system functions and their subfunctions?

The relational arrangement of the key functions and their subfunctions constitutes the FIRST SYSTEMS MODEL of the future system. Figure 10.6 represents a model of key functions and Figure 10.7 a model of subfunctions.

3. Evaluating the Model

The functions model is a conceptual model. It is tested conceptually through a line of inquiry which evaluates its adequacy. "There are no valid models and invalid ones, only defensible conceptual models and ones which are less defensible" (Checkland, 1981, p.173). The criteria for testing the model come from the statements of mission and purposes and the specifications. Questions that drive the inquiry include the following:

- Did we provide for all the functions necessary to satisfy the core definition of the system? Are there any redundant functions?

- Will carrying out the functions empower the system to obtain the systems specifications as described?

- Does the system have a functions-based capacity to learn and engage in continuing design?

In exploring these questions, we move into the design evaluation, which most likely will lead to a redesign of the model.

FIGURE 10.6. AN EXAMPLE OF A MODEL OF KEY FUNCTIONS

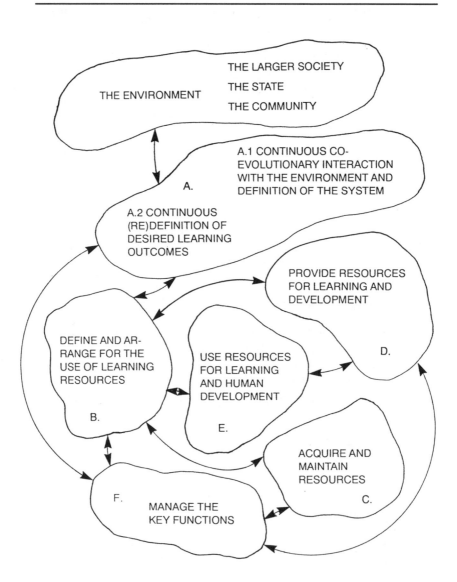

A.1 and A.2 represent the outcomes of Spirals 1 and 2 of the design inquiry.

FIGURE 10.7. COMPONENT FUNCTIONS OF SYSTEM B

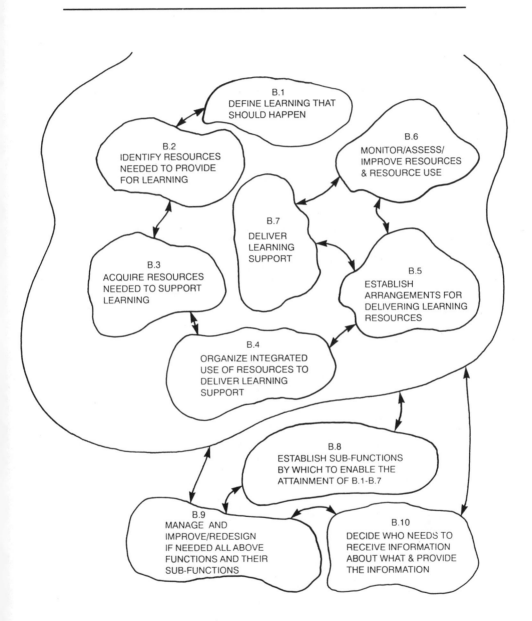

B.8, B.9 and B.10 are relevant to all of B.1-B.7.

SPIRAL FOUR: DESIGNING THE ENABLING SYSTEMS

The system complex of functions tells us what activities have to be carried out in order to attain the mission and purpose and meet systems specifications. In the course of the next design spiral decisions will be made as to who or what will carry out those functions. (See Figure 10.8.)

During spiral four, the inquiry involves the design of the NOUN-BASED version of the functions model as designers create systemic arrangements ENABLING the attainment of functions. The inquiry focuses on the questions: What components have the capacity and capability to carry out the functions identified in the functions model? and, What should be the arrangement of these components? Two NOUN-BASED models will be constructed: (a) a model of a system that has the capacity and capability to MANAGE the functions, and (b) the model of the ORGANIZATION that will carry out the functions. These models portray the two enabling systems (Ackoff, 1981).

A. DESIGNING THE MANAGEMENT SYSTEM

The first NOUN-BASED model that should be designed is the model of the MANAGEMENT SYSTEM that will have the organizational capacity and staff capability to guide the educational system and ensure that the functions will be carried out as specified in the

FIGURE 10.8. THE SPIRAL OF ENABLING SYSTEMS

EXPLORE ⟶ FORMULATE ⟶ CREATE ⟶ DESCRIBE

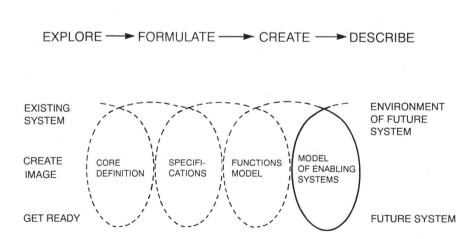

| EXISTING SYSTEM | | | | | ENVIRONMENT OF FUTURE SYSTEM |

| CREATE IMAGE | CORE DEFINITION | SPECIFI-CATIONS | FUNCTIONS MODEL | MODEL OF ENABLING SYSTEMS | |

| GET READY | | | | | FUTURE SYSTEM |

functions model. The question designers ask at this point is: What design (of the management system) will enable it to:

- Conceive a plan to initiate action that provides appropriate response to carrying out the functions and guide the action taken?

- Motivate and energize for individual and collective performance?

- Interact with the environment and collect and analyze information which is of value to the system and which enhances the accomplishment of functions?

- Identify actual and potential problems, threats, and opportunities?

- Engage the system in continuous organizational learning and redesign it whenever appropriate? and

- Acquire and manage the resources needed by the system?

In Chapter Four organizational implications of changed societal characteristics were explored and examples of those implications provided. In designing the management system, as well as the organization, those implications will provide a useful knowledge base.

B. DESIGNING THE ORGANIZATION THAT CARRIES OUT THE FUNCTIONS

The design of the organization builds the second and major NOUN-BASED model of the new system. The challenge of designers is to model a system which will have the organizational capacity and the staff capability to carry out the functions as specified in the functions model. Questions that drive the design inquiry include the following:

- What organizational and personal capabilities are required to carry out the identified functions?

- What system components and people will have those capacities and capabilities?

- How should we organize the selected components in relational(vertical/horizontal) arrangements?

- What authority/responsibility should be assigned to whom?

- What resources should be allocated to what component?

The design is now completed by synthesizing the products of all the spirals into a comprehensive statement of systems description of the future educational system.

III. THE PRODUCTS OF DESIGN AND THEIR TESTING

The outcome of design is products that designers have created in the course of their inquiry. A description and presentation of these products can be arranged by the use of the three general systems models introduced in Chapter Two (Banathy, 1973). They will also prepare a PLAN for DEVELOPMENT and IMPLEMENTATION. This plan includes strategies to be used for the transformation of the model into the real-life development and implementation of the new system.

Using the SYSTEMS-ENVIRONMENT MODEL, designers first characterize the systemic environment, that part of the general environment with which the new system will constantly interact. The SYSTEMS-ENVIRONMENT MODEL enables designers to describe the NEW SYSTEM in the context of the community and the larger society. The model will describe systems-environment relationships, interactions, and the dimensions of mutual interdependence. A set of inquiries will guide designers in assessing the environmental adequacy and responsiveness of the new system and, conversely, the adequacy of the responsiveness of the environment toward the system.

The FUNCTIONS/STRUCTURE MODEL is used to describe the NEW SYSTEM at a given moment in time. It guides designers in presenting the mission and purpose of the system, the functions that must be carried out in order to attain the mission and purpose, the relational arrangement of those functions (the functions model), the components of the system complex that engage in attending to the functions, and their relational arrangement(the structure of the new system). Coupled with this model is a set of inquiries that enables designers to assess the functions/structure adequacy of the new system.

The PROCESS/BEHAVIOR MODEL concentrates on what the new system does through time. It portrays how the system behaves as a dynamic societal system in interaction with its environment: how it receives/screens/assesses and processes input, transforms input into output, assesses and processes the output, makes adjustments and systemic changes, and, if necessary, transforms itself based on information coming from within the system and from the environment.

Another set of inquiries helps designers to evaluate the process/behavior adequacy of the new system.

The three models, also called "lenses," are used by the designers to provide a comprehensive description of the new system and its systemic environment. This description also includes elements that provide opportunities to make a first comprehensive assessment of the system.

In addition to the inquiry-based evaluation of the new system to be accomplished by the use of the three models, another form of testing is also useful. This form is testing by arranging small-scale—real-life—implementation of the integrated design. The findings of this testing, and the assessment made with the use of inquiry built into the three general models, will lead us to assess readiness to develop and implement the system. Or it will lead us to initiate the redesign of the system. The process of testing and revision will reach a point at which designers will have enough confidence to move into systems development and implementation. This point can come quite early, due to the fact that we have designed a system that is capable of continuous learning and redesign. Learning never ends. Neither does design.

IV. SYSTEMS DEVELOPMENT AND IMPLEMENTATION

In the case of the design of new systems designers can move into systems development at once. Based on the outcome of their testing, they might decide that development should proceed. In the case of redesign, however, they need to establish a base-line from which to depart in implementing the design. This base-line is a systems description of the existing system. They will describe the existing system in the same terms they used in describing the new systems, namely, with the use of the three general models. With this description in hand, they can now identify the DISCREPANCY between WHAT now IS, namely, the existing system, and WHAT SHOULD BE, namely, the new system. The specifications of this discrepancy become the basis for planning the means and methods (of development) by which they can close the gap between the existing system and the future system.

At this juncture, designers move into the larger inquiry context which was introduced in Chapter Two, as a model of a COMPREHENSIVE SYSTEM OF ORGANIZATIONAL INQUIRY. Figure 10.9 displays the model. It is reintroduced here for two reasons. First, to show the relationship of design to the larger organizational inquiry context, and second, to discuss the unique contribution of design, beyond producing a model of the new system.

FIGURE 10.9. A COMPREHENSIVE SYSTEM OF ORGANIZATIONAL INQUIRY

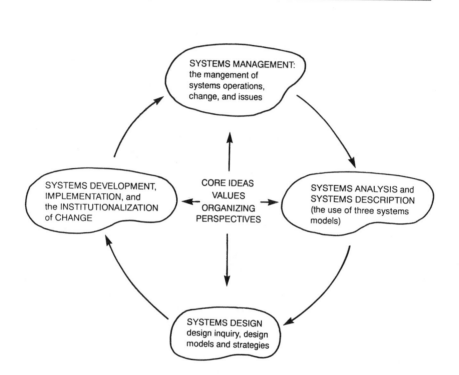

We now place design in the context of the comprehensive system of organizational inquiry. Having completed design, the inquiry moves on into development and implementation. And once implemented, management comes into focus. However, the inquiry does not end here, but it moves again into analysis and, if needed, design.

Working in the design domain of the comprehensive system of organizational inquiry has yielded significant benefits that go beyond the boundaries of design inquiry. These include the following:

- The core ideas and core values generated in the course of the inquiry STAY IN THE CENTER of the larger space of organizational inquiry, becoming a shared guidance to all domains.

- Design has provided a most unique and powerful opportunity to people in the system to learn how to learn as an organization.

This learning will be most beneficial in all the other domains of the inquiry.

- Participation in design has built a strong bond and shared identity among members of the organization. This bond becomes ever stronger as people continue to participate in the life of the system.

- The management of design inquiry can now fold into the management of the system as a mature and well-tried-out organizational capability and arrangement.

The above areas of organizational benefits can be best attained by the kind of design inquiry described in this work. The attainment of these benefits is of value in itself, even without having the value of the creation of the new system.

REFLECTIONS

Chapter Nine introduced the territory of the design journey. In this chapter the journey has led us into a more detailed mapping of the process of design inquiry and has provided a description of the products of design. This chapter can certainly serve as an orientation to those who wish to know more about systems design and find out what the scope of design inquiry is. The various sections of the chapter have guided the reader through the four "creative" spirals of design and discussed strategies that implement design. In conclusion, design was "mapped" back into the larger context of comprehensive organizational inquiry and the special benefits of design—which go beyond the attainment of the model of a new system of education—were briefly mentioned.

In the Appendices examples are introduced that portray work accomplished by design scholars in education.

REFERENCES

Ackoff, Russell L. (1981). *Creating the Corporate Future*. New York, NY: John Wiley & Sons.

Argyris, Chris (1982). *Reasoning, Learning, and Action*. San Francisco, CA: Jossey-Bass Publishers.

Banathy, Bela H.(1973). *Developing a Systems View of Education*. Salinas, CA: Intersystems Publications.

Banathy, Bela H. (1980). "The School: An Autonomous or Cooperative Social Agency." In Louis Rubin, ed., *Critical Issues in Educational Policy*. Boston, MA: Allyn and Bacon, Inc.

Banathy, Bela H. (1987). "Instructional Systems Design." In Robert M. Gagné, ed., *Instructional Technology: Foundations*. Hillsdale, NJ: Lawrence Erlbaum Associates, Publishers.

Banathy, Bela H. (1988a). "A Systems View of Development" in *Goals of Develpment*. Paris: UNESCO.

Banathy, Bela H. (1988b, No. 1.). "Systems Profile: The Evolution of a Systemist." *Systems Research*.

Banathy, Bela H. (1988c, No. 1.). "Matching Design Methods to System Types." *Systems Research*.

Banathy, Bela H. (1988d, June). "Systems Inquiry in Education." *Systems Practice*.

Banathy, Bela H. (1989, No. 4.). "The Design of Evolutionary Guidance Systems." *Systems Research*.

Banathy, Bela H. & Lynn Jenks (1990a). *The Transformation of Education by Design: An Orientation Guide for Educational Decision-Makers*. San Francisco, CA: Far West Laboratory.

Banathy, Bela H. & Lynn Jenks (1990b). *The Transformation of Education by Design: Leadership Guide for Educational Decision-Makers*. San Francisco, CA: Far West Laboratory.

Banathy, Bela H. & David W. Johnson (1977). "Cooperative Group Interaction Skills Curriculum." In Louis Rubin, ed., *Curriculum Handbook*. Boston, MA: Allyn and Bacon, Inc.

Barth, Roland S. (1990). *Improving Schools from Within*. San Francisco, CA: Jossey-Bass Publishers.

Bell, Daniel (1976). *The Coming of Post-Industrial Society*. New York, NY: Basic Books.

Botkin, James (1979). *No Limits to Learning*. London: Pergamon Press.

Boulding, Kenneth E. (1956). *The Image*. Ann Arbor, MI: The University of Michigan Press.

Boulding, Kenneth E. (1985).ʹ *Human Betterment*. Beverly Hills, CA: Sage Publications.

Boulding, Kenneth E. (1989). *The Three Faces of Power*. Beverly Hills, CA: Sage Publications.

Branson, Robert (1988, No. 4.). "Why Schools Can't Improve: The Upper Limit Hypothesis." *Journal of Instructional Development*.

Capra, Fritjof (1982). *The Turning Point: Science, Society, and the Rising Culture*. New York, NY: Bantam.

Carnegie Forum on Education and the Economy (1986). *A Nation Prepared: Teachers for the 21st Century*. Report of the Task Force on Teaching as a Profession. Washington, DC.

Chaisson, Erick J. (1987). *The Life Era*. New York, NY: The Atlantic Monthly Press.

Chaisson, Erick J. (1988, No. 4.). "Our Cosmic Heritage." *Zygon*.

Checkland, Peter (1981). *Systems Thinking, Systems Practice*. New York, NY: John Wiley & Sons.

Churchman, West C. (1982). *Thought and Wisdom*. Salinas, CA: Intersystem Publications.

Csanyi, Vilmos (1982). *General Theory of Evolution*. Budapest: Akademiai Kiado.

Curtis, Richard K. (1982). *Evolution or Extinction*. New York, NY: Pergamon Press.

Elmore, Richard F. and Associates (1990). *Restructuring Schools*. San Francisco, CA: Jossey-Bass Publishers.

Ferguson, Marilyn (1980). *The Aquarian Conspiracy*. Los Angeles, CA: J.P. Tarcher, Inc.

Gleick, James (1987). *Chaos*. New York, NY: Viking.

Harman, Willis (1988). *Global Mind Change*. Indianapolis, IN: Knowledge Systems Inc.

Harvey, Glen & David P. Crandall (1988). "A Beginning Look at the What and How of Restructuring. "In *The Redesign of Education*. San Francisco, CA: Far West Laboratory.

Havel, Vaclav (1990). Speech presented to the U.S. Congress.

Heath, Shirley Brice & Milbrey Wallin McLaughlin (1987, April). "A Child Resource Policy: Moving Beyond Dependence on School and Family." *Phi Delta Kappan.*

Hobbs, Nicholas (1979, Vol. 79). "Families, Youth, and Communities: An Ecosystem for Children." *Teachers College Record.*

Huber, George P. (1986). "The Nature and Design of Post-Industrial Organizations." General Systems, XXIX, *Yearbook of the Society for General Systems Research.*

Hutchins, Larry C. (1990). *A⁺ chieving Excellence.* Aurora, CO: The Mid-Continent Regional Laboratory.

Hutchins, Robert (1968). *The Learning Society.* New York, NY: Praeger.

Huxley, Aldous (1945). *The Perennial Philosophy.* New York, NY: Harper Brothers.

Jantsch, Erich (1981). *The Evolutionary Vision.* Boulder, CO: Westview Press.

Johnson, David W. & Roger T. Johnson (1982, Spring). "The Study of Cooperative, Competitive, and Individualistic Situations." *Contemporary Education: A Journal of Reviews.*

Kniep, Willard M. (1989, Sept.). "Global Education as School Reform." *Educational Leadership.*

Leonard, George (1984, April). "The Great School Reform Hoax." *Esquire.*

Markley, O. W. & Willis W. Harman (1982). *Changing Images of Man.* London: Pergamon Press.

Mitchell, Douglas (1989). Alternative Strategies for School Reform (working paper). San Francisco, CA: Far West Laboratory.

Morgan, Gareth (1986). *Images of Organization.* Beverly Hills, CA: Sage Publications.

Mumford, Lewis (1956). *The Transformation of Man.* New York, NY: Harper Brothers.

Naisbitt, John & Patricia Aburdene (1990). *Megatrends 2000.* New York, NY: William Morrow and Company Inc.

National Commission on Excellence in Education (1983). *A Nation at Risk: The Imperative for Educational Reform.* Washington, DC: U.S. Government Printing Office.

National Governors' Association (1986). Time for Results: The Governors' 1991 Report on Education. Washington, DC: National Governors' Association Center for Policy Research & Analysis.

National Task Force on Educational Technology (1986). *Transforming American Education: Reducing the Risk to the Nation.* A Report to the Secretary of Education. Washington, DC: U.S. Department of Education.

Peccei, Aurelio (1977). *The Human Quality.* Oxford: Pergamon Press.

Perelman, Lewis J. (1987). *Technology and Transformation of Schools.* Alexandria, VA: National School Boards Association.

Polak, E. (1973). *The Image of the Future.* San Francisco, CA: Jossey-Bass Publishers.

Reigeluth, Charles M. (1988, No. 4.). "The Search for Meaningful Reform: A Third-Wave Educational System." *Journal of Instructional Development.*

Roszak, Theodore (1977). *Person-Planet: The Creative Disintegration of the Industrial Society.* New York, NY: Doubleday.

Salk, Jonas (1983). *Autonomy of Reality: Merging of Intuition and Reason.* New York, NY: Columbia University Press.

Schlechty, Phillip C. (1990). *Schools for the 21st Century.* San Francisco, CA: Jossey-Bass Publishers.

Schorr, Lisbeth B. (1988). *Within Our Reach.* New York, NY: Doubleday.

Sculley, John (1987). *Odyssey.* New York, NY: Harper & Row.

Simon, Herbert (1989). *The Sciences of the Artificial.* Cambridge, MA: MIT Press.

Smith, Elise & Clement B.G. London (1981, Vol. 16). "A Union of School, Community, and Family." *Urban Education.*

Sorokin, Pitrim (1941). *The Crisis of Our Age.* New York, NY: Dutton.

Toffler, Alvin (1980). *The Third Wave.* New York, NY: Bantam Books Inc.

Toynbee, Arnold (1947). *A Study of History.* Oxford: Oxford University Press.

Vickers, Geoffrey (1983). *Human Systems Are Different.* London: Harper & Row Ltd.

Webster's New Collegiate Dictionary (1979). Springfield, MA: G. & C. Merriam Company.

Zigler, Edward & Heather Weiss (1985). "Family Support Systems: An Ecological Approach to Child Development." In Robert N. Rapoport, ed., *Children, Youth, and Families.* Cambridge: Cambridge University Press.

APPENDICES

INTRODUCTION

The Appendices introduced here are examples that—in the context of the book—represent various design configurations and design options. The three examples are characterized here on the three dimensions of an educational design option: (1) the scope of the inquiry, (2) the focus of the design, and (3) relationship with other systems in the environment.

APPENDIX A: A THIRD-WAVE EDUCATIONAL SYSTEM by Charles M. Reigeluth represents a design option which places the LEARNING EXPERIENCE in the FOCUS of the system complex to be designed. It does not elaborate on the educational function or the learning agenda of the information age, but indicates the absolute necessity to design the system from a LARGER SOCIETAL PERSPECTIVE. On the choice of relationships dimension, Reigeluth indicates COOPERATING RELATIONSHIP with other systems of the community.

APPENDIX B: THE APPLICATION OF DESIGN TO SCHOOL PLANNING by C.L. Hutchins makes a commitment to the SYSTEMS DESIGN choice in educational reform. The other two, Hutchins says, are: increasing the efficiency or increasing the effectiveness of the old design. He suggests that only a new design will enable us to achieve excellence. He describes the process of a design program that is based on (a) SOCIETAL ANALYSIS, and (b) FOCUSES on the LEARNING-EXPERIENCE LEVEL, and identifies with a strong orientation toward SYSTEMS THEORY and its APPLICATION in education.

APPENDIX C: EXPERIENCE-BASED CAREER EDUCATION by Lynn Jenks reports on the outcome of a SYSTEMS DESIGN of education that represents a LEARNING-FOCUSED approach and COORDINATION with other systems in the community. Jenks provides a detailed description of how a learning-focused approach operates in a variety of learning territories that provide experiential learning. When we designed this system in the early seventies, that effort represented the first comprehensive systems design effort for us.

APPENDIX A

A Third-Wave
Educational System

Charles M. Reigeluth

Indiana University

This appendix describes a preliminary "blueprint" outlining the systemic characteristics that a "third-wave" educational system might have. The first-wave educational system was the one-room schoolhouse, which was created for an agrarian society—the first wave (Toffler, 1980). The second-wave educational system is our current system, which was created for an industrial society—the second wave. A new educational system needs to be designed to meet the needs of an information society—the third wave.

Many people look back to the one-room schoolhouse with a good deal of longing and nostalgia. As with most things from the "good olde days," the one-room schoolhouse was not everything that we, our parents, or our grandparents remember it as being. There were, however, several educational advantages that the one-room schoolhouse had over our present schools. The teacher worked individually with most students, in contrast to our present group-based system. Students progressed at their own pace, as opposed to our current lock-stepped or tracked system. Students were not promoted to learn new skills and knowledge until they had mastered the current ones (nor were they held back once they had already mastered the current ones), in contrast to our present time-oriented, graded system. The teacher was responsible for the child (as opposed to a content area), was concerned with the whole child (as opposed to just one aspect of his or her intellectual development), and was often a partner with the child's parents and thereby responsive to their desires and able to draw on their influence.

Also, there were considerable benefits from having children of a variety of ages in the same room, such as opportunities for peer tutoring and role modeling. A teacher was able to work with each child over a period of years and, therefore, a thorough knowledge of each child and a consistency in monitoring and follow-through existed that is often lacking in today's schools. In the present, second-wave school system, where children usually rotate from one teacher to another each day and completely change teachers each year, the teachers often just begin to know and understand most of the children by the end of the school year. This results in many needs going unmet and a great deal of inefficiency in meeting those that are eventually met. And perhaps most importantly, the reduced knowledge and understanding of each child usually results in a great deal less caring than existed in the one-room schoolhouse. The negative effects of this problem have been made even more severe by today's large and impersonal school environments, which have done much to foment alienation and violence in our youth.

We do not in any way believe that a third-wave educational system should merely be a one-room schoolhouse with modern paint. Our society and its needs have changed too much for that. But we do believe that we should carefully consider the positive and negative structural characteristics of our present and past systems in attempting to develop a structure that will be appropriate for a third-wave educational system.

In 1983 we formed a small design team of researchers and practitioners, parents and teachers, to work for four months on the initial development of a blueprint for a third-wave educational system. We decided to focus our attention on the systemic components of an educational system, both because there was so much evidence that the current problems lie primarily in the structure of the system and because we felt that the people of a community should decide on the other aspects of education: the goals and content.

I. Overview

In our third-wave educational system, the teacher's role has changed from one of disseminating knowledge to one of motivating, advising, and managing the child's learning. Well designed resources (including interactive computer and videodisc systems), peer tutors, projects, and learning centers are used to convey most of the skills and knowledge. A teacher is responsible for a child for a period of three to five years. And the school district contains a variety of small, competing "schools" for parents to choose from (all at no cost to parents, and with no power for any school to turn any child away, thereby providing a degree of diversity and, simultaneously, accountability that are both sorely lacking in the present system).

These and other aspects of the structure of a third-wave educational system are described next. However, it is important to keep in mind that this blueprint is one possible vision of a third-wave system. We hope it will help to encourage new ideas for the design of a better school system for a rapidly changing information society.

Teachers as Guides

People learn at different rates. Yet the current system "teaches" a fixed amount of content in a fixed amount of time, and then compares the students with each other by giving A's and F's. It is as if the current educational system were designed more for selection than for learning, to separate the managers from the laborers in an industrial society.

If the new system is to focus on learning, rather than selection, then it must allow time to vary so that achievement can be held constant at a mastery level. But time cannot be allowed to vary unless we have a personalized system rather than a group-based system. And we cannot have a personalized system unless we rely much more on well designed resources and change the teacher's role from lecturer (dispenser of information) to facilitator and manager (coach). This is why most people who have advocated systemic redesign of our schools have called for a different role for teachers, a role that is more professional and that relies more on technology to free the teacher from routine tasks and drudgery. Accordingly, in our third-wave educational system the relationship between the teacher and the child is not one of dispenser and receiver of information.

In an information society, more and more learning occurs outside of schools; the parents and the community are important sources of learning. Therefore, one of the teacher's roles is to orchestrate and coordinate efforts by parents, community, and school. And within the school, most knowledge is conveyed through well designed resources (including real objects, printed materials, and interactive computer-based instruction), inexpensive assistants (including apprentice teachers, senior citizen volunteers, parents, and peer tutors), projects, discussion groups, learning centers, and resource people.

Hence, the teacher is more a *guide* than a teacher, as is the case in the Montessori system, which has functioned well in this mode. The role of the guide is one of motivating, advising, and managing the child, rather than dispensing knowledge. The guide is a conductor rather than a musician. She or he is an instructional manager and facilitator who helps the child and parents decide upon appropriate instructional goals (within limits) and then helps identify and coordinate the best means for the child to achieve those goals. And those goals go beyond the intellectual development of the child; they may extend to the child's physical, social, moral, emotional, and psychological development, depending on the parents' wishes. And they extend to all of Howard Gardner's seven intelligences (Gardner and Hatch, 1989).

Guides work individually and in small groups with children to insure that they reach their goals. Therefore, there is no such thing as a "class" in the sense of a group of children who learn the same material in the same place at the same time for a whole term or academic year. (There are, however, occasional discussion groups and seminars, which are especially useful in such areas as literature; and some mini-courses utilize class meetings when better alternatives are not available.) Each child has personal educational goals, and a unique combination of resources is prescribed with the help of a computer-based advisement and management tool. The cost-effectiveness of this system is very promising and is discussed later.

Developmental Levels as Grade Levels

In the agrarian society, there was the extended family in which grandparents, aunts, and uncles did much to raise the kids. In the industrial society, it was replaced by the nuclear family in which the mother stayed home and raised the kids and made sure they got their homework done. Now in the information era the single-parent home has become the norm, and in the majority of two-parent homes both parents work outside the home. Parenting has changed greatly, and in many homes there is little time for a meaningful, caring relationship between parents and children.

To compensate for this, in our third-wave educational system a guide is responsible for each of his or her students for a period of approximately 3 to 5 years: one of the developmental stages of the child's life. On the basis of work by Piaget, Erikson, and others, we currently conceive of four stages as being relevant to the school system: approximately ages 3 to 5, 6 to 9, 10 to 13, and 14 to 18. The school organization is structured around these four levels, enabling each guide to work with a child for an average of four years. Either the parents or the guide can request a change before the child enters the next developmental level, but there is a "test period" of, say, 6 months during which no changes are allowed. The process whereby parents request a guide is described next.

Parents Choose Guides

Parents request a guide for each of their children. On the basis of information made available by an independent "consumer support" type of district-wide office and on the basis of word of mouth and interviews with guides, the parents request in order of preference about three to five guides (depending on the size of the school district). The "consumer support" office also provides diagnostic testing and interviews to help parents make the best decision, or to make it for them if they are not interested. Each guide decides how many children to accept each year, but does not decide which children to accept — that is decided by a formula that maximizes the number of first choices filled district-wide, within the constraints of racial and socio-economic balance guidelines.

"Clusters" as Independent Schools

In other professions like medicine and law, professionals often have more of an opportunity to consult with each other and even work together on common problems rather than always working in isolation. And, unlike teachers, they maintain a high degree of decision-making participation in, and control over, their organization. In a similar way, even though parents choose an individual guide, that guide does not work independently, but is a member of a "cluster" of guides. A cluster usually consists of about 4 to 10 guides, their assistants, their students, and a leader, who is a "master guide."

Like a lawyer in a law firm, each guide has considerable responsibility for the success of the cluster, *and* considerable incentive to meet that responsibility (see next paragraph), *and* considerable power to meet that responsibility. In the present system, teachers are given the first but not the last two! Is it any wonder that the structure of the system works against good results! Just as the "administrator" of a law firm is a practicing lawyer, so the master guide is an active teacher. But the master guide also has a variety of other responsibilities, foremost of which is instructional leadership for the cluster. Ultimately, the master guide has the major (but not the only) responsibility for the climate and success of the cluster.

Incentives and Rewards

One of the characteristics of an information society is the rapid rate of change. Our current educational system is highly resistant to change, so that a crisis is necessary before any significant change can take place. To design a third-wave system that is also highly resistant to change would be to ensure another educational crisis at some time in the not-too-distant future.

A third-wave system should be self-designing, so that change is continuous and crises are avoided. Therefore, change is demand-based (user-based) rather than bureaucracy-based (administrator-based). A cluster's success depends on how satisfied the parents and children are, because its budget depends in part on the number of first-, second-, and third-choice requests for all of its guides. As its budget grows, a cluster in high demand can grow and provide its services to more students, whereas a cluster in low demand will have to take fewer students. With incubation policies to encourage the formation of new clusters, the educational system will constantly evolve to meet the needs of a changing society.

But competition can have negative effects, unless the system is designed in such a way as to avoid them. Therefore, the budget of each *cluster* varies with the demand for its guides, not the income of each *guide* directly. Each guide's "full-time" salary is determined by the cluster guides (similar to law firm partners), within the constraints of their budget, for it is the guides themselves who decide how to spend their budget. Each guide's salary is then adjusted according to the percent of a full-time load (number of students) he or she has. Hence, there is considerable incentive to help any guides in one's cluster who are not doing well. This results in a nice combination of *competition* among clusters (providing incentives for excellence and responsiveness to the community's diverse desires and needs) and *cooperation* within each cluster (providing support and encouragement among guides), not unlike that characterizing most other professions.

With respect to competition, the dependence of cluster resources on parental satisfaction makes guides very accountable for what they do or don't do. If a cluster is doing a bad job of meeting parental expectations, its budget will fall, as will the income for each of its guides. With respect to cooperation within each cluster, the fact that a guide's income depends not only on his or her own efforts, but also on the success of the other guides in the cluster results in a much greater incentive to cooperate and help each other to insure that all the cluster's children do as well as possible.

Learning Centers

In the fields of law, accounting, and medicine, the general practitioner has access to specialists in different areas. In a similar way, the guide has access to various learning centers (as well as other specialists). A learning center provides instruction in a specific focus area. It can be a traditional, discipline-oriented area such as biology or a cross-disciplinary, problem-oriented or thematic area such as pollution. These learning centers operate completely independently of the clusters. All children in the school district receive a certain number of passes that entitle them to use the learning centers (and they can earn additional passes). The centers in turn receive their resources (budgets) on the basis of the number of passes that they collect, so there is considerable incentive to attract students and satisfy cluster guides' needs. Again there is a nice combination of competition among centers and cooperation within a center. We currently envision three types of learning centers: "shopping mall" centers, community centers, and mobile centers. They are described in some detail later.

In summary, the major aspects we currently envision for this third-wave educational system are the following:

1. Teachers are guides who, in cooperation with the child's parents, motivate, advise, and manage a child's education for 3 to 5 years.

2. Educational resources (including well-designed materials, peer tutors, projects, discussion groups, learning centers, and resource people) are used to effect most of the learning.

3. There are no traditional "classes," but each child has individual goals, and a unique combination of resources and approaches is prescribed to reach those goals.

4. Guides work cooperatively within an educational cluster with about 4 to 9 other guides, including a master guide.

5. The master guide sets the school climate and philosophy, hires guides and assistants, provides professional development for guides and assistants, and provides direction and leadership for the whole cluster.

6. After a trial period, parents are free to request to move their child to another available guide and cluster if they are not satisfied with their child's progress. Hence, individual guides and clusters are very accountable for what they do or don't do, and they have considerable incentive to work with parents.

7. Guides have a great financial incentive to cooperate and work together for the success of the whole cluster.

8. Guides can send children to learning centers of various kinds to receive the best available instruction in selected focus areas.

The following is a more detailed description of the various aspects of the structure of this third-wave educational system.

II. Cluster Operations

Because the guide is the hub of this educational universe, the structure of the system is further described on that level. As was mentioned above, every guide must belong to a cluster, which is much like a small law firm or medical clinic. Also, a guide is responsible for children for one complete level of development (approximately four years). In an exceptional case, a guide might prefer that his or her students be spread out over two or even three levels, rather than just one. In such cases it is probably advisable that children switch to a different guide upon transitioning to the next level.

Each guide often uses apprentices (training to become guides), advanced students, and volunteers (including parents, senior citizens, and other members of the community) as assistants to help further the learning and development of his or her students. Many receive credits for their services, rather than money. Those credits entitle them to personal use of the learning centers for continuing education or the child care center for care of their own children. Tutoring is also a valuable experience for students. There is an apt adage that "the best way to learn something is to teach it." Students are a very much overlooked resource that can save a school system much money, improve learning, and result in even greater benefits for the tutors. But they must have proper training and guidance to be most effective (Frey and Reigeluth, 1986).

At this point, our best guess is that in Level 1 (ages 3 to 5) each guide is responsible for about 25 children, in Level 2 (ages 6 to 9) about 35 children, in Level 3 (ages 10 to 13) about 45 children, and in Level 4 (ages 14 to 18) about 55 children. These differentials reflect the increased use of learning centers as the age level increases. The services of apprentices, advanced students, and volunteers considerably increase the number of students each guide can handle. However, these figures are our best guess at present, and experience may reveal better figures.

As mentioned earlier, each guide decides how many children to accept; that is, what portion of a "full load" to accept. The importance of parent satisfaction keeps this figure from becoming too large, and the guide's personal income needs keep it from being too small. But if a guide wants to work half time on, say, writing a book or educational software, then he or she can do so by accepting fewer students (and receiving a lower income from the district).

Anywhere from about 4 to 10 guides can comprise a cluster. With 4 guides in each cluster, there would be one guide on each of the four developmental levels, assuming that the cluster elects to serve all four levels. Such a cluster would have about 160 children spread out over the ages of 3 to 18. This means that there would be an average of about 10 children of any given age within the cluster. If the cluster serves only two developmental levels, there would be an average of about 20 children of any given age within the cluster. This size allows the children to get to know most other students in the cluster fairly well, resulting in a more friendly and caring environment and more cross-age interaction.

Specifics by Level

In Level 1 the guides are very similar to Montessori teachers (Standing, 1962). They introduce children to well-designed educational resources as the children become ready for them, and the resources do most of the teaching of knowledge and skills. The guides also arrange activities that help develop the child socially, emotionally, and physically (motor coordination). Children are exposed to a variable environment in which caring guides and assistants nurture their development and encourage them to alternate regularly between learning activity, social interaction, free play, exercise, and rest.

Most learning at this level takes place within appropriate cluster facilities, but field trips are occasionally taken so that the outside environment can influence the children's development. Mobile learning centers (discussed in the next section) and other outsiders (including parents) occasionally come and put on a program to enrich home-room activities.

Parents can leave their child in the cluster facility as long as they wish, but there is a charge if the child is left for more than six hours per day. This charge can be paid in money or in time contributed to the cluster.

The more advanced children occasionally participate in activities in a Level 2 group. This facilitates their transition into the next level with a minimum of anxiety (even if the child advances to a different cluster). The timing of the full "graduation" to the next level is made in consultation with the parents and is based on a combination of the child's intellectual, social, and emotional development, including level of learning skills and degree of self-directedness and responsibility.

In Level 4, the opposite end of the developmental spectrum, the cluster facility is more of a conference room than a home room and activity room. Almost all content learning occurs in the learning centers, including center-sponsored seminars, projects, and tutoring sessions. Also, intellectual scavenger hunts entailing interdisciplinary problem solving are widely used. Guides spend much time monitoring and motivating the children and just plain caring. Much time is also spent in individual conversations, for the guide is more a counsellor (an educator in the true sense of the word) than a teacher. In the domain of cognitive development, those conversations are often directed at higher levels of knowledge, including synthesis and evaluation in Bloom's (1956) taxonomy and cognitive strategies (or generic skills) in Gagné's (1977) taxonomy. Service projects are often required of students.

The guide also works closely with the parents on such other concerns as the child's emotional, social, artistic, moral, and psychological development. This entails (1) identifying with the parents any aspects of development that need work or any obstacles to further development that need to be removed, and (2) developing with the parents an appropriate plan that entails certain parental actions, as well as certain guide actions of which the parents approve. The design team, as parents who had occasionally felt as if we were at our rope's end with one of our children, thought that it should also entail providing advice—when desired by the parents—on how to handle behavior problems and how in general to increase the quality of home life.

On the intervening levels (2 and 3), the guides serve both roles described above (for Levels 1 and 4). The degree to which each role is played by the guide progresses as the child develops from a Level 1 person to a Level 4 person.

At whatever level, district policy requires each guide to abide by a "renaissance approach" that establishes a certain balance of development in each of a broad range of basic areas, including thinking skills. Students' quarterly contracts (described later) require them to advance by a certain number of levels of development in each area every month. The contracted levels vary depending on the general ability level of the child. For example, a child with an IQ of 50 is not expected to advance the same number of levels as one with an IQ of 150. Benjamin Bloom (1976) has evidence to suggest that the differences in rate of learning that currently exist in our schools are more a function of differences in accumulated skill and knowledge deficiencies than of differences in "intelligence." If this is true, then there will not be large differences from one student to another. In any event, the emphasis in our system is on each child's achieving according to his or her potential. For "late bloomers" the levels are adjusted to represent more rapid advancement.

As long as the contracted number of levels of development is attained in all areas, the students may study whatever they want, whenever they want. Students tend to exceed the contracted number of levels in focus areas that they like. And for a focus area that they don't particularly like, they decide when to work on it and they are motivated to get it done as quickly as possible. In a cluster there might be a big chart on which advancements in each focus area are posted for each student. And points might be given for each advancement, with students in the cluster belonging to teams that compete to get the highest number of team points.

A guide maintains an achievement profile for each of his or her students on a computer-based advisement and management system. Grades are not given, because in an information society, a profile of the kinds of abilities and knowledge one has is more important than a letter grade or a general rank in class.

There are cluster-wide and district-wide interest groups and clubs, dealing with such interests as computers, drama, photography, woodworking, music, chess, and dance. There are also cluster-wide and district-wide social events and athletic events. A major benefit of this structure is a much higher rate of student participation in athletics and other interests. Opportunities for leadership and exercise of responsibility are also increased (Brandt, 1981). Volunteers (parents, senior citizens, and other community members) and older students do much of the supervision, as is presently done with Little League baseball and Scout programs.

III. Learning Centers

It was mentioned earlier that learning centers provide specialized expertise and learning resources in different focus areas; and we explained that the older the child, the more the centers are used. A learning center can be for a traditional, discipline-oriented area such as biology or for a thematic, cross-disciplinary, problem-oriented area such as pollution. And it can be for an intellectual area such as philosophy or for a technical area such as automobile maintenance and repair. In all cases, centers are encouraged to incorporate instruction on thinking skills and other higher-order skills into the focus area instruction, and a guide is responsible for helping the student to put together a program of study that represents a good progression of such higher-order skills instruction. Resources are allocated to the centers on the basis of their usage, providing a combination of cooperation and competition similar to that for the clusters.

We mentioned earlier that there are three types of learning centers: mobile centers, community centers, and "shopping mall" centers. The mobile centers are centers on wheels that travel around from one cluster to another and even from one district to another. The community centers are located at the organizations which sponsor them, such as museums and businesses. Tax deductions are an important incentive for the creation of such centers. The "shopping mall" centers are centrally located, with easy access from all of the clusters. They range from a one-room, one-person (part-time) "craft shop" operation to a nationwide operation (the "Sears" of the shopping mall centers). There tends to be continuous (although not too frequent) turnover as the "offerings" adjust to changing times and changing demands. Also, there are cooperative arrangements whereby children may use centers located in another school district.

All learning centers must be approved and periodically recertified by the school district's Center Management Organization (described later). Learning centers can be started by almost anyone in any focus area, including cross-disciplinary areas, but certain training and standards (especially regarding character) are required. A learning center director runs the center; and depending on the nature of the center, the director finds out about and makes available top-quality resources, plans good activities, makes arrangements for community-based experiences, hires, trains and monitors assistants (apprentices, advanced students, parents, and other members of the community) to help teach, and interacts personally with children to motivate, advise, and manage their learning within that focus area. Teachers refer their students to specific learning centers and even to specific personnel in a learning center. Many learning centers are run by part-time amateurs/hobbyists and retired people at very little expense to the school district.

Logistically, the shopping mall centers are usually located at the "hub of a wheel" in which the clusters are located in separate buildings out on the "rim," attached by enclosed walkways ("spokes"). This arrangement eliminates the need for transportation and allows for district facilities such as libraries, auditoriums, child-care centers, and food services to be easily accessible to all clusters, while still maintaining some physical separateness for each cluster. Although food preparation could be done centrally, each cluster should have its own cafeteria to help build cluster cohesion. Very large districts might have several such "wheels" at different locations within the district. Although such a logistical arrangement might be ideal, existing school buildings can be used with relatively few modifications to meet the same needs.

How a Student Uses the Learning Centers

At the beginning of each quarter (three month period), each student in the district is allocated a certain number of learning center passes. The exact number depends on the child's level of intellectual development—the higher the development, the more passes awarded, because more of their learning occurs in learning centers. Also, each child can earn additional passes through such activities as tutoring, helping with the preparation of displays and materials, and supervising extra-curricular activities.

Some of the passes are "restricted" passes and some are "open" passes. The restricted passes must be used for the advancement of learning and development specified by the child's quarterly contract, whereas the open passes can be used to study anything the student wants. This results in a balance of structure and flexibility.

Each pass must be filled out and signed by the student's guide, who indicates the center in which it is to be used. This helps the guide to influence and keep track of the child's learning. The child hands in the pass to the center, so that the center can then cash it in for payment from the Center Management Organization (described later). The passes could be implemented electrically with magnetic ID cards and electric time clocks that feed data on student and center usage into the district-wide, computer-based, advisement and management system. Guide approval is entered into the computer system, and the system rejects any child who tries to log in to a center without a valid restricted or open pass. Each center allows each student a minimum of one hour of free "browsing" every quarter for purposes of seeing if there is anything he or she would like to learn in that center. Of course, the center receives remuneration from the school district for such browsing.

Having a limited supply of passes to use in a quarter, the children are more concerned with making the most of each one — that is, not wasting precious time "hacking around." Also, having the flexibility to study what they want when they want (within the structure of the minimum requirements and the other goals specified in a child's quarterly contract) provides heightened motivation and increased self-determination and self-management that are so important in an information society.

IV. What the Student Does

At the beginning of each quarter, the guide sits down with each of his or her students and the student's parents, either in the cluster or at the student's home. Together, they prepare a plan or contract for the student's learning and development goals and activities for the quarter. As a result of this plan, a checklist of required goals and activities is prepared (probably with the help of the computer-based advisement and management system), and the use of restricted passes is planned. Some time is allocated for students to pursue their own interests with their open passes, whose use is also discussed and informally planned at the beginning of each quarter.

The intent here is to establish a balance between structure and flexibility. Each cluster may establish its own policy (or lack thereof) with respect to the balance between requirements and options, except that the district may establish certain minimum levels of development in different focus areas for different age groups (perhaps adjusted by individual limits to rate of development as measured by, say, IQ or some better indicator).

At this time, the guide and parents may also have a private conversation about any problems the parents are having with the child so that the guide can give advice and/or take steps to help out. The guide also identifies things the parents can do or need to do to help the child achieve his or her quarterly goals (not just intellectual, but also emotional, social, artistic, and physical).

At the end of each quarter, the guide sits down with each child and the parents and reviews the child's achievements in relation to the contract for the quarter. This provides part of the basis for planning the next quarterly contract, which usually occurs at the same session. Since parents choose guides, they are much more inclined to work with them. And since guides' income depends on parental satisfaction, they have much more incentive to work with parents.

V. Extensions of the Present System

The present educational system is extended in two important ways, in addition to the concern for nonacademic aspects of the child's development: (1) it is open longer and (2) it is open for use by adults. It is open longer in three ways. It is open more hours per day, until, say, 9:00 p.m.; it is open on weekends; and it is open during vacations, including all summer long. These are all done at little extra expense because guides and other personnel, like their students, work at staggered times and heavy use is made of volunteer and nonprofessional help.

Students can take vacations whenever their parents want, due to the personalized structure of the school. Similarly, guides and staff can take their vacations pretty much whenever they want because of the multiple-leveled staffing structure of the system (apprentice guides, volunteers, and older students). Guides feel less of a need for a long vacation in their new roles, and this eliminates the need for teachers to find summer employment at what are often not very rewarding jobs (professionally or financially). Hence, it makes education a year-round profession, like law and medicine, with flexible opportunities for vacations.

Adults (people over 18 years old) can buy or earn passes to use the learning centers, making the school system a place where young and old can learn together. It also provides an extra source of income and labor for running the school system. Finally, children can start school earlier than the traditional kindergarten age. The school district's child care services are simultaneously educational services and are available from birth. Prenatal consultation and guidance are also available. In fact, many of the community's social service agencies are integrated with the educational system.

VI. District Organization and Administrative Systems

All school tax revenues, block grants, and state aid go directly to the school district office for district-wide distribution. The district office establishes a budget for clusters by establishing an amount per pupil and multiplying by the number of pupils anticipated for that year, and a budget for the Learning Center Management Organization by establishing an amount per pass and multiplying by the number of passes anticipated for that year. These budgets are then approved by a vote of the community members, who simultaneously approve a local tax rate to supply the community's portion of the educational costs.

The budget for clusters is allocated to each cluster based to some extent on the demand for its guides. The budget for the learning Center Management Organization (CMO) is allocated to each center in accordance with the number of passes it receives, except that a certain percent is kept to meet the CMO's administrative expenses. Finally, the Consumer Support Agency receives a flat percentage of the total school district budget (around one-half of one percent); and the district office keeps a flat percentage (much lower than current levels) for its administrative expenses.

Cluster Organization and Administration

A new cluster can be started by anyone who meets the requirements, but a cluster can be disbanded if it ever fails to meet minimum standards set by the school board (and individual personnel can be "disbarred" if they are found by the district review board to be negligently unprofessional). It is probably wise to specify a minimum of three or four guides for forming a cluster. Training and certification are required for anyone who wants to be a guide. The training and certification are provided by schools of education that have been certified by a National Institute for Third-Wave Education. Some local training may also be required regarding the district's computer-based advisement and management system and current learning centers. The master guide is chosen by the guides that comprise the cluster, and a 2/3 majority is required to replace the master guide.

For an established cluster, the hiring of new guides is decided by a 2/3 majority of the cluster's guides. The firing of a guide would be based on standards that are clearly laid out in the charter of the cluster or school district regulations, but those standards should allow a sufficient length of time for new guides to improve and for older guides to reform their ways. Because of the importance of cluster cohesiveness and cooperation among guides, a simple majority is sufficient for a cluster's guides to decide whether or not the criteria for release have been met. There is no grievance or appeal procedure, again because of the importance of cluster cohesiveness and cooperation among guides. There is no standard grievance procedure when a lawyer or doctor is released from a law firm or medical clinic, but that is extremely rare.

An administrative person from the district office is in charge of the accounting, reports, and logistical aspects for all clusters within the school district, but the cluster decides how its budget will be spent. This frees the head guide to concentrate on instructional concerns and school climate. In general, the central administration's role is to facilitate rather than control the activities of the small, relatively autonomous operating units, because the accountability system is vested in the users of the system rather than in a bureaucracy.

It was mentioned earlier that each cluster's budget is dependent to some extent on the total demand for its guides. A point system is used whereby each guide receives 3 points for being the first choice of a "new" student, 2 points for being the second choice, and 1 point for being the third choice. A "new student" is one entering a new level of development, one entering the school system for the first time, or one requesting a new guide after the six-month trial period. The "budget rate" for each cluster is determined solely by the cluster's total points divided by the number of guides in the cluster. The cluster's budget is then determined by multiplying that budget rate by the actual number of students the cluster will accept for the next year.

In turn, the guides' salaries are determined by the guides within the limitations of the cluster budget. They are also adjusted based on the individual load each guide decides to assume for the year. The guides know that if they increase their own salaries too much, their other budget categories will suffer, parents will be displeased, and the cluster's points—and budget—for the next year will be lower. Hence, the only real way guides can increase their salaries, as in a law firm or medical clinic, is to increase the demand for themselves. In this way, there is a tremendous incentive to cooperate within each cluster. This kind of budget flexibility is also very important for allowing the professional educators to decide whether their students will be better served by hiring different types of personnel, such as two more assistants instead of one more guide.

Some districts may want to allocate a certain minimum dollar amount per student to each cluster's budget, regardless of demand for its guides, to partially even out the expenditures per student across clusters. However, it should be understood that the more the cluster (and center) budgets are influenced by demand for them, the easier it will be for superior ones to grow and thereby offer a better education to more students in the district. It will also be less necessary for the district office to close down weak clusters (or centers) by executive mandate, which is likely to be politically difficult, if not impossible. This will be less necessary because insufficient personal incomes will lead the guides in less successful clusters to seek more lucrative positions on their own initiative. In the long run the community will be better off by rewarding excellence and not encouraging mediocrity to linger on.

Learning Center Management Organization

There is a Learning Center Management Organization which has the following responsibilities:

- It surveys the needs of the clusters for external instructional support (from centers) and prioritizes those needs.

- It contracts new learning centers. These may be (1) part-time individuals (e.g., a retired biologist who lives in the community and is willing to devote a part of her time to the school district), (2) part-time organizations (e.g., a local museum or business which is willing to devote a part of its time to the school district), (3) full-time individuals (e.g., a mechanic who would like to leave his job and work full-time with kids), and (4) full-time organizations (e.g., a publishing company that has established a subsidiary for running learning centers in schools across the country).

- It trains center directors whenever necessary, and provides professional development support services to the centers upon request.

- It distributes money to the centers according to the amount that each center has used.

An administrative person in the district office is responsible for the accounting, reporting, and logistical aspects for all centers within the school district, but again each center decides how its budget will be spent.

VII. Consumer Support Agency

The district-wide Consumer Support Agency which was mentioned earlier serves (1) as a placement counseling service for matching children with guides and (2) as a watchdog service for providing "consumer reports" on clusters, guides, and learning centers (explained below). This Consumer Support Agency is run by parents (many on a volunteer basis) but receives a permanent fixed budget (something like one-half of one percent of the total district budget) as part of a system of "checks and balances."

The Consumer Support Agency's counseling service helps parents to decide which guide will be best for their child. It maintains extensive data on each guide's characteristics and accomplishments, and it diagnoses a child's needs if parents so desire, so as to enable them to select the guides which seem most likely to meet those needs. Such people-categories as "intuiter" and "thinker" may be very useful for part of this function.

The Consumer Support Agency's watchdog service has responsibility for collecting and disseminating information about the quality of performance of the clusters, guides, centers, and Center Management Organization.

Given that some parents do not care enough to choose a guide for their child, the placement service diagnoses each such child's needs and applies for the most appropriate guides. However, such applications are not included in the point count described under "Cluster Organization and Administration" above, to avoid the temptation for dirty politics. Federal, state, and local supplements for disadvantaged children would be passed through the district office directly to the clusters' budgets.

VIII. Cost-Effectiveness

No thorough cost analysis has been performed as yet, but preliminary indications are that this system would cost approximately the same per student as our present system, yet would be considerably more effective. Although guides are paid more than present teachers, their various assistants (apprentice guides, volunteers, and older students) cost considerably less. Their use enables a much higher student-guide ratio, but with increased human contact and caring. Furthermore, administrative costs currently count for up to half the cost of education in many districts. This expense would be much lower in our third-wave system.

The learning centers are an important cost factor. The number of centers and relatedly the number of passes provided to students each quarter will influence the cost. Also, the extent to which the centers are staffed and/or directed by volunteers or semi-volunteers (those who accept nominal payment to supplement retirement or other income) will also influence the cost.

In a small school district, it might be wise for each guide to also serve as a center director, with fewer students to guide. We presently anticipate that this entire system can be run within present school budgets, especially given that local businesses, foundations, and individuals would be considerably more inclined to sponsor learning centers, including basic-skill and focus-area shopping mall centers, as well as more application-oriented and problem-oriented community centers.

Conclusion

This is but one vision of a third-wave educational system, and much work remains to further develop, field test, and refine this "blueprint." It is hoped that it will provide a stimulus for local school districts' efforts to design creative alternatives to our current system that are more appropriate for meeting the needs of an information society.

Given that many teachers, administrators, and parents in any school district are not interested in change, a good change strategy might be to design and implement a parallel system in the district. Identify teachers and other stakeholders who want to change, give them the opportunity to form a design team for each cluster, allow them to collectively design an administrative system to support their clusters, and allow them to implement the third-wave system alongside, but completely independently of, the current system. Separate state policy could even be designed. And community service agencies could be integrated with the third-wave system. Then, as problems are worked out of the new system and other teachers and parents in the district see the advantages of the new system, additional clusters and learning centers could be formed. This would provide a gradual, nonthreatening method for the district to slowly evolve into the new paradigm with a minimum of disruption and resistance.

This appendix is based on an article published by the *Journal of Instructional Development.* This revision is printed with permission from the Association for Educational Communications and Technology.

Author's Note:

I am deeply grateful to Ruth Curtis, Bonnie Keller, Bonnie Lang, Don Parks, and Joe Powell for their considerable input into the development of the ideas presented in this Appendix.

References

Bloom, B.S. (1956). *Taxonomy of Educational Objectives, Handbook I: Cognitive Domain.* New York: David McKay.

Bloom, B.S. (1976). *Human Characteristics and School Learning.* New York: McGraw-Hill.

Brandt, R.M. (1981). *Public Education Under Scrutiny.* Washington, DC: University Press of America.

Frey, L., and Reigeluth, C.M. (1986). Instructional Models for Tutoring: A Review. *Journal of Instructional Development*, 1986, 9 (1).

Gagné, R.M. (1977). *The Conditions of Learning* (3rd edition). New York: Holt, Rinehart and Winston.

Gardner, H., and Hatch, T. (1989). Multiple Intelligences Go to School: Educational Implications of the Theory of Multiple Intelligences. *Educational Researcher*, 18 (8), 4-10.

Standing, E.M. (1962). *The Montessori Revolution in Education.* New York: Schocken Books.

Toffler, A. (1980). *The Third Wave.* New York: Bantam Books.

APPENDIX B

The Application of Design to School Planning

C. L. Hutchins

Mid-continent Regional Educational Laboratory

For the past several years, the Mid-continent Regional Educational Laboratory has been developing a program intended to assist school planners and decision makers in the design process. The work has culminated in a program called A$^+$chieving Excellence which is published by the Laboratory. It is divided into four parts. One part deals with the implementation process itself. A second and third focus on increasing the efficiency and effectiveness of the existing design, and the fourth section relates to the process of redesigning schools. This appendix will focus on the experiences of the Laboratory in dealing with the school redesign unit of A$^+$chieving Excellence.

This fourth component of the program is organized into three parts. The first deals with strategic analysis, the second with design, and the third with implementation or, as it is called in the program, "empowerment."

Strategic Analysis

The strategic analysis section is predicated on the belief that the current design of schools is no longer functional in the context of the changing environment. For example, the populations served by schools have changed dramatically, particularly in urban areas; furthermore, the performance requirements for students graduating from high school have changed dramatically as a function of the shifting nature of the work place.

The old design emerged from the development of the "Common Schools" of New England in the early 1800's and the curriculum reforms of the Committee of Ten in 1893. The environment of the twentieth century no longer fits with the primary features of the historical design.

The key to getting a commitment to redesign is to get local policy makers to agree that there is a misfit between schools and their environment. Based on several dozen field tests of the A$^+$chieving Excellence program, its developers have concluded that the best way to create a consensus that a new design is needed is to involve the community and policy makers of the school in a "strategic analysis" of the situation.

Initially, it was assumed that the process of strategic analysis needed to be highly original; that is, that each site had to discover for itself all of the major factors that defined the discrepancy. Thus, early versions of the A$^+$chieving Excellence materials provided detailed instructions as to how to conduct an "environmental scan" by collecting economic, demographic, social, cultural, and educational trends. Sources for this data were even identified so that each community could gather this information for itself.

Over time, however, it became clear that such an undertaking was not only too costly for most schools, but unnecessary. By presenting local communities with a tightly worded scan of trends at the national level and then asking them to derive the implications of these trends for their local community as well as identify variances found at the local level, the process could be significantly shortened without reducing the participant's commitment to the conclusion that change was necessary.

Once sufficient conviction had developed that the match between the environment and the current design of schooling was no longer functional, the A$^+$chieving Excellence program guided participants through the development of a strategic mission statement. The developers of the program found that most traditional mission statements were too general and lacked meaningfulness for most people. As a result, they developed a much more prescriptive procedure for insuring that mission statements carefully addressed such issues as the client groups served by the school, the outcomes its clients expected, services that the school was expected to provide, partners with whom they could work, and the competitors they had.

The development of a tight mission statement then permitted an in- depth, "internal audit" of the extent to which there was a discrepancy between the new mission and existing practice. Once again, the developers assured that these audits would need to be quite specific to each locale, and that a lot of data would be needed to convince the policy makers that a discrepancy existed. In field trials, however, it was found that most participants would quickly acknowledge that their current practices were at a high level of discrepancy with the new mission and, hence, were ready to move on. Some of the data that was necessary, however, had to do with disaggregating achievement by socioeconomic, gender and race data to show the extent to which certain student populations are underserved. The usual practice involved in strategic planning is to undertake the internal audit simultaneously with or just after the completion of the environmental scan but prior to the development of a new mission.

The developers of A⁺chieving Excellence found that the risk of following that order was that if the old design of schooling was used as a basis for the scan rather than the new one, the extent of the discrepancy between the desired state and the current state was minimized.

Based on actual experience with schools that have used the strategic analysis process, the developers of A⁺chieving Excellence have concluded that this process can produce significant requirement for change in the design. The end result is a set of specifications for a new design.

Design

The specific approach used by A⁺chieving Excellence for design was adapted from *Systems Thinking, Systems Practice* (Checkland, 1981) and *Systems Design of Education: A Journey to Create the Future* (Banathy, 1991).

One feature of the design process outlined by Checkland is to ask the user to adopt a general system model of the system in order to remove the process from the specifics of the existing design. The general model used by A⁺chieving Excellence is a modification of Miller's General Living System (Miller, 1978). After convincing users that such a model is appropriate, the user is asked to identify general functions that such a system would require of education without being so specific as to identify the means. A simplified form of the Miller subsystem functions that McREL has found most participants in the design process can understand and use is based on this list of what a well-educated person should be able to do:

- Access information.

- Interpret or decode that information so as to produce understanding.

- Process that information so as to reason and solve problems.

- Produce a broad range of outcomes and use technology.

- Develop his/her own "executive" or "self-regulating" function
  to: make decisions about himself/herself, set goals, create a
  positive self-image, monitor and learn from his/her past performance, experience enjoyment, pleasure, excitement, accomplishment, etc.

- Work well with other people and things in his/her environment.

Another characteristic of the design process used by A$^+$chieving
Excellence was the model adapted from Banathy (1991) that has to
do with designating the starting point for the learning level as the
primary level of the system. It's here that the Miller model can be seen
as the most appropriate general system model to use in education.

Another feature of the A$^+$chieving Excellence design process
adapted from Checkland is the use of English language verbs to define
the outcomes of the system. Participants in the program are provided
with a comprehensive list of outcomes organized into the modified
list of Miller subsystem functions. They select those that match the
functions that they have accepted as a result of their review of a general
systems model.

Up to this point the design process is very analytical. However, there
is a point at which the user must shift into a very creative generation
of an alternative or ideal design. That is done in A$^+$chieving Excellence
by the use of a "story writing process." This procedure requires that
participants generate a series of key words that describe their ideal
vision of a redesigned school; a journalist converts these into a story
of what it would be like in that school if those features were found.
The stories are narrative in character and have been found to be very
powerful tools, much more powerful than traditional planning
models in persuading both participants in the program as well as
outsiders in the community that the new design is feasible and
desirable. These stories, in effect, become the vision which, in
Banathy's words, "pulls the designer to the future."

The final step in the design process is to "backward map" to the support systems necessary to operationalize the design. These backward mappings progress from the instructional level (that is, what teachers must do to create the behavior they seek in the learner) through to the administrative and governance levels of a system to indicate the kinds of conditions and resources that these levels must provide to drive and support the instructional and learning levels.

Under field conditions where this backward mapping process was not used and participants could move immediately to the design of the instructional or administrative levels, developers of A⁺chieving Excellence found that a complete redesign did not occur. Instead, superficial changes were envisioned for the design that were not capable of producing true change at the learning level.

Creating a new design is not sufficient. A well thought-out process for implementing the design is necessary. Traditional long-range planning models can be used here; however, given the open and complex nature of the school system, the authors of A⁺chieving Excellence have focused much more on a contingency and empowerment approach. For example, clients are urged to conduct what the program calls an "opportunities analysis," during which they are asked to look at events that are predictable in the near future — events which can be seen as opportunities to bring about key elements of the design without creating new tasks. Only those things that can't be brought about through such contingency arrangements are then systematically planned.

For example, a good deal of time is spent in the A⁺chieving Excellence program helping clients understand the complex process of change including such things as:

- Access to revelant information.

- Policies that facilitate and do not block the adoption of the characteristics of the model.

- Decision-making structures for involving teachers and students in the implementation process.

- Statements of outcomes that can be used as milestones for judging progress.

- Conditions that ensure that the process is self-regulating and self-organizing.

- Partnerships that access resources necessary to implement the change.

There is no empirical evidence at this time that the A$^+$chieving Excellence program's approach to design produces better schools. It has been available for less than one year outside the initial field test sites, and in those field test sites (none of which have been in place longer than two years), the design process is still unfolding. But clearly, testimonial evidence from clients and changes that they have made already in their existing design suggest that the design process may be the key to the "restructuring" called for by such groups as the National Governors' Association.

The rationale for the design process embedded in the A$^+$chieving Excellence program is a rationale for existence in that all calls for improvement, reform, and restructuring are impotent unless the systemic nature of school design is considered and a drastic alteration of that design occurs. The old design of schools is no longer working for the majority of today's students and only a radical redesign, implemented in an evolutionary way, is likely to create schools that meet the needs of the future.

References

Banathy, Bela H. (1991). *Systems Design of Education: A Journey to Create the Future.* Englewood Cliffs, NJ: Educational Technology Publications.

Checkland, Peter (1981). *Systems Thinking, Systems Practice.* New York: John Wiley & Sons.

Miller, James (1978). *Living Systems.* New York: McGraw-Hill.

APPENDIX C

Experience-Based Career Education:

A Secondary School Program

C. Lynn Jenks

Far West Laboratory

Its Purposes

Experience-Based Career Education (EBCE) was designed as an alternative form of secondary education that attempts to link learning and experience.[*] It takes students outside the school walls into the community and workplace of adults. This alternative approach rests on the following key assumptions: education should be experience-based, career-oriented, student-centered, and it should expose students to the ideas, skills, and personalities of working adults.

The broad purpose of EBCE is to produce graduates who are:

- planful—not only about their long-range futures, but about how they intend to accomplish more immediate goals and tasks;

- self-reliant and able to set their own goals: plan activities, manage their time and other resources; work independently;

---

[*] EBCE was designed by the Far West Laboratory for Educational Research and Development, San Francisco, CA. This brief description was compiled from our extensive program documentation.

recognize when they need help and how to seek it; evaluate their own behavior and learn from it; and accept the consequences of their own decisions and actions;

- capable of interacting with adults as equals: know what is expected from them as adults; be able to communicate on an adult level; to make and keep realistic commitments; and have reasonable expectations of others;

- capable of making realistic and satisfying career choices: more informed about career options and requirements and more aware of their own values, needs, goals, strengths, and limitations;

- independent learners: are able to identify what is worth learning; to identify and use effective resources and methods of acquiring information; and to analyze, evaluate, and incorporate new information into their own knowledge and experience base.

At a somewhat more specific level, the following EBCE program goals represent areas in which student progress is expected:

Career Development

- Career Awareness. Acquiring a broad understanding of the world of work—how people perform tasks, deal with one another, solve problems, and derive satisfaction in their daily lives—and understanding the particular nature and requirements of specific careers.

- Self-Development. Learning about one's own interests, abilities, values, and goals, and using this knowledge to weigh options and make informed decisions about post high school plans.

Basic Skills

- Developing reading, writing, oral communications, and computational skills essential for acquiring and communicating information in daily life.

Life Skills

- Interpersonal. Learning to relate to others on an adult level; recognizing the needs and expectations of others; handling interpersonal conflicts; and contributing productively to group endeavors.

- Inquiry. Learning to interpret and critically analyze information and its sources, draw generalizations, develop and test hypotheses, and evaluate data and ideas.

- Problem-Solving. Learning to analyze situations, define problems, identify and use appropriate sources of information, evaluate alternatives, and employ effective solutions.

- Decision-Making. Learning to recognize decisions that need to be made, to identify options and probable outcomes, to examine personal values and goals affecting decisions, to make informed choices, and accept responsibility for decisions made.

Who Makes It Work?

IN THE COMMUNITY

The EBCE learning process—an interaction between the students, the Learning Coordinator, and the resource volunteer—depends first of all on various people in the community who offer their time, ingenuity, work facilities, and practical knowledge to students.

Resource Persons (RPs) are adults from all walks of life who volunteer to share their seasoned knowledge and special skills with interested students in a one-to-one relationship. The RP's primary role is to help students become adults, to learn how to think for themselves, make responsible decisions, relate maturely to others, and carry out their own learning projects.

The relationship is voluntary on both sides, and is defined by a set of mutually understood expectations and consequences. Its scope, objectives, and duration are negotiable—depending on the RP's availability and the student's educational needs and interests.

By providing direct experience in a variety of social and economic settings, RPs help students:

- acquire firsthand information about what people actually do in their daily work, how they feel about what they do, and what kinds of knowledge and skills are needed to enter and succeed in particular careers;

- learn more about who they, the students, are and what they want to become by testing their values, interests, and abilities through actual experience;

- improve reading, writing, and computation skills by using them to solve real problems in everyday life situations, and by challenging them to employ these skills on an adult level;

- integrate learning in ways not possible in the traditional classroom by seeing how career skills, academic concepts, and social issues converge in the need to solve practical problems; and

- develop some technical skills through hands-on experiences in real or simulated work tasks.

While the core of the EBCE learning experience is this one-to-one relationship between a student and an adult interested in his education, two other kinds of resources are used in the program:

Resource Organizations (ROs) range in size from fewer than ten to more than several hundred employees, and open most of their operations to students. Activities at these sites typically include pre-planned group briefings, tours, and observations and discussions with individual employees. Resource Organizations give students exposure to a total organization: the nature of the business; its relationship to the community; the kinds of jobs performed there; how particular careers interlock; the working conditions and environment; and educational prerequisites for job entry.

Community Resources (CRs) are institutions or organizations open to the public, such as museums, libraries, aquariums, parks, courts, and city council meetings. Students use them when working on projects and to supplement information available from other resources. At these Community Resource sites, and at Resource Organizations, students may identify RPs who are willing to work with them on individual projects.

Resource Development. Individuals and organizations are recruited to form a balanced pool of resources that can accommodate student interests and high school graduation requirements, and which provide a representative mix of career fields.

Resource sites are analyzed for their learning potential in career awareness, academic subjects and issues, and the application of basic skills. A range of on-site learning activities, from which students can choose in designing their projects, are mutually agreed upon by the Resource Person and EBCE staff, and conveyed to students in the form of Resource Guides.

STAFF ROLES

While students will spend a major portion of their time at learning sites in the community, a school center serves as a home base where they plan projects, schedule appointments with resources, and return to digest and share their experiences in the community. Located in a school or in a separate facility, the EBCE center is where students use supplementary resources such as tutorials, workshops, and programmed instructional materials, coordinated by a Skills Specialist. Here students also come in contact with the Program Director, who serves as administrative coordinator and staff supervisor, a Records Clerk, and the Resource Analyst, who is responsible for recruiting, analyzing, and maintaining the pool of resources. The key staff role, however, is that of the Learning Coordinator (LC).

Like all adults involved in EBCE, the LC plays a multi-faceted role as helper, facilitator, and resource. Each LC works with 20 to 30 students to help them:

- formulate long-term goals consistent with their own interests and educational needs, and decide what steps are necessary to achieve them;

- determine what's worth learning, focus areas of inquiry; identify resources, and develop project plans;

- refine their interests, clarify values, and assess needs, based on cumulative experience;

- integrate what they know about themselves with information about career and educational opportunities; and

- monitor their own learning progress, articulate problems, devise appropriate solutions, and modify strategies to incorporate new insights and emerging interests.

The LC coordinates the student's total learning program and monitors on-site learning experiences through counseling sessions and regular contact with resources in the community. LCs are teachers in one important sense—working with students individually and in small group sessions, they can teach inquiry, problem-solving, planning, and decision-making skills necessary for independent learning.

LCs also provide students with the kind of feedback that can help them make sense out of what they are doing and learning in the community. This process of consolidating and interpreting their diverse experiences, of reinforcing and further stimulating learning, pervades all the staff's daily interactions with students.

ROLE OF THE STUDENT

Within the framework of EBCE goals and clearly specified account- ability procedures, the student acts as planner, decision-maker and self-evaluator. Students are allowed to pursue their own particular needs and interests, at their own pace, and according to learning methods best suited to their purposes and capabilities.

Projects. Students plan and carry out their learning through in- dividual projects, using goals and evaluation criteria they help specify. Designed to blend growth in academic subjects, career development, and basic and life skills, each project:

- is organized around a topic or issue relevant to a career or discipline;

- is focused in terms of significant questions that require for their answer planned learning experiences at resource sites and the use of other information sources such as related readings;

- includes activities that require the student to apply communica- tions, interpersonal, and/or computations skills in practical, career-related situations; and

- results in demonstrable growth toward stated goals, and in tangible products for which credit is awarded.

Organizing the Curriculum

Because EBCE departs from the conventional classroom approach to content and instruction, the Far West program has developed curriculum guides, called project planning packages, tailored to the unique aims of the model.

A package is not a curriculum, but rather a structure within which an individualized curriculum can be planned and carried out in the form of projects. Each package unites under a single heading a broad area of study and its related professional and technical careers, and enables a student to focus his learning on an academic subject area, a significant issue, or a career field, while simultaneously learning about all three.

Prototype packages have been developed in the following areas: Social Science, Commerce, Physical Science, Communications and

Media, and Life Science. Easily adaptable to local needs, each package contains the following essential parts:

- Package goals define the package scope and range, set minimum requirements, and identify significant underlying concepts and process skills of the career/discipline area.

- Sample projects demonstrate how students can pursue their own interests while meeting minimum requirements for credit, and learn those skills, concepts, and principles considered basic to the package career/discipline area. They also serve as exemplary samples of completed program planning forms (the project Sketch and the Student Project Plan), while offering project suggestions for students to pursue.

- The annotated list of resources describes resources available for learning activities relevant to the study area.

In addition,

- A statement about required group discussions explains their nature and purpose. Students working on projects within a career/discipline area meet regularly to broaden their exposure to the field by discussing what each of them is doing and learning.

- A step-by-step description of how to plan and complete a project provides guidance on how to plan projects and a reminder of the tasks involved.

Other sections not as critical to the package concept, but time-savers for students and staff, include an introduction; a bibliography; project ideas; careers to explore; and a list of courses for which students could seek subject matter equivalency credit, depending on the content and focus of the project they design. Within this flexible structure, students can plan more ambitious projects to earn more credit, or can plan two or more smaller projects to meet the minimum requirements.

Using the package and working with staff, the student selects the resources to visit in getting a fix on a project topic. Students are allowed to explore several possible topics and resource sites if necessary before clarifying and narrowing their theme for a full-scale project plan. The student interested in rent control, for example, might visit Resource Persons at the housing authority, the legal aid society, and a city councilman's office, only to become involved in a more interesting topic, such as affirmative action employment programs and how they are working.

Before long, however, the student must firm up his project plan. (While students may explore as much as they want, they earn credit only for completed projects or other work such as tutorials.) With the assistance of the Learning Coordinator and chosen resources, the student identifies on a project planning form:

- a focus of theme for the project;

- questions for which answers are being sought;

- Resource Persons and Organizations to work with;

- related reading;

- an estimate of time required in visiting resources, doing related research, and developing at least one product; and

- project goals and indicators—what the student wants to learn about or learn how to do through the project, and how what was learned will be known by the student and demonstrated to the staff. In addition to spelling out how work will be evaluated, the student designates who the evaluators will be and sets deadlines for completion of goals.

The student also negotiates with the Learning Coordinator the amount and kind of credit to be earned if the project is satisfactorily completed. The package goals provide a standard for use in negotiating credit. If a student's project meets the minimum package goals, a specific amount of credit will be received.

The package provides the structure and the student's project provides the mechanism for integrating learning of process skills with subject matter content.

The package design emphasizes to students that growth in life, and in basic and career skills, is a natural part of every learning project, whatever its particular content.

INDEX

A

Aburdene, Patricia, 63
Ackoff, Russell L., 136, 140
Administrative focus model,
    89-91
Argyris, Chris, 80

B

Banathy, Bela H., 23, 26, 32,
    33, 35, 37, 45, 78, 79,
    86, 108, 111, 120. 165,
    225, 226
Barth, Roland S., 8
Bell, Daniel, 64, 66, 68, 69,
    70, 72-73
Bloom, Benjamin S., 210, 211
Botkin, James, 78
Boulding, Kenneth E., 26,
    42-44, 67-68, 164
Brandt, R. M., 211
Branson, Robert, 7

C

Capra, Fritjof, 63
Chaisson, Erick J., 61, 64
Change
    inactive style of perception
        and management, 140-142
    interactive style of
        perception and management,
        145-148
    preactivist style of
        perception and management,
        143-145
    reactivating or reactive
        style of perception and
    management, 137-140
    systemic vs. piecemeal, 149
    taking charge of, 135-136
Checkland, Peter, 225
Churchman, West C., 45
Closed systems, 35, 36
Communication systems,
    addressing educational
    function, 109
Community agencies, addressing
    educational function, 109
Complex systems, 35, 36-37
Conant, James, 15
Consciousness
    creating aspect of, 27
    evolutionary, 25-26
    self-reflective cognitive
        aspect of, 26-27
Cooperation with external
    systems, 49, 106
Coordinating option, 49, 106,
    110-111
Core ideas
    derived from societal
        characteristics, 81-83
    to guide design of learning
        society, 128
    for learning focus model,
        102-103
    for learning society,
        120-121, 126, 127-128
    for New System, 120-121
Core values
    derived from societal
        characteristics, 81-83
    for learning focus model,
        102
    for learning society,
        120-121, 125-126

for New System, 120-121
Crandall, David P., 6
Crisis in education, 5-9
  irrelevance of old design to
    current needs, 15
  new image needed, 30, 41-42,
    46-47
  old design preventing
    attainment of excellence,
    15
  restructuring recommended,
    7-8
  school improvement not
    affecting, 7
  school reform approach to,
    9-12. *See also* School
    reform approach
  sources of, 9-12
  systems design approach
    proposed, 8-9. *See also*
    Systems design
Csanyi, Vilmos, 25
Cultural evolution. *See*
  Societal evolution
Curtis, Richard K., 22, 63

D

Design
  See also Systems design
  as a journey, 153-164. *See
    also* Design journey
  compared with planning,
    150-151
  definition of, 162-164
  designing for the future
    vs. designing the future,
    151
  developing capability and
    competence in, 165-167
  developing design action
    teams, 167
  developing design
    leadership, 166
  developing organizational

capacity for, 167-168
  generating willingness in
    community to support, 168
  tasks of, 163
  user-designers, 165-166
  vs. planning, 150-151
Design action teams, 167
Designing the future
  vs. designing for the
    future, 151
Design inquiry
  defining desired system,
    169-170
  formulating organizing
    perspectives for, 168-169
  organizing, 170
  planning, 168-171
  planning implementation of,
    170-171
  selecting design methods,
    170
  spirals of, 176-190
Design journey
  dynamics of, 162
  map of, 154-158
  mapping between start and
    end, 157-158
  mapping development of
    design solution, 158-159
  mapping knowledge base,
    158-159
  mapping terrain of
    departure, 155-156
  mapping terrain of
    destination, 156, 157
  mapping territory of design
    evaluation, 161
Design leadership, 166
Design process
  organizing perspectives for,
    174-175
  overview of, 173-174
Design products, 190-191
Design thinking and design
    action, 26-28

Deterministic systems, 36
Double-looped organizational
   inquiry, 143-144
Double-trek approach to
   organizational inquiry,
   150

E

Education
   See also Learning
   administrative focus model
      of, 89-91
   boundaries of current
      system, 112
   broader basis needed for,
      106-108
   choice of organizational
      model, 95
   as closed system, 112
   core values and core ideas
      derived from societal
      characteristics, 81-83
   current crisis in. *See*
      Crisis in education
   current system of, 111-112
   defined from systems
      perspective, 31
   dynamics facilitating
      transformation of, 46-47
   emerging learning agenda
      for, 77-79
   emerging role in
      spearheading societal
      evolution, 61
   emerging societal functions
      of, 75-76
   fragmented study of, 9-10
   implications of cultural
      evolution for, 24-25
   implications of societal
      characteristics for, 73-83
   implications of use of
      organizational models for,
      95

important role of, 30
institutional focus model
   of, 88-89
instruction focus model of,
   91-93
integration with all social
   service fields proposed,
   107-108
irrelevance of old design to
   current needs, 15
learning focus model of,
   93-95
new image of humankind
   needed for, 46-47
new system proposed for,
   112-120. *See also* New
   System
and organizational
   implications of societal
   characteristics, 80
organizational models of,
   88-95
rationale for a broad-based
   system, 106-108
reflecting society, 29-30
re-imaging needed for, 30,
   41-42, 46-47. *See also*
   Framework for educational
   images
as societal system, 108-109
systems complex of, 86-87
systems involved in, 109-111
systems thinking needed for,
   30-31
third-wave system proposed
   for, 14, 201-220
Educational reform
   boundaries of existing
      system restricting, 11-12
   focusing on existing system,
      7-8, 9-12, 41-42, 47
   handicapped by piecemeal and
      incremental approach, 11
   ideas for solutions not
      integrated, 11

new and different questions
to be answered, 16-17
old mindset hindering, 9-10,
17
school reform approach to,
7, 9-12
system design approach to,
12-13
Educational systems
See also entries beginning
Systems
boundaries of, 112
systems inquiry applied to,
37-38
Elmore, Richard F., 7-8
Evolution
See also Societal
evolution
changed by human race, 24-25
Evolutionary consciousness
need for development of, 26
power of, 25-26
Excellence in education, old
design preventing
attainment of, 15
Experience-based career
education, 229-236
community resources used in,
231-232
organizing curriculum for,
234-236
purposes of, 229-231
staff roles in, 233-234
student role in, 234

F

Ferguson, Marilyn, 63
Focus of inquiry, 48, 50-51,
85-104
and organizational models of
education, 88-95
Formal educational systems,
addressing educational
function, 109

Framework for educational
images, 47-56
constituents of dimensions
of, 50-53
dimensions of, 48-49
focus of inquiry dimension,
48, 50-51, 85-104
illustrated, 53-55
implications of use of,
53-55
patterns that connect
dimension of, 49, 52-53
scope of the inquiry
dimension, 48-49, 51-52,
59-83
uses of, 49-50
Functions/structure model, 34
products of, 190

G

Gagné, R. M., 210
Gardner, H., 204
Gleick, James, 63
Governance system, for the New
System, 115, 117

H

Harman, Willis H., 29, 30, 44,
46, 63, 120, 125,
Harvey, Glen, 6
Hatch, T., 204
Havel, Vaclav, 18
Heath, Shirley Brice, 107
Heuristic systems, 36-37
Hobbs, Nicholas, 107
Huber, George P., 71
Hutchins, Larry C., 15, 78
Huxley, Aldous, 44

I

Image
aesthetic dimension proposed

for, 45
central characteristics of,
44-45
creation as an ongoing
process, 43-44
dimensions of, 42-43
dimensions proposed for,
45-46
economic dimension proposed
for, 45
educational dimension
proposed for, 45
emergence of, 44
invariants in, 44-46
lacking for education, 43
moral dimension proposed
for, 45
new image needed for
education, 46-47
New System and existing
system compared, 129-131
political dimension proposed
for, 46
public, 43
resistant to change, 42
role in societal
development, 42-46
scientific dimension
proposed for, 45
social action dimension
proposed for, 45
sources used in creating,
44-46
technological dimension
proposed for, 45
wellness dimension proposed
for, 45
Image creation for education
See also Framework for
educational images
need for, 46-47
Information exchange, 49, 105
Institutional focus model,
88-89
Instructional focus model,

91-93
compared with learning focus
model, 99-102
Integration with other
systems, 49, 106, 109-111
new system created by,
112-120. *See also* New
System
rationale for a broad-based
system, 106-108
reinforcement of rationale,
108-112

J

Jantsch, Erich, 25
Jenks, Lynn, 165
Johnson, David W., 79
Johnson, Roger T., 79

K

Kniep, Willard M., 7

L

Learners' system, for the New
System, 115, 117-119
Learning
See also Education
new agenda for, 77-79
organizing society's
resources for, 105-121
society as territory for,
108-112
systems complex for, 109-111
Learning agenda
acquiring competence in
cooperation, 79
competence for technological
age, 78
competence in systems
thinking and action, 79
emerging, 77-79
higher order learning

content needed, 77
managing and shaping change,
    78-79
Learning focus model, 93-95,
    96-103
  compared with instructional
    focus model, 99-102
  core ideas about learning
    and human development for,
    103
  core ideas about the learner
    for, 102-103
  core values for, 102
  expanded base for, 97-98
  key conditions for, 97
  key propositions for, 96-97
  organizing perspectives and
    systems requirements for,
    96
Learning resources, for the
    New System, 114
Learning resources
    information, planning, and
    control system
  for the New System, 115, 118
Learning society, 120-121
  core ideas about functions
    and purposes for, 127
  core ideas about the learner
    and learning for, 127-128
  core ideas and values for,
    120-121
  core ideas to guide design
    of, 128
  creating a new image for,
    128-129
  creating a vision for,
    124-125
  defining sets of core ideas
    for, 126
  example of an image for,
    129-131
  examples of core values for,
    125-126
Learning territories and

resources systems, for the
    New System, 115, 119-120
Learning territory, defined
    for the New System, 114
Leonard, George, 7
London, Clement B. G., 107

M

Management system for system
    design, 188-189
Markley, O. W., 29, 30, 44
McLaughlin, Milbrey Wallin,
    107
Mechanistic systems, 35, 36
Miller, James, 225
Mission statement in system
    design, 177-179
Mitchell, Douglas, 11
Models and model building,
    183-185
Morgan, Gareth, 25, 63
Mumford, Lewis, 63

N

Naisbitt, John, 63
New System, 112-120
  boundaries expanded for,
    113-115
  components of, 115-120
  connections needed within,
    113
  core ideas and values for,
    120-121
  example of an image for,
    129-131
  experience-based career
    education as an example
    of, 229-236
  governance system for, 115,
    117
  image compared with existing
    system, 129-131
  learners' system in, 115,

117-118
learning-experience focus
of, 113
learning resources for,
114-115
learning resources
information, planning, and
control system in, 115,
118
learning society as,
120-121. *See also*
Learning society
learning territories and
resources systems in, 115,
119-120
learning territory defined
for, 114
resource acquisition and
control system in, 115,
110
tentative model for, 115-120

O

Occupational and work systems,
addressing educational
function, 109
Open systems, 35, 36-37
Organizational
characteristics, affecting
societal transformation,
71-72
Organizational implications of
societal characteristics,
80
Organizational inquiry
design in context of, 192
domains of, 37-38
single-looped vs. double-
looped, 143-144
single trek vs. dual-trek
approach, 150
systems design in, 37-38

Organizational models of
education, 88-95
administrative focus, 89-91
choice of, 95
implications of use of, 95
institutional focus, 88-89
instructional focus, 91-93
learning focus, 93-95,
95-103

P

Patterns that connect, 49,
52-53, 105-106
cooperation, 49, 106
coordination, 49, 106
information exchange, 49,
105
integration, 49, 106,
107-111
Peccei, Aurelio, 24
Perelman, Lewis J., 7, 14
Piecemeal change, 149
Planning vs. design, 150-151
Pluralistic systems, 35, 36-37
Polak, E., 30-31
Primary social groups,
addressing educational
function, 109
Process/behavior model, 34
products of, 190-191
Purpose-seeking systems, 37
Purposive systems, 36

R

Reigeluth, Charles M., 7,
13-14
Resource acquisition and
control system, for the
New System, 115, 119
Restricted systems, 35, 36
Rigidly controlled systems, 36
Roszak, Theodore, 63

S

Salk, Jonas, 25
Schlechty, Phillip C., 8
School planning, application
    of system design to,
    223-228
School reform approach, 7
    See also Educational
    reform
    handicapped by fragmented
    study of education, 9-10
    traditional inquiry
    prevailing in, 10
Schorr, Lisbeth B., 107
Scientific inquiry,
    characteristics affecting
    societal transformation,
    70-71
Scope of inquiry, 48-49,
    51-52, 59-83
    exploring emergent societal
    features, 62-63
    options in, 48-49, 60
    rationale for selecting a
    broad scope, 60-62
Sculley, John, 63
Simon, Herbert, 162
Single-looped organizational
    inquiry, 149
Single-trek approach to
    organizational inquiry,
    150
Smith, Elise, 107
Social image. *See* Image
Societal characteristics
    and core values and core
    ideas, 81-83
    emerging learning agenda
    implied by, 77-79
    and emerging societal
    functions of education,
    75-76
    organizational implications
    of, 80

Societal development, role of
    image in, 42-46. *See
    also* Image
Societal evolution
    cut off from evolution of
    education, 61-62
    evolutionary markers for, 24
    evolution of global culture
    needed, 61
    gap between technological
    and cultural intelligence
    in, 60-61
    implications for education,
    24-25
    increasing speed and
    intensity of, 23-24
    planetary ethics needed, 61
    time scale of, 22-25
Societal features
    characteristics of, 63-66
    exploring, 62-63
    industrial age and current
    era compared, 64-66
Societal functions
    emerging for education,
    75-76
    relational, 75-76
    relevant to learning and
    development, 76
Societal systems
    congruence with society,
    29-30
    education as, 108-109
    impact of new eras on, 28-29
    with potential for serving
    learning, 109-111
    transformation of, 28-29
Societal transformation, 63
    characteristics of
    scientific inquiry, 70-71
    implications of, 164
    implications of, for
    education, 73-83
    organizational
    characteristics, 71-72

socio-cultural
characteristics, 67-68
socio-economic
characteristics, 69-70
socio-technical
characteristics, 68-69
Society, reflected by
education, 29-30
Society as learning territory,
108-112
new system proposed for,
112-120. *See also* New
System
Socio-cultural
characteristics, affecting
societal transformation,
67-68
Socio-economic
characteristics, affecting
societal transformation,
69-70
Socio-technical
characteristics, affecting
societal transformation,
68-69
Sorokin, Pitrim, 63
Standing, E. M., 209
Statement of purposes for
system design, 179-180
Systemic change, 149
Systemic systems, 35, 36-37
Systems
closed/open, 35, 36
deterministic, 36
heuristic, 36-37
map of types of, 36-37
mechanistic/systemic, 35,
36-37
purpose-seeking, 37
purposive, 36
restricted/complex, 35,
36-37
rigidly controlled, 36
types of, 35-37
uniqueness of, 34-37

unitary/pluralistic, 35,
36-37
Systems complex of education,
86-87
See also Education
administrative level of, 87,
89-91
choice of primary systems
level for, 87
institutional level of, 87,
88-89
instructional level of, 87,
91-93
key systems entity for, 87
learning-experience level
of, 87, 93-95
levels of, 87
normative dimensions of, 87
purpose, input and output
in, 87
Systems design
See also Design
application to school
planning, 223-228
designing enabling systems,
188-190
designing first model,
183-185
designing management system,
188-189
designing organization to
carry out functions,
189-190
designing system of
functions, 182-187
developing system
specifications, 180-182
establishing boundaries of
ideal system, 182-183
formulating core definition
for, 177-180
getting ready for, 165-171
mission statement for,
177-179
products of, 190-191

significance of, 28-29
statement of purposes for,
    179-180
systems development and
    implementation, 191-193
system specifications for,
    180-182
testing the new system, 191
understanding, 165
Systems design approach, 12-13
    design thinking and design
        action, 26-28
    journey as metaphor for,
        18-19, 153-171. *See also*
        Design journey
    need for, 13-17
    preparing for, 17-19
    transportation metaphor for,
        14
Systems development and
    implementation, 191-193
Systems-environment model,
    33-34
    products of, 190
Systems inquiry, 31-32
    application of, 32-33
    applied to educational
        systems, 37-38
    systems methodology aspect
        of, 32
    systems philosophy aspect
        of, 31-32
    systems theory aspect of, 31
Systems methodology, 32
Systems models
    to examine
        functions/structure of
        systems, 34, 190
    to examine process/behavior
        of systems, 34, 190
    to examine systems-
        environment relationships,
        33-34, 190
    use of, 33-34
System specifications for

system design, 180-182
Systems philosophy, 31-32
Systems theory, 31
Systems thinking, 30-31
    application of, 32-33
Systems view, defining
    education, 31

T

Third-wave educational system,
    14, 201-220
    budgeting for, 206-207,
        217-218
    child care services
        associated with, 215
    cluster operations in,
        208-209
    cluster organization and
        administration in, 216-218
    clusters as independent
        schools in, 205-206
    community learning centers
        associated with, 212
    Consumer Support Agency
        functions, 216, 218-219
    cost-effectiveness
        anticipated with, 219-220
    developmental levels as
        grade levels in, 204-205,
        209-211
    district organization and
        administrative systems
        for, 215-216
    extending present system,
        215
    guides' salaries for, 217
    guides' training and hiring
        for, 216-217
    incentives and rewards in,
        206-207
    interest groups
        supplementing, 211
    Learning Center Management
        Organization in, 216, 218

learning centers in, 207, 212-214

mobile learning centers, 212

parents choosing guides for children, 205

planning for student learning in, 214-215

responding to changes in parenting, 204

responsiveness to change essential to, 206

role of learning centers in, 207

self-designing nature of, 206

"shopping mall" centers, 212, 213

social and athletic activities supplementing, 211

student contracts for learning in, 211, 214-215

student passes to learning centers, 213-214

student use of learning centers, 213-214

summarized, 207-208

support services for, 213

teacher's role in, 202-203, 210

teachers as guides in, 203-204, 208, 209

transition between levels, 210

Toffler, A., 13, 63, 201

Toynbee, A., 63

U

Unitary systems, 35, 36

V

Vickers, Geoffrey, 70

W

Weiss, Heather, 107

Z

Zigler, Edward, 107